Reflections in a Farmhouse Window

A Prairie Memoir

Marilyn Frey

Reflections in a Farmhouse Window

© 2023 Marilyn Frey

All rights reserved. No part of this book, including images, may be reproduced, stored in any retrieval system, or transmitted in any form or by any means (electronic, mechanical, photocopying, recording, or otherwise) without permission of the copyright holder, except for brief quotations in printed reviews.

First Edition

Printed in Canada

ISBN: 978-0-9813803-4-6 (Paperback)

Cover illustration & book design: Christina Weese
Editing: Kay Petryk, Little Details Editing

Disclaimer: This book reflects the author's present recollections of experiences over time. Some events have been compressed and some dialogue has been recreated. Some names have been used with permission and others have been changed.

CONTENTS

Leaving A Mark 5

The Long Walk 8

The Games Children Play 11

Surviving The Winter. 15

The Strap 19

Woman's Work. 22

Flying Salamanders. 26

Riding A Pig 29

No More Peas, Please 33

Rock Picking. 37

Sunday Ball Games. 43

The Idiosyncrasies Of Mr. Fulmann 46

A Winning Situation. 51

Running Of The Bull 55

Moving Cows 58

More Luck Than Brains 62

A Chance Encounter 67

The Big Lie. 70

Crop Circles 74

Our First Home 79

Bear Encounter................83
Life On The Farm..............89
Deer Hunting..................93
Reflection...................101
So, You Think You Can Dance..107
Walking The Dog..............111
Just In Time.................113
Black Day In July............118
Teacher's Call...............125
Hospital Visit...............130
Size Matters.................132
Fear Lives Here..............135
Tough Lesson.................139
Devil Lake...................142
The Little Chick And The Fox.147
Oh, Christmas Tree...........150
Close Call...................155
Elvis........................161
The Hangings.................164
Christmas Premonition........169
Acting On A Dare.............174
Assaulted....................179
Leaving The Acreage..........189
The Train Ride...............195
Answer To A Prayer...........201

Friends	204
Moving Day	210
The Door Is Always Open	214
Neighbourhood Watch	216
On A Whim	221
Gone Too Soon	224
Winter Roads	232
Doggone	237
The Break-In	246
Going Home	252
The Man In The Van	254
Pandemic Christmas	258
Road Trip	262
Martins Lake	266
Farmhouse Window Reflections	271
About the Author	273

For Mom

Leaving A Mark

I crawled through the labyrinth of my mind, searching out the corners, the dead ends, struggling through the cloud and murk, rummaging for my first conscious recollection. My first memory emerges like a ship floating through the vast expanse of fog, silently becoming more defined, advancing on me until it is there, right in front of me – not so much a memory as a story my mother shared with me many times over the years and for which I brandish a scar on the back of my hand. The details that my mother provided made it hard to distinguish her account from my memory.

A toddler, recently having mastered the skill of walking, I wore a cotton dress with puffy sleeves and a Peter Pan collar, the waist of the dress gathered with ties that formed a little bow at my back. I had socks on and little black shoes that clicked when I walked across the worn linoleum floor. I felt a shiver as I looked around at the walls of my home. Our old house, made partly of logs and wood, had sparsely insulated walls that beckoned to the wind and mice, both of which came freely through the cracks, uninvited. One day my mother saw a mouse scurry across the kitchen floor and into a box of macaroni that sat on a bottom cupboard shelf. In one swift movement, she snatched that macaroni box and threw the whole thing – mouse and all – into the woodstove so the fiery flames could lick it to death. Once I got over the shock of what happened, I felt pride in my mother's actions. She acted without hesitation, doing what she needed to keep her home safe from intruders.

That same hot woodstove burnt an indelible mark on me. My mother stood at the stove frying pork chops for supper, the fat crackling and spitting, and the heady aroma floating through the kitchen. Like a big girl, I wanted to help my mom by taking care of my baby sister, Sharon. Only a few months old, Sharon lay in a navy-coloured baby carriage, the type with the big metal wheels with hard rubber tires. Its large metal handle curved up at just the right height for an adult, but was far above my head as a toddler.

My sister squirmed and fussed in the carriage, making squeaking noises as babies often do. I stood on my tiptoes and reached up to grab the carriage handle. From this uncertain stance, I pushed as hard as I could back and forth to rock the carriage, hoping it would quiet my little sister as I had seen my mother do so many times before. This rhythmic motion worked fine for a short while until the carriage wheels caught on an uneven plank in the floor. I pulled and pulled with all the strength my stretched-out arms could manage. After a particular hard tug on the handle and a sudden jerk, the carriage rolled backward, pinning my hand that held the carriage handle against the hot wood stove. Trapped and not strong enough to push the carriage away, I screamed out in pain as the stove's heat seared the back of my hand.

My mother rushed to me, grabbing me away from the hot stove. With me in her arms, she hurried to the pail of water on the counter and plunged my hand into its depths. The water's cooling effect calmed me down until all that remained inside of me were a few painful whimpers. Once I took my hand out of the water, the pain intensified again. I wailed. Mom spoke to me in soft, comforting murmurs, spreading butterfly kisses over the back of my hand which was red and blistering.

She assured me I was a big girl, a brave girl. She told me how helpful I was in taking care of my baby sister. Perched on her lap, holding my hand out so she could carefully apply ointment, I glanced at the carriage that held my sister, sound asleep.

In the years that followed, my mother repeated the story of what happened and the bravery I had shown. The mark I brandished on the back of my hand became a badge of honour for me. I took pleasure in showing it to everyone and re-telling how I had gotten it. I don't remember the pain anymore, but I remember the comforting way my mother took care of me, calming me and reassuring me that everything would be all right.

The Long Walk

The wolves howled in the pre-dawn light of that October morning in 1963, shadows everywhere, darting furtively as I made my way down our long, winding driveway. Eyes watched from behind the trees, yellow and wicked. The wind howled a devilish cry, and the willow trees reached their craggy arms to the sky, swaying them back and forth in a mournful demonstration. Agonizing moans filled the air. I turned and fled back to my home.

Running up the hill toward our house, I saw my mother watching from the kitchen window. I knew she worried that I would be too afraid to traipse down the road alone to catch the school bus. And she was right. Sobbing and stumbling up the steps to the house, I fell into my mother's arms. I was only six years old and used to my father driving me to the end of the driveway and sitting with me in his truck until the school bus came to pick me up, but he wasn't there this morning. He had left when it was still dark to drive an hour so he could help Grandpa build a fence. I missed my dad being there with me.

"You're a big girl now. In Grade 1. It isn't so bad. You can walk to the bus by yourself, can't you?" Mom asked.

I shook my head no.

"Marilyn," Mom said more firmly, "I can't leave your four younger brothers and sisters alone in the house so I can go with you. What if something happened to them while I was gone?"

I looked at her doubtfully.

"I'll be watching from the kitchen window to make sure you get to the bus," she promised. "There's nothing to be afraid of. You can do it."

I stared down at my feet, not feeling brave at all, but slowly nodded. "Okay, you've got to get going. The bus will be here soon."

Bolstered by her reassurances, I set out once again. Walking across the yard, I headed for the driveway, turning to wave to my mother, or more accurately, to see if she stood at the window watching me as she had promised. I was relieved to see her there, and she motioned with her hands for me to hurry. I trudged along, wandering down the hill and around the slight curve in the driveway. I looked back. The hill and the evergreens blocked my view, and I could not see her or the house anymore. Once again, fear gnawed at me as I imagined all the evil things lurking around waiting to devour me. The wolves were back and so were the ghosts and monsters. They were moaning and chortling their evil laughs. The wind in the spruce trees whooshed, and the willow branches rubbed together, making an eery sound. A muskrat scuttled across the road in front of me. The sudden unexpected movement alarmed me.

Once again, I turned and hightailed it back to where the glowing orange house lights beckoned to me, offering safety and warmth, where I knew my mother waited. This time when I reached out for her, I could tell she was trying to hide her impatience. I sobbed, upset because my mother was mad at me, and I was too terrified to make that quarter mile walk down the driveway by myself.

Mom risked it, threw on her coat, tied a scarf around her head, and hurried me out the door. My mother left her four preschool children in the house to escort me down the road to the waiting bus. She ran beside me, hollering for me to hurry. We could see the bus making its way down the grid road. Now, it stopped at the end of our driveway. We had to hurry. We ran, me panting, trying to keep up with my mother. I complained that my schoolbag and lunch kit were heavy, but Mom told me to keep running. We finally made it.

Mr. Fischl, the school bus driver, threw open the bus doors, and Mom kissed me goodbye and waved to the driver. He smiled and waited for me to settle into the first seat right behind him. My mother ran back to the house where the other children waited for her.

    I slumped in my seat, feeling ashamed and upset that I had not been brave enough to walk to the bus alone. I hoped Mom wasn't mad at me and that she knew how scared I was. I missed her. A tear slowly leaked out and spilled down my cheek as the school bus pulled away.

The Games Children Play

Growing up on our farm west of Middle Lake, Saskatchewan in the '60s and '70s, we did not have computers or gaming systems. We didn't have cell phones or smart TVs either. Instead, we had our ingenuity and creativity in devising new challenges and games to play with our siblings and friends. Sometimes we played games passed down to us by our parents or older brothers and sisters. Sometimes we invented games to play. Never bored or short on ideas to keep ourselves amused, we knew if we complained we had nothing to do, our parents immediately produced a long list of chores to counter any boredom we might be experiencing.

Early on, I remember playing simple games like Hide and Seek or Tag, but we improvised to make it entertaining. We called one of them One-Legged Catch, where each child held up one leg and hopped on their free leg trying to catch the other children who were also hopping on one leg. As a young child at school, I remember playing one of our favourite games at recess where we all joined hands and chanted, "Ring around the Rosie, pockets full of posies, husha, husha, we all fall down," and collapsed on the ground, giggling, before once again rising to repeat the singsong. Red Rover and Crack-the-Whip were both more physically demanding and therefore had a higher risk of someone getting hurt. Often as little girls, our parents and teachers told us these games were for boys and we should content ourselves with playing hopscotch and jacks. Happy with that, I much preferred these quieter games.

As I grew older, dodgeball became popular for passing time during the summer. We all formed a big circle with one child in the middle.

Each child took turns throwing the ball at the individual in the centre of the circle, trying to hit them and make them out so they could take their turn in the middle of the ring. We played Fox and Goose in the winter, stomping out a pie-shaped formation in the freshly fallen snow. Everyone was a goose trying to make their way to the centre of the pie to overtake the fox who stood there guarding it. We soon learned that by buddying up with the other geese, we could distract the fox long enough for another goose to gain entry to the fox's den. This great winter game got us outside to enjoy the crisp air.

King of the Castle was another winter game that could get quite rough as we formed two teams. One squad would be on top of a high snow pile chanting, "I'm the King of the Castle. You're the dirty rascal." The other team charged up the snowy mountain and attempted to push the first team down the slope. If they succeeded, the advancing team could then rightfully claim that they were now Kings of the Castle. This involved lots of physical activity and afterward, we lay in the snow gazing up at the brilliant blue sky, panting, and taking in all that Mother Nature offered.

During the winter, we built massive snow forts on the school playground, as well as at our home on the farm. Depending on the complexity of our structures, building forts kept us occupied for days, sometimes weeks, before we completed them. Our elaborately created snow forts included rooms, hallways, and tunnels leading through the deep snow. We had hidden rooms and passageways as well as windows and escape routes. Many times, the Grade 11 and 12 boys came with shovels to help us complete our masterpiece, adding to the fun of creating such an engineering feat.

In summer, during our adolescent and teen years on the farm, we played Anti-I-Over, using our granaries to cast the ball over before we ran to search out the opposing team. Our farm had many granaries in a row between which we could hide and escape. Another popular game we always played when visitors came over was Kick the Tin Can. This game became a real cat-and-mouse challenge, as one person sought the other players before they could rush home and kick the tin can. You had to be cagey and daring to win this game. Playing it in the evening just before the sun fell on the horizon made it even more challenging and fun.

During the summer, our week was not complete without our regular Sunday ball games. All the neighbours gathered at our farm to play softball. We created a make-shift ball diamond in the cow pasture where everyone came together, both adults and children. These fun ball games acted as a tremendous stress relief after a hectic, work-filled week.

To stave off boredom during the winter, skating parties replaced ball games. With the blade attached to the front of his tractor, Dad cleared snow from the slough. We all piled out of the house with second-hand skates adorning our feet, making our way to the slippery ice in the pigpen. The one problem we encountered involved the string of electric wire Dad had stretched across the pond. Most times, those of us who were taller remembered to duck as we sailed under the wire. But sometimes, in our excitement, we forgot. On one occasion, I skimmed by, failed to duck, and hit the wire across my forehead. It felt like it had nearly taken my head off as I fell backward on the ice. Wailing all the way to the house, I felt relieved when Dad immediately checked me over. Seeing nothing physically wrong with me, he commented with a grin, "It's a good thing you got hit in the head. Nothing serious." That was the end of that.

When it was too cold or too dark to venture outside to play, we always had board games in the house to keep us occupied. One year, we received a game that held a dice in a bubble. This new technology drove our mother crazy listening to the hollow popping sound of the dice on the board as we played it non-stop.

Television helped while away the hours after supper, but it did not resemble today's modern flat-screen TV with cable or satellite bringing multitudes of channels. No, we had large box-like designs that usually took at least two men to move. We had two stations on our TV, making it considerably easy for a family of eight to decide what they wanted to watch. Either we watched this channel or that one. Ultimately, Dad got to choose, and we all spread out on the floor sitting cross-legged, fanned out in a semi-circle to watch the show he selected. Undoubtedly, if we complained about his choice, the other option included an earlier-than-usual bedtime.

    I grew up in a pleasant time, a simpler time, where we played together and challenged each other, learning comradery and team spirit. We knew how to be gracious winners and even better losers, and this helped build and mould us into caring and enterprising adults. I worry about today's children when I see them with their heads bent, maneuvering through a video game or on their phones, texting their friend who is sitting across the room from them. What will they become? Am I too cynical, or do I have cause for concern?

Surviving The Winter

My childhood home stood like a sentinel at the top of a hill overlooking our farm and the buildings that skirted the house in almost every direction. Its two-story prominence with a multitude of windows watched us as we played. The orange lights at night beckoned, bringing us back within the confines of its four walls, keeping us safe.

In winter, this bulwark withstood many harsh storms that descended on us in a fury of snow and glacial winds, with three-day winter blizzards being common back then. At the storm's end, it usually took another three or four days to fully dig ourselves out from the banks of snow that crowded our farmyard and the roads leading to it. I remember some of our older family members talking about the 1947 storm, where so much snow fell that many people could only get out of their houses by crawling out the second-story windows.

After a storm, Dad needed to shovel a path to the well and the barns so that he could tend to the animals, a laborious task that took the better part of a morning. Our farm animals found the long, cold winters taxing. Dad had a barn for the milk cows, but the remaining herd stayed outside. My father tried to protect his herd of thirty cattle by building a lean-to with a straw roof for them. This meagre structure helped shelter them from the wind and snow, but I recall many times seeing those gigantic animals shivering in the cold with a build-up of frost on their backs. The ten pigs Dad had on the farm were more fortunate: they had a barn into which they crowded to escape the cold.

Having a source of water for the animals was always a challenge in winter. Dad chopped the frozen water in the oblong metal trough so they could drink. In later years, he purchased an electric submersible water heater that helped keep the water from freezing. This did not come without its dangers because Dad had to run the wire from the electrical outlet in the wall across to the heater floating in the water trough. There was always the risk of someone tripping over it, or, worse yet, getting electrocuted. Every day my dad, siblings, and I guided the cows out of the fence and directed them to the trough for a drink. We stood there shaking in the cold and stamping our feet, trying to stay warm while the entire herd took turns at the tank consuming the frigid water.

During this time, the only equipment the rural municipalities had to remove snow was snowplows with blades that pushed the snow high along the sides of the road. These high banks of snow encouraged even more snow to drift in, filling in the roads and accumulating in even higher banks. My father belonged to a snow club, a group of neighbours who hired someone with a tractor and snowblower to help clear the roads after a storm. The snowblower was better than a snowplow because it could blow the snow further instead of piling it high along the roadside. During my childhood, I remembered several snow club meetings held at our house in the evenings where the men gathered to discuss whom they would hire and what they would pay him to clear the roads.

Despite their best efforts, snow piled high, especially at crossroads. One winter at a rural intersection two miles west of our farm, the snow piled as high as the telephone lines. Many mornings my father was worried that the school bus would not make it through the tunnel of snow at the crossroad. He followed the bus to make sure it navigated that intersection successfully. If it got stuck and Dad was not there, the bus driver had to leave the children unattended to walk a mile to the nearest neighbour. Once Dad knew the school bus had successfully navigated the bend at the intersection, he turned his truck around, often getting stuck in the deep snow himself. Many times, he spent hours digging the truck out before he could return home.

Heating the house during winter also presented its challenges. As a child, I vaguely remember my father bringing home truckloads of coal that he picked up from the grain elevator in town. He shovelled the pitch-black chunks through the chute and into the coal bin near the furnace in the basement of our house. Our furnace burned both wood and coal, but because the coal burned longer than wood and kept the house warmer, Dad preferred it to wood.

Over the years, coal became increasingly difficult to come by. My father converted the furnace to oil. He purchased a large tank that stood on the west side of our house to hold the heating oil. I remember my father crawling up on top of the tank and inserting a stick to measure the depth so he would know how soon to call for the truck in town to deliver more heating oil. You could not risk running out of oil in the dead of winter or the middle of a storm. The thick heating oil often froze in the pipe's joint that led from the tank to the house. My dad wrapped old rags around the joint to keep it as covered as he could from the bitter cold. I remember many times his hands nearly froze as he worked to fasten those rags around the pipes.

Vehicles presented another problem during the fierce prairie winters. Batteries, not of the quality they are today, had to be brought into the house every evening if you had any hopes of starting either the car or the tractor the next day. Despite taking this precaution, there were many times my dad had to crawl under the tractor with a torch to warm the oil so it would flow smoothly through the engine. The tractor had to run so he could clear our driveway and push the snow aside to access the barns to tend to our animals.

I remember playing indoors one winter morning with my brothers and sisters during a storm. The angry wind lashed at the outside of our house, but we felt snug and secure in the refuge of our home. The sound of one long ring alerted us to a general call coming in. In the

'60s, everyone had a large rectangular box mounted on the wall with a crank on the side: our telephone. Usually, about six to eight neighbours belonged to one phone line, which meant they could listen to or "rubber" on each other's calls.

Many housewives who could not drive or did not have a vehicle felt isolated. The ability to listen in on others' phone conversations offered a way for them to stay connected with other women outside their homes. I can honestly say my mother, busy with her brood of six small children, did not have time or the inclination to run and grab the phone to listen in on someone else's conversation and she scorned those who did.

A general call announced an important message, such as a quota opening, which meant farmers could haul their grain to the elevator. The one long ring called out again. Our father picked up the phone. This time the call announced no school today because the buses could not run.

My brothers, sisters, and I cheered and happily settled down for a day at home. We chuckled to ourselves as we watched our father frantically check all his jacket and shirt pockets for any bits of tobacco he could find. His empty tobacco pouch meant he could not roll any fresh cigarettes. Without cigarettes, we understood Dad might become a little testy. For that reason, we knew it would be a long storm in more ways than one.

The Strap

In a two-storey schoolhouse, with bathrooms in the basement and three classrooms for Grades 1 to 3 on the main floor, my Grade 3 classmates and I sat at our desks. Our backs were straight, our arms with elbows kept together, and our hands held in a prayer-like fashion, pointing straight ahead on the desks in front of us. Our teacher, Mrs. Wimmer, demanded we sit in this manner. Before class, we heard rumours floating around the school that some boys had shot holes in the school water jug the night before. Petrified, we knew there would be retribution.

Mrs. Wimmer, tall and slender in her black pencil skirt and starched white blouse that looked as stiff as her unyielding face, marched to the front of the classroom. Her jet-black hair and painted-on eyebrows were a sharp contrast to the paleness of her skin. Small, beady bird eyes did not miss a thing as she scanned the room, her thin lips drawn together, forming pinch wrinkles around her mouth. Her long, skinny arms had her elbows jutting out like bones without skin as she placed her hands on her hips, preparing for a showdown.

"I want the three culprits to come to the front of the class and own up to what you did."

No one moved. We were all too terrified.

"I know who you are. Three of you brought BB guns into the school and shot holes in the water jug last night. Come forward."

Still, no one moved.

"So, now you are cowards on top of being hooligans," she continued, her voice rising in anger.

Mrs. Wimmer slid open the top right drawer of her desk and brought out a thick brown piece of leather. She slapped it on the edge of her desk. We all jumped. One girl behind me began to cry. I bit my lip, willing myself not to do the same.

Having lost patience, she pointed to three little boys.

"You, you, and you. Come up here."

The three nine-year-old boys she identified slowly left their seats and shuffled to the front of the room, their eyes huge and filled with terror.

"If you think you can get away with that kind of mischief and not pay for it, you have another thing coming."

She grabbed the first boy's hand and made him hold it out while she raised her arm and brought the strap down hard on his palm with a smacking sound. Twice more she struck him. The boy trembled and sobbed as his punishment ended. She directed him to return to his seat.

The second boy held back, looking for a means of escape. The teacher dragged him forward, intent on making an example of the boys. The strap snapped three times across the little boy's hand as he wailed in pain. When she finished, he rubbed his stinging hands together and walked down the aisle to his desk.

Michael, my third little classmate, looked horrified at what he had just witnessed.

"Come here," Mrs. Wimmer demanded of him.

"But I didn't do it. I didn't shoot holes in the jug," Michael cried out.

"Now you are a liar as well as a hoodlum. I said come here."

"But I didn't do it."

"Come here."

Mrs. Wimmer strode to where Michael stood, grabbed his hand, and brought the leather strap down as hard as possible. Michael winced, but he did not make a sound. Repeatedly, she strapped him. He never took his eyes from hers, refusing to give her the satisfaction of making him cry. Michael endured more strappings than the other two because he refused to let her break him. When she finished punishing him, he buried his burning hands deep inside his pants pockets and walked down the aisle past my desk. He glanced at me. I saw the hurt and determination in his eyes. Mrs. Wimmer screeched at him to return to his desk. Instead, he walked to the classroom door, opened it, and then closed it softly behind him. I believe he left the school and went home.

* * *

"Marilyn, is that you?"

Standing in a line-up at Timmy's, I turned to the voice behind me.

"Michael! How are you?" I asked the man with greying hair dressed in business pants, a shirt and tie, and a black leather jacket.

We briefly caught up on each other's lives, not having seen each other for nearly forty-five years. He was a consultant and gave me his business card, and I shared that I was a District Manager for a bank. We had both gone on to make something of ourselves. We talked about our families, and too soon, I was called up to place my order. Before I did, Michael touched my arm and said, "You know, I didn't do it."

I faced him, looking straight into his eyes and said, "I know."

Woman's Work

Turning over in bed, I raised my hand over my eyes to block out the sun's rays that teased my eyelids. My younger sister, Sharon, slept beside me. Careful not to disturb her, I slipped from under the warm blankets, found the clothes I had worn the day before, and hastily dressed my nine-year-old body. It was the beginning of another day on our farm in central Saskatchewan.

Quietly, so as not to awaken my four sleeping brothers and sisters, I slowly descended the stairs, my hand gliding along the wall as I went. Before I reached the last step, I heard a metallic clang and bump. My father let out a roar, followed by a chain of swear words. I stopped with my foot in mid-air.

"What did you do?" my mother cried out.

"The handle broke."

"Oh, for Gawd's sake! Look at this mess," my mother shouted.

"It's not my fault. The handle broke."

I scrunched up my nose. A putrid smell invaded the house, and I held a hand over my nostrils to block out the stench. Making my way into the porch, I saw my father and mother peering down the basement stairs, Dad holding a pail handle.

We did not have indoor plumbing. The bucket Dad had held was our toilet, a five-gallon metal pail that sat behind the furnace. A toilet seat balanced on top of the pail added a bit of comfort while we perched. After we finished, we closed the lid. When the pail filled, my father carried it and its reeking contents up the entire flight of stairs and disposed of the matter by dumping it in the pigpen.

This morning, the handle had broken loose from the bucket. The half-rusted pail bounced down the stairs, spewing its contents over the walls, the ceiling, the stairs, and the floor. The brown soupy excrement clung and dripped everywhere.

I inched forward.

My mother, spying me out of the corner of her eye, yelled, "Stay back."

I stopped. I did not move so much as a finger. Whenever Mom used that tone, I knew it was best to obey.

"What happened?" I asked in a small voice.

"Your father dropped the toilet pail down the stairs."

"I didn't drop it. It broke," he reiterated, holding up the pail handle and pointing to the rest of the pail lying on its side at the bottom of the stairs.

Dad walked to the kitchen, sat down on his chair at the head of the table and reached for a box of cornflakes. He shook some cereal into a bowl, added milk, and grabbed the sugar bowl.

"How can you eat?" my mother pressed. "Who's going to clean up this mess?"

My father plunged his spoon into the bowl of cereal and raised it to his mouth, ignoring her question. His silence suggested that it would not be him.

How could Dad eat with that horrible smell creeping through the rooms?

Mom stomped to the kitchen, dug around in a bottom cupboard, produced a large kettle, and pumped water into it from the hand pump in the porch. She carried the kettle to the stove and turned on the burner. While she waited for the water to heat, she searched for rags to use in the clean-up.

Dad chomped on his cornflakes, one hefty spoonful after another. Mom slammed around the kitchen, waiting for the kettle to heat. My younger brothers and sisters awakened and began their descent down the stairs.

"Marilyn, keep them back," Mom ordered.

"I have to go to the bathroom," my younger brother, Ronnie, whined.

"You'll have to go outside," Mom snapped.

"But I don't want to go outside. I want to use the potty downstairs."

"Not right now. Can't you see there is a mess to clean up? You can't go down into the basement."

"But Mommy, I have to go," Ronnie persisted.

I knew I had to deal with this situation quickly or my mother might explode. I grabbed my brother's hand and asked the others to follow me outside. We used an outhouse for emergencies, which this was. In the small wooden structure, I assisted my four-year-old brother, taking his pants down and holding him over the gaping hole in the bench so that he could have his morning pee. My other brothers and sisters followed suit, careful not to fall in.

Cautiously, we made our way back into the house. Mom was scrubbing everything in sight, repeatedly twisting her rag in the brown water with her bare hands. Chunks floated in the tub she carried outside to dispose of its contents. She filled the bucket once more with hot water from the stove and then balanced precariously on a chair at the top of the stairs as she stretched to wipe the ceiling before climbing down to clean the wall along one side, gagging from the smell. The excrement was under her fingernails and stuck to her skin. I even saw some in her hair. I don't know if it dripped on her head from the ceiling or if she unknowingly left it there after pushing her hair back with dirty hands.

My younger brothers and sisters crowded around the top of the basement stairs, watching Mom wash the wall along the stairwell. They wanted a good view of the fiasco below them.

"Marilyn, get them back before they fall," Mom growled at me from her spot halfway down the basement stairs. Her tub was once again full of brown water and floating chunks.

"Ew," Audrey said, wrinkling her nose in disgust when our mother picked up the bucket to take it outside and empty it again.

After ushering my younger brothers and sisters into the living room and turning on the television, I tiptoed back into the kitchen. Dad had finished his breakfast and now slurped his coffee. He looked up when I edged toward the basement stairs.

"Better not go down there," he said, noticing my intent before raising his cup and drinking his last bit of coffee.

Dad pushed back his chair and stood up. He walked to the porch, grabbed his cap off the hook, and headed outside. The screen door slammed behind him.

Flying Salamanders

As part of a Grade 4 and 5 split classroom in a one-room school, I fidgeted at my desk. The morning stretched on. I hated arithmetic. Unfortunately for me, that is all my teacher, Mr. Winkel, wanted to explain this morning. Fractions. I hated fractions most of all.

To make matters worse, it was raining. I let out a deep sigh and studied the rivulets of water coursing down the windowpane, wishing it would stop. The rain could ruin all our plans. I watched others in my class glancing toward the window and knew they felt the same.

Every noon hour, the boys and a handful of girls played softball. If the rain kept coming down, it would be too muddy to play, and the ball games were the highlight of the school day. Just as I was about to give up hope that we'd be able to play outside, the rain stopped and gave way to a bright and inviting sun.

As the noon hour crept closer, we waited impatiently, counting off every minute until we could gobble down our sandwiches and fruit before clambering out through the schoolhouse doors on our way to the ball diamond. Finally, that time arrived. We grabbed the bat and ball and headed for the diamond, hollering as we ran.

When we reached the ball diamond, we milled around as the two captains chose their teams. This time, unlike other days, I noticed something was not as it should be. The boys did not immediately take up their positions in the field. Instead, they scrambled around in the grass that grew up around the fence behind home plate. The boys had their heads down, conspiring about something. I, along with the other girls, edged closer to see why. Suddenly, the boys began flinging things at us. At first, we thought it was mud. All too soon, we realized the boys had captured salamanders they found scurrying in the weeds and now hurled in our direction. The boys flung the animals at us as we screamed, trying to get away.

Shock and horror slammed through me when I saw a boy running toward me with evil intent in his eyes and something in his hand. I turned to run but I did not get very far, slipping and sliding in the clay-like mud. The boy raised his hand, and I cried out as I felt a thud on my back, just below my hair and between my shoulder blades. I could feel the toenails digging through my shirt onto my back. I knew I had a salamander clinging to me. Nearly hysterical and screaming, I squirmed and jumped around trying to dislodge the six-inch-long creature from my clothes. One of my friends found a stick and used it to pry the amphibian off my back.

Together, we ran toward the school and away from the pesky boys. We knew better than to make a big deal of what the boys had done. If we did, the boys would see it as encouragement to torment us further. We spent the remaining recess making sure no boy got close enough lest they had another salamander to chuck our way.

The bell rang, announcing the end of the noon hour break. We all plodded to the school with heavy mud caked to our shoes. Our teacher scowled as we traipsed into class, leaving muddy footprints behind.

News of the lunch hour antics reached Mr. Winkel. He demanded to know who had instigated this abhorrent behaviour. We all refused to either admit to it or rat out our classmates. Reluctantly, he turned to write our social studies assignment on the blackboard. Behind his back, we looked at one another and tried not to giggle.

Mr. Winkel didn't know that a boy had placed a salamander in the teacher's top right-hand desk drawer. I imagined the long-toed animal crawling over his books and paper, waiting to be discovered. Collectively, in nervous anticipation, we held our breath. His finding the trapped animal would be a hoot. We could hardly wait for him to open the drawer and hear him shriek when he saw the intruder.

Much to our disappointment, this never happened. Mr. Winkel never opened the drawer during that class or the one after that. When the end-of-day bell rang, Mr. Winkel reminded us of our fraction homework, which evoked a loud groan. We hurried to the cloakroom and grabbed our coats and lunch kits before scrambling out the door to catch our waiting school buses for the ride home.

Eventually, we forgot about the poor creature locked away in the teacher's desk drawer. I don't know if Mr. Winkel found it and quietly disposed of it or if it died in the confines of that desk. To this day, I don't know what became of it. But I will remember what it felt like having a salamander digging its toes into my back, hanging on for dear life.

Riding a pig

On our small farm west of Middle Lake, my brothers, sisters, and I learned to work hard at an early age. For us, summer holidays did not include a trip to the lake or a visit to the mountains. Instead, we picked rocks, hauled bales, butchered pigs, cut up meat, hoed the garden, and canned berries. We all understood that if we wished to partake in the bounties of our farm, we had to do our share of the work to bring them to the table.

One summer, Larry, our sixteen-year-old cousin from Saskatoon, came out to help our dad with some of the more physically demanding chores that my siblings and I, too young, could not yet manage. Larry lived in the city but was a farm boy at heart. Not afraid to get dirty, he enjoyed a day of good, hard work to spur on his robust appetite. He loved working alongside our father, learning new things on the farm. He also enjoyed our mother's cooking, especially when she served up home-grown vegetables fresh from the garden or raspberries plucked from the bushes and served with sweet, thick cream straight from the cow.

One hot summer day, Larry boasted to my four younger brothers and sisters and me that he could ride a pig. I, eleven years old, and my younger siblings stood in complete awe. In our minds, being able to ride a pig elevated a person to the stature of a Greek god. No one could ride a pig. Larry, handsome in his clean work clothes, brushed back his shoulder-length wavy hair and stood by his words. He offered to prove it to us.

We all trudged behind him, heading to the barn that held our pigs.

A dark, smelly, rat-infested place, the pig barn also held a chop bin for easy access to feed the animals – hence the rats. Rats love chop. Most of us would not enter the barn if we didn't have to, but to see Larry ride a pig would be worth it. The barn had a connecting pigpen outside where the hogs rooted around, making themselves even dirtier and more disgusting.

All five of us climbed up on the fence that separated one pigpen from the other so we could better see the feat Larry was about to perform. Larry leaned on the fence and first one leg went over and then the other. His rubber boots sank into the deep, liquid mire. With each careful step he made, we could hear the suctioning sound of his boots in the pig manure. He warily made his way to one sow standing in the corner, suspiciously ogling him with her head down and her big droopy ears hanging on each side of her dirty snout. You could tell by her demeanour she did not like the looks of this human advancing on her. The other pigs had long rushed out of the inside pen to the adjoining outside pen, so she stood alone, just her and him. She could not escape.

Larry, arms stretched out on either side of him, slowly made his way toward the animal, muttering to her, almost as if to lull her into a trance. Warily, she watched him, uncertain of what this teenager was up to. When Larry grabbed for one of her ears, she let out a squeal and ran to one side of the pen, splaying muck in every direction, hitting Larry's face and clothes. Undeterred, he wiped his face with his sleeve and continued to croon to the frightened animal until she once again calmed down.

We sat on the fence, holding our breath. We watched Larry gain more confidence and he once again approached the pig. In one slick manoeuvre, Larry was astride the pig's back. We could not believe our eyes.

We all cheered and clapped for the short-lived victory. The raucous noise we made only frightened the animal more. The squealing, indignant pig plowed through the smelly manure with Larry flopping like a rag doll on her back. She spied her one true means of escape – the four-foot-high opening at the end of the pen. She thundered straight for it. Larry, realizing too late that he was in trouble, slammed into the barn wall above the door. The pig rushed outside, free of the burden she had born on her back.

Larry, the wind knocked out of him, fell on his back into the evil-smelling manure. It covered his hair and clothes and even began creeping into his ears. He struggled to stand up but kept slipping in the muck, filling his boots with pig excrement.

He reached out his hand and called for one of us to give him a hand. We all backed away.

Smelly manure covered every inch of Larry's body. He kept slipping and falling then struggling to get up again.

My siblings and I scrambled down from the fence and scattered in every direction. Loyalty to our cousin only went so far. Knowing the reaction our mother would have when Larry made his way to the house kept us at a distance as that part of the scene played out. My brothers hid in the pump house and my sisters hid in the trees while I hid behind the house. From our various vantage points around the yard, we witnessed Larry dive into a slough near our house. We saw him splash around in the murky water before resolutely climbing out, only marginally cleaner and dripping wet with the odd blade of grass hanging from his face. He traipsed toward the house. Funnily enough, he looked nothing like a Greek god now. As he opened the porch door and stepped inside the house, we could hear our mother's loud outbursts and admonishments.

"Oh, my Gawd!" she cried out. "What is that smell? Larry, you're soaking wet. Get changed out of those clothes," we heard her screech. "And don't you dare leave those stinking clothes in your room. Take them outside," she added.

We children quietly went about our business of trying to be invisible.

We could only assume the trouble that would follow for us, too.

At supper time, Larry, properly bathed and freshly clothed, had a persistent smell that seemed to ooze from every cell of his body and permeate the entire house. We all sat down at the table, not daring to look up.

Dad, at the head of the table, said, "Let's pray."

We clasped our hands, bowed our heads, and prayed out loud together.

With the meal prayer over, our father glanced around the table and, with a smirk on his face, said, "Does anyone care to tell me what that horrible smell is?"

Dad's chuckles filled the air and we realized we were not in trouble. We all began speaking at once, extolling Larry's amazing feat. Larry did not say a word. Mom sat there, shaking her head.

No More Peas, Please

6:00 a.m.

My mother, younger sister Sharon, and I stood with pails in hand, surveying the expanse of the vegetable plot before us. At fourteen, I knew that a workout, a marathon in the blistering heat, awaited us. Just two short months earlier, the fresh young plants lined up in the garden, lifting their leaves in a salute to the sun. Now, the dry corn leaves rustled in the early morning breeze. The broad leaves of the bean plants almost seemed to wave at me. Tired and ready to give up their bounty, the peas slouched under the weight of the plump pods clinging to the vines.

Wearing my customary shorts and halter top, I made my way to the first row of peas, damp with lingering dew. The snowy blossoms promised more to harvest in the coming days. Bending over and pushing the blighted leaves aside, I began plucking one pea pod after another, dropping them into the five-gallon pail resting before me on the ground. The plunking sound as the first pods hit the bottom of the plastic container seemed to startle the robins into song. Their sweet trill in the early morning made our job a little easier to bear.

After an hour, I no longer bent over the pea plants but squatted, my back sore as I searched for a more comfortable position to carry on my task. I brushed aside the leaves looking for the pods underneath. Groping for the thicker pods to pick, I felt something unusual, something bigger and not as hard, something that now moved. My breath caught and my heart pounded. A muddy-coloured salamander with its elongated body and sharp, finger-like toes scuttled away to hide under the next plant. I shrieked loud enough to awaken the dead. My mother ran toward me, hopping over the rows of peas to where I stood, trembling.

"What's wrong? What happened?" she asked, her eyes doing a quick once-over to ensure I wasn't hurt.

"Th-there's a salamander," I sobbed.

"Oh, that's all …" She turned to walk back to where she had left her pail two rows over and bent to resume picking.

I dashed to the house. Running hot water, I scoured my hands with soap to rid myself of the sensation of having touched the amphibian. Returning to the garden, I trembled as I reached for the next plant in case the salamander hid there. It took all my courage to continue as the heating rays of the sun pushed me forward. I knew how important it was to get as many peas picked before the sun's intensity became too great.

My back cried from the constant bending. Two hours had passed. We were about half finished with the pea patch. We laboured on. After another two hours, we were in the home stretch, but I did not feel like we were winning. The green expanse of the unpicked rows of peas mocked me, daring me to give up. I continued picking row after row, pod after pod. Down on my knees, I bent and picked. Sweat built on my brow and trickled down my back. The black dirt on which I knelt scorched my skin. My hair dripped and salty water ran into my eyes. I swiped at my forehead with the back of my hand, leaving a dark smudge near my temple. Glancing at Sharon, I noticed she too crawled on her hands and knees, pushing her pail full of peas ahead of her.

I persevered, dragging my pail behind me. This pail, the one I had emptied many times already that morning, was filling for the last time. The end was near. We hurried to finish that last row of peas. I met up with my mother and sister.

Done.

Finally.

I slowly brought my aching body to an upright position, leaning backward to stretch the tension out of my back. A sense of accomplishment washed over me. I looked over and saw my mother and sister doing the same. I grasped the pail by the handle to lift it. We made our way through the garden and walked a short distance to the house. Inside, my four younger brothers and sisters sat in a circle around the square galvanized wash tub. We emptied pail after pail of peas, filling three or four washtubs in total. Each child held a dish in their lap, methodically popping pea pods open and running their fingers along them to push the peas from the pods into their dish. The children sat like that for hours. When their dish filled with peas, they emptied it into a larger dishpan and then returned to their chair and began filling their bowl all over again.

The children welcomed the sight of the three of us returning from the garden. This meant they had more hands to help with the shelling. It also meant the pea picking was over for the day. They finished shelling all the peas in the washtub and dashed outside to play.

Mom went to the kitchen, ran a sink of water, and began washing the peas. Bent over the sink, she scooped one green handful after another, scanning them for broken pea pods, little bugs, or other debris that may have gotten into the peas. Mom placed a dishtowel over the dishpans filled with freshly washed peas. The dishtowels helped keep flies off. The large pots of water on the stove reached the boiling point. Mom poured four cups of peas into the pot and let them cook precisely twelve minutes before hastily pouring the water and peas through a colander. Once the peas cooled enough, we packed them into previously washed one-litre milk containers. We blanched and packaged peas most of the afternoon.

Because the pea picking usually began the last week of July and extended into August, the warm weather and the boiling water on the stove increased the humidity and heat in the house. Flies buzzed lazily in the kitchen looking for a place to land, their efforts thwarted by the dishtowels Mom used to cover everything to keep them off.

By the end of the day, even though her back and legs ached, Mom always wore a look of satisfaction on her face after she packed another nineteen one-litre cartons of peas neatly inside her large freezer.

Tomorrow would be raspberry picking. The day after, it would be pea picking again. And so, it continued for two or three weeks until the pea vines and the raspberry bushes, depleted of their bounty, had Mom satisfied that she could do no more. Daily, she tracked everything in her food journal, so she knew how much she had put away. This tracking allowed her to compare it to previous years to make certain she had enough to feed her family over the long winter months.

Rock Picking

The early morning sun poured through our second-story bedroom window, washing our faces and kissing the night away. Outside a robin twittered. We heard the repeated clanging of the bell around our lead cow's neck as she and the other three cows clambered their way to the barn for their morning milking.

Sharon and I snuggled deep under the rough woollen blanket, trying to push the sun away and pretend we hadn't heard Mom's soft call from the bottom of the stairs.

"Girls, it's time to get up," she called again.

We groaned simultaneously.

"Come on, girls. The longer you take, the hotter it'll get."

We knew Mom was right. Moms have a way of always being right.

Together we crawled out of bed and tugged on our work clothes – long dark pants and long-sleeved shirts. Yes, it would be hot today, but we needed the material on our legs and arms to protect us from the sun and the bruises and scratches that were sure to come.

We knew we'd better hurry before Mom had to call us again. Even this early in the morning and with the boundless energy of youth, we made a game of bouncing down the stairs, stepping to the left, then to the right, missing this step, catching the other. We practiced our movements to see which one could reach the bottom of the stairs without hitting a step that creaked. We felt that perfecting this manoeuvre would be handy in the years to come when we began going out with friends or on dates and perhaps missed a curfew. Little did we know Mom had an uncanny ability to hear a cotton ball hit the floor and a door squeak even before it opened. Nothing wrong with Mom's hearing.

In the kitchen, Mom stood in front of the stove stirring the cream of wheat as it *bluck-blucked* in the white enamel pot on the stove.

"Good morning, girls."

"Morning. Ah, Mom," we complained. "Why do you always make that stuff?"

"Because your father likes it."

"But we don't. Do we have to eat it?"

"You should. It'll give you lots of energy."

We sat down on our chairs and waited for the porridge.

Dad and our brother, Murray, came up the front steps into the house, and the screen door slammed behind them as they each set down two pails of milk beside the cream separator.

"It's going to be a hot one," Dad said as he dragged his red hankie from his pocket and mopped his face. He and my brother washed their hands before sitting at the table where Mom quickly dished out the cream of wheat to everyone. I think she purposely gave my sister and me a smaller helping, knowing that neither of us had a taste for it. Dad immediately reached for the box of cornflakes and began shaking out the contents onto his cream of wheat.

"Ugh. Dad! How can you eat that stuff?" we cried.

"Just like this," he said as he mushed it all together and, with a devilish grin, raised it to his mouth to devour a huge spoonful.

Murray, three years younger than I, always looked for ways to imitate our father, to be just like him. Gauging our reaction, he did the same, and together my dad and brother polished off their respective bowls of cream of wheat and cornflakes.

Mom poured the pails of milk into the top bowl of the cream separator. It hummed as milk spewed out of one spout and cream from the other. The tranquillizing whir of the cream separator almost lured us back to sleep as we all sat at the kitchen table with our elbows up and our hands propped on our heads. Hypnotized by the soothing sound of the cream separator, we ate the disgusting cereal in the bowls in front of us. When all the milk had run through the separator, Sharon and I would have the unenviable task of washing all the spouts and the thirty-two discs that made up the separator. I hated how the dishrag got that slimy feeling as we scrubbed each disc clean and then dried them one by one so they would be ready for the suppertime milking.

Mom sat down next to Dad, and in a moment, Dad's hand rested softly on hers. He smiled at her. It was an action so simple and yet so tender that when I look back now in later years, I am grateful for our wonderful, loving parents. Mom's sitting down cued my sister and me to get up from the table and begin preparing lunch for all eight of us: two parents and six children. After breakfast, Mom directed our three younger siblings to dress for the day as my dad and Murray went outside to check over the tractor. Sharon and I finished packing lunch, then quickly washed and dried the dishes.

Today we picked stones just as we had done every day for the past week and a half. We continued to do so until we had the fields clear of the obtrusive objects that greatly irritated our father. He had his pride, and an excellent farmer did not have his black summer-fallowed fields spotted with stones. Besides looking bad, rocks wrecked his machinery.

By the time we made our way outdoors, Dad and Murray had the tractor greased and filled with diesel. Proper maintenance was important to Dad, and he took good care of everything he owned. And those he loved.

As he started up the tractor, my sister and I ran to him and begged, "Can we ride in the bucket? Ple-a-s-e."

Dad told us to stand back as he lowered the bucket of the tractor's front-end loader so that we could scramble into it. Murray hesitated before deciding to ride on the tractor with Dad. Sometimes our father let Murray work the levers or turn the steering wheel. Dad lifted the front-end loader with Sharon and me in it as he drove past the kitchen window. He gave Mom a cheery wave to let her know with that signal that he had the three oldest children with him as we made our way to the "other quarter." We owned four quarters of land, three of which were together in one section and another a couple of miles away, which we labelled the "other quarter."

We lumbered down the road, Dad and my brother behind the steering wheel and Sharon and I in the bucket, picking up speed as we bounced along the gravel road, making our way to our destination. After ten minutes, Mom, along with our three youngest siblings, caught up to us in the half-ton truck and followed us to the field.

Dad drove the tractor to a central spot in the field, and then we all fanned out, picking up as many rocks as we could carry before stumbling back to the tractor with our load and heaving the stones into the bucket. We made these trips back and forth, time after time, our shoes filling with dirt, our fingers slamming between rocks, our faces burning in the blistering heat. We worked hard.

A creative bunch with a good sense of humour, we made games of it such as who could make the most trips to the tractor, who could carry the most rocks, who could spot a rock the furthest away, who could get to the stone first before Dad had to point out that we missed it. We sang songs and rhymes to lessen our load, and when so exhausted we thought we would drop, Dad called out, "Dinner."

Mom opened the truck's end gate, and we all piled into the back of the truck as she doled out jam-soaked sandwiches. Meat sandwiches only went bad in the heat, and we did not own a cooler. A real treat was the two-quart jar filled with an orange drink Mom mixed up. Dad raised the old metal syrup pail filled with milk-diluted coffee, long gone cold and sour, consumed the contents and then wiped his mouth on his shirt sleeve.

We enjoyed this time sitting together discussing the progress we made and how much more we needed to do by the end of the day. Dad praised us for how hard we worked. That little piece of recognition, along with food and drink, went a long way in getting us going again for the afternoon.

Sometimes a neighbour drove by and we all waved, as neighbours did. Dad told us later how his friends envied our family. They said Dad's kids knew how to work and never complained. What Dad may or may not have known was his children only followed the fine examples laid out by him and our mother. Always working hard. Together. Never complaining. Mom worked the hardest and the longest. Up each morning before any of us, she was always the last to crawl between the sheets at night.

With another day of picking stones ending, Mom stood at the stove preparing supper for the eight of us. Believe me, after picking stones all day, she had a ravenous crew to feed. Sharon and I tried to keep the younger children amused because we knew the more time Mom could devote to cooking, the sooner we could eat. She always whipped up a full two-course meal in no time at all.

Exhausted, our leg and arm muscles crying from overuse, our heads pounding from the heat, we basked in our overriding sense of accomplishment. Supper over, it was now time to relax as we crowded in front of the TV.

"Kids, come here."

We all rose from our spots on the floor and joined our parents in the kitchen. Dad sat on his chair in the centre of the room with Mom standing behind him, her hand gently resting on his shoulder. We knew, or at least suspected, what was coming next. We gathered around them.

"You all worked hard today. We got a lot done." Dad would pause as his eyes teared up slightly and he smiled his gentle, loving smile. Mom squeezed his shoulder, and he continued.

"All of you line up, oldest to youngest. We have something for you."

With that, we all found our position and formed a line in order of age. One by one, we accepted the small payment Dad handed out to each of us. Not much, maybe a few quarters, but it meant the world to us. We had very little money of our own. The look of appreciation on our parents' faces meant the most. We were a little army of pleasers, content to make our parents happy.

We all scurried off to our bedrooms, excitedly talking about what we would do with our newfound wealth. As we closed our eyes and succumbed to sleep, we knew that with the dawning sun, a day much the same as today awaited us. It would be just as dirty, just as long and hot, just as backbreaking. We knew that the work had to be done. We didn't complain. This intensive labour continued summer after summer until Dad could finally afford to purchase a rock picker.

Alleluia!

Sunday Ball Games

Sundays were great! We got home from church and gobbled down the home-cooked meal of fried chicken, mashed potatoes, home-grown peas, and fresh garden salad. For dessert, we had cream puffs stacked high with whipped cream and freshly picked raspberries or warm crab apple pie fresh from the oven. Oh, yes. Sunday dinners were great.

We ate a lot because we needed our strength and endurance for what lay ahead. With the meal over, my sisters and I jumped from the table and washed the dishes. The sooner we completed the task, the sooner we could begin.

Like clockwork, promptly at one o'clock, the first neighbour's vehicle arrived, sometimes a car, sometimes a half-ton truck with everyone in the truck box. We could hear them talking and laughing above the sound of the motor and the blatant horn honking that sent our dog, Sporty, into a frenzy. He loved these weekly events as much as anyone. He raced around and barked, and no one got angry at him or pushed him away.

A second vehicle arrived and sometimes a third. On a sunny warm day, neighbours occasionally walked to our farm by cutting across a field. We met them out in the yard before we all strolled to the ball diamond in the pasture. No one seemed to mind the odd cow pie if it wasn't in the way or still steaming.

They all came, young and old alike. Everyone knew the rules. The captains chose their teams by picking the youngest ones first so they did not feel left out. We lacked enough ball gloves for everyone, and only those holding key positions enjoyed the luxury of padding on their hands. Those less fortunate took up their positions with nothing but bare hands to catch the ball.

Dad umped every game. No one disputed this. Once positioned soundly behind the catcher, he rumbled the words "Play ball!" and the game began.

"Ste-e-e-rike!" Dad yelled with all the zest of a professional ump and a cheer went up from the outfield.

Our neighbour and long-time friend, Leonard, pretended to knock the umpire on the head with his bat. The game was on with lots of cheering, laughing, trying, and encouraging. The older ones helped the younger ones. There was no fancy equipment, only a sense of fun and sharing.

As the afternoon wore on, the rules of the game slackened even more. Perhaps someone trying to slide into third base noticed too late that it was gone. The umpire, a man of rules, insisted that third base needed to be touched before the runner could advance to home plate. The pursuit began. All the members of one team chased the opposing team members, the one in possession of third base. As the keeper of the game, the umpire knew when to end this folly and call the teams back to the game.

We thought of ourselves as skilled ballplayers, but size limited some. My youngest sister, Cindy, came up to bat. She concentrated so hard on hitting the ball that she did not see the teenage neighbour boy, Danny, standing between her and the catcher. The ball sailed across the plate. Cindy struck down with the heavy bat, however, Danny's bat connected with the ball and sent it flying. Thinking she had hit the ball; Cindy ran as fast as her legs could carry her to first base with the older boy right behind. Someone in the outfield threw his body in front of the hurling missile and redirected it back into the ball diamond. Danny, sensing the urgency, picked up Cindy. He ran to second base, carrying his round-faced, pink-cheeked teammate to safety. Cindy giggled, demanding he put her down. Did he not know the seriousness of the game?

Occasionally, a grazing cow wandered into our makeshift ball diamond. We called time-out so we could chase her back behind the barn. Sometimes the bigger guys hit the ball so hard that it landed in the slough. No problem. We simply took off our shoes, rolled up our pant legs, and waded in to retrieve it. One time the ball landed in water so deep that we could not get to it. That summer, we had to wait for the slough to dry up. It also meant a cancellation of our Sunday ball games for several weeks until we could get our ball back.

These summer ball games became the highlight of each week. Growing up, family and neighbours shared in the hard work, so it only followed that everyone shared in the fun times as well.

Now, many years later, we all share fond memories of those warm summer Sundays when we gathered at the mound and the ump roared, "Let's play ball!"

The Idiosyncrasies Of Mr. Fulmann

I attended school in Middle Lake, a small town nestled next to Lucien Lake, which was established as a regional park in 1967. Even after the designation, neighbouring farmers continued letting their cattle wander down to the lake for a drink. The village of Middle Lake, with a population of approximately 250 people, prided itself on being a close-knit community. Its residents consisted mainly of German or Hungarian descent. Most families numbered five to nine offspring, sometimes more, and the majority lived on farms just like I did.

As children, closed off from the rest of the world, we did not learn acceptance of others different from us, different from our parents. When it came time to hire new teachers, the school unit office in Humboldt sometimes struggled to find ones willing to move to our small town. Some teachers could not imagine living so secluded with few amenities.

Most of our parents wanted only for their children to learn to read and write and do arithmetic. Many of the boys missed school to help on the farm during seeding and harvest time, much more important than school since the family's livelihood depended on it. Similarly, not all parents felt it necessary for girls to have a Grade 12 education. Many girls dropped out of school early to work at home or get low-paying jobs with little prospect of bettering themselves.

Into this environment, short, stocky Mr. Fulmann lumbered his way into our classroom and our lives. When he walked, he shifted his weight from one foot to the other, his brown shoes squeaking in protest as his weight came down. I say brown shoes because he wore those same brown shoes every day no matter what colour suit he had on. It did not seem to matter to him if his shoes matched his clothes or not. It must have been the only pair he owned. When he returned to his classroom after supervising outside on the playground, we would find him at his desk polishing those brown shoes with a cloth he kept in his desk drawer. He rubbed those shoes until they gleamed. Classes could not start until he finished polishing them. We all sat and waited. And watched. Mesmerized. Trying not to giggle.

The top of his squarish head shone from his lack of hair and the moisturizing cream he liberally applied each day during class. He kept the navy jar of lotion in his top right-hand desk drawer. After assigning us our work, he would saunter to the back of the classroom, where he had a rectangular mirror mounted on the wall to look at himself as he massaged the cream into his scalp. Round and round his hands went, working the lotion into his skin. When he finished applying the cream to his head, he rubbed the excess over his round, pudgy hands before giving himself one last look in the mirror. The smell of this lotion permeated the classroom. We students held our books over our noses, trying to block out the smell and cover our smirks.

I don't know if he saw in his reflection what others saw – a huge, wrinkled face with dark eyes that gave nothing away. His sagging Nixon-like jowls shook when he moved his head and his thin lips seemed to be drawn in as if holding back something he wanted to say. I will never know why he studied the mirror so closely every day. Perhaps he suffered from OCD or maybe his insecurity had him doubting his value. I don't know. Whatever the reason, our pubescent tendencies had us quietly poking fun at him behind his back and jeering as he made his way slowly back to the front of the class.

Mr. Fulmann's suit jackets always fit him snugly. The one button strained around his middle so that the open pleat in the jacket's back always spread open. His skinny shirt ties led a path from his thick neck, over his round chest, and disappeared behind the buttoned lapel, only to resurface again somewhere near his waist.

Mr. Fulmann refused to call students by their first names. Ever. He always called his students by their last names. It immediately sounded harsh, almost military-like. I often wondered if using last names distanced him from his students. I think it did. He did not develop a connection with any of us. He remained aloof. We seldom saw him smile. While he called us all by our last names, he demanded we call him Mr. Fulmann as a show of respect. Years later, I can imagine how difficult it must have been for someone new to the community trying to find acceptance in our town and school.

Mr. Fulmann collected many issues of the National Geographic magazine over the years. One thing he loved to have his class do was tear them apart, losing the distinctive yellow border of each glossy cover. He insisted that we reconstruct every article inside the magazine into a little booklet. He wanted us to make a new front and back cover using Bristol board. We carefully illustrated the covers to reveal the contents of the newly created manuals. We seldom studied or even talked about the magazine contents, but he seemed to derive endless pleasure from having us create these new volumes. I enjoyed this project because it allowed me to be creative and scrutinize the contents of this time-honoured publication. Our family could not afford such a luxury as this magazine, so having it at my fingertips in school became a real treat.

The school year with Mr. Fulmann unfolded, and our social studies class became one of interest, especially to the boys. During this time, each classroom had a world map rolled up at the top of the blackboard. One tug of the faded pink ribbon that bound it had the map tumbling to display brightly coloured countries all around the world. A wooden rod ran along the bottom of the map to help weigh it down. It seemed funny that even if Mr. Fulmann did not refer to it during class, he always wanted the map down. Perhaps he enjoyed looking at it, or maybe the reason was a little more depraved than that.

One day, toward the end of the class, before the bell rang, Mr.

Fulmann walked to the back of the room.

"Kramer, roll up the map," he commanded from his vantage point.

Karen Kramer, the prettiest girl in the class, also wore the most fashionable clothes. Most of us wore hand-me-downs or home-sewn clothes. Karen had the privilege of wearing store-bought miniskirts, a new trend in the late 1960s. She loved her miniskirts, and it appeared Mr. Fulmann did too. Karen relished her status as a fashion icon in our school but looked uneasy as she left her desk and made her way to the front of the class.

She bent over, rolling the map around the wooden rod at the bottom. Mr. Fulmann and the boys in the class ogled Karen, struggling to roll up the map. Her arms reached up, her short dress rising higher. She tried to hold one side of her skirt down with one hand while using the other hand to continue rolling the map. Of course, this did not work. She let go and the map dropped. She began rolling it again, reaching the point where she stretched up to tie the map in place with the ribbon, her skirt riding up, but was not able to manage the task.

Frustrated with everything that was going on, Mr. Fulmann's perversion and the boys snickering, I rose from my desk to help her.

"Krenn, sit down," he barked at me from the back of the room.

"But I was just …" I began.

"SIT DOWN!"

Obediently, I slid back into my desk.

Karen let the map fall for the third time. She turned to face him, tears brimming in her eyes. She glared at him.

"We are waiting," Mr. Fulmann jeered at her.

Karen brazenly stared back at him before she walked to her desk and sat down.

"Kramer. I told you to roll up that map."

"Do it yourself," she responded.

At that moment, the girls in the class seemed to erupt in a silent cheer.

United in an unspoken sisterhood, secretly admiring our classmate who dared to stand up to our teacher, we collectively held our breath. Karen remained seated at her desk, staring straight ahead, until the bell rang, announcing the class was over. Mr. Fulmann never said another word.

After that, Karen continued to wear her miniskirts and Mr. Fulmann continued to rub lotion over his head and hands. Thinking back on this unfortunate event, Karen's defiance stirred a little sexual revolution in our school. Over time, more girls began wearing miniskirts, albeit they were homemade. Hotpants became the rage in the 1970s and I had one or two that I convinced my mom to sew for me, though not as short as the other girls. A few girls choosing to go without bras had their mothers dismayed. While the adolescent and high school boys continued to push the boundaries with their sexually inappropriate comments and gestures, the girls became less tolerant and stood up to them.

The winds of change blew in our small town, but it would take a worldwide hurricane to have the impact needed for girls and women to be considered as more than sex objects and second-class citizens.

But it had begun.

A Winning Situation

Attending school during my adolescent and teen years, nothing made me feel more uncomfortable and self-conscious than our physical education classes. I remember scanning the six-day school calendar only to discover that I had physical education three times in a six-day cycle, three times too many for my liking.

I hated everything about that class. It began with the initial time before class spent in the girls' change rooms where we all had to get out of our regular clothes and into our green shorts and white t-shirts, our school colours. Mom always taught us modesty. We did not even change in front of our siblings, let alone our classmates. My shyness made me rush for one of the two toilet stalls where I changed into my gym gear. Struggling within the cubicle's confinement usually made me late for class. My tardiness inevitably evoked comments from our gym instructor and brought me unwanted attention.

In those years of adolescence transitioning into teenage years, I didn't seem to fit into my skin. My hormones took hold and shook my body up. During this time, all students had to complete a physical assessment presided over by our gym teacher. First, he recorded my height on a graph laid out on his clipboard. He then got me to step on a scale. He hollered my weight from one end of the gym down to the other for the entire class to hear. Next, I had to run around the gym, stopping every few minutes to take my pulse and record it on the same clipboard as my height and weight. With that complete, my heart pounded like a jailbird trying to break free, and I felt weak from exhaustion.

Without a break, I next had to do chin-ups on a bar I could not reach even if I jumped. The gym teacher asked some of the stronger boys to lift me. Once I had my hands wrapped tightly around the cold metal bar, I dangled there like a rag doll, unable to pull my chin up to the bar. This last exercise hammered away what remaining ounce of self-respect and dignity I had left. Humiliated, I crept back to the changing room, refusing to strip naked and take a public shower alongside my classmates. Instead, I changed back into my bellbottom jeans and shirt and hoped I didn't smell too bad.

Spring's arrival brought our physical activities out to the school grounds as we all began preparing for the school track and field event. I always liked the idea of competing in broad jump. I stood in line with the other girls in my age group. When my turn came, I ran as hard as I could, pounding my foot down on the board and propelling myself through the air before landing in the sand. Because I could not balance myself properly when I jumped, my span didn't compare to the other girls because my hands plunged into the sand behind me, preventing my fall backward. This tactic, of course, significantly reduced my score. I failed at this challenge.

Well, if I couldn't run and jump, perhaps I was better at throwing things. I tried discus. Striking the half-bent pose with the metal disc in my hand, I sought to master the pirouette; releasing the disc in a magnificent sailing motion for it to land meters away from where I stood. That did not happen. Often, my carefully orchestrated spins failed. The disc landed on either side of me or sometimes even behind me. It never landed in front of me where it should. The same thing happened with shot put. Throwing the heavily weighted metal ball, I swear half of my shoulder blade attached itself and flew out of its joint along with the ball. I remember the gym instructor crossing his arms, looking down at his sneakers, and shaking his moustache-encumbered face.

Time for the races. I tried the short sprints and then the longer dashes. I tried the relay races and the hurdles. Time after time, I brought up the rear or fell over the roughly constructed hurdles. In an exercise in diplomacy, the team tried to tell me they wanted someone else, someone who could run.

I went home determined to make it in whatever competition I could. I had watched a friend, one with long legs, run and throw herself in an effortless glide over the bar of the high jump. She made it look so easy. I resolved that I could do it too.

After school one sunny afternoon on our farm, I found two boards and pounded them into the ground to create a high jump stand. Instead of a cushioned pad to land on, like at school, I substituted with a pile of straw. My younger brother and sister volunteered to move the bar up each time I successfully cleared it. The first few times at the lower bar, I made it over rather effortlessly. But the bar steadily moved up. Running faster to launch myself higher, I leaped into the air and pushed myself over the bar. I came crashing down into the straw, landing with a thud and felt my thumb twist in an unnatural direction. I cried out as the piercing pain made my thumb immovable. Through tears, I glanced down and noticed my hand beginning to swell.

Seeing me injured, my younger siblings galloped to the house, yelling as they ran. I brought up the rear, tenderly holding my hand as I wandered to the house, sobbing. My mother looked at my thumb. She tried to move it but that only solicited a piercing scream from me. She summoned my father to drive me the thirty minutes to see a doctor.

Several hours later, I returned home brandishing a cast where only the tips of my fingers peeked out. It stretched right up to the middle of my forearm. My thumb still throbbed, but the hard enclosure held my finger in a place that made it feel a little better. The unyielding plaster around my hand captivated my brothers and sisters and they could not get enough of touching it.

The next day at school, my classmates exhibited the same amount of awe and respect for the cast as my siblings had. Realizing this as my way out, I proclaimed to everyone at school that I had suffered a sports-related injury. In doing so, I sounded like an actual athlete. This impairment provided me with an escape from competing in any sports events in the upcoming track and field meet. I maintained my self-respect and the regard of my classmates. I no longer had to attend gym classes or practice for the field meet. Instead, I remained in my classroom, reading a book. I much preferred that pursuit over physical activity any day. I had fallen into a winning situation all around.

Running Of The Bull

It was a brilliant day in July 1970 when my brother Murray, ten years old, and I, on the verge of becoming a teenager, made our way through the cow pasture. The sun splashed down on the two of us as we slowly picked our way through the dense undergrowth. Even though we had called for the cows, they had not come back to the barn on their own, forcing us to set out and look for them. The cows probably lazed in the shade of the trees in the far northwest corner of the pasture. We followed the cow trail in that direction, hoping to find them.

We chatted as we strolled along, Murray on the lookout for gophers and I absorbing the day's beauty. Meandering down the path, I spied a patch of buttercups, their sunny heads swaying in the breeze. I walked closer, taking in the magnificence of the lemon-coloured solitary flowers with the fuzzy stems and leaves. I picked a few and stuck them in my hair. Only later, as an adult, did I learn how poisonous buttercups are for cattle. On this day, the only thing that concerned me was picking some of the buttery-coloured flowers as my brother called for me to hurry.

Rising to my feet from having knelt amid the flowers, I heard my brother yell, "Run, Marilyn!"

Looking in the direction Murray pointed, I froze with fear. Two thousand pounds of heaving, trembling muscles thundered through the undergrowth. The bronze-coloured bull had his massive head down, his nostrils flaring as he charged toward us. We saw how easily he mowed down the brush and shrubs as if they were nothing. His russet hair glinted in the sunlight, and his robust frame and sheer size and strength threatened to end our young lives.

"RUN!!" Murray cried out again. "Climb the tree."

I ran for the tree my brother pointed to and scraped and skinned my arms and legs, trying to pull myself up into it and out of the path of the charging bull. Murray pushed on my bottom, providing me with some leverage.

Sitting on the branch and out of harm's way, I called down to my brother, "Murray, climb up! Quick!"

I reached down for his hands to pull him up. The tree bough groaned as I tried to lift my brother to safety. We could hear the angry animal snorting and breathing only a few feet from where my brother stood. In one last combined effort, we got Murray up into the tree beside me. Just in the nick of time. The tree's branch sagged under our combined weight and threatened to snap. Had it broken, we would have toppled right on top of the burly beast that stomped the earth below us. We sat in the tree, watching the brute shake with irritability and fury, in awe of the immense physical power of this animal. We braced ourselves and clung to the branch, waiting for the powerful beast to ram his head into the trunk of the tree, at which point we would have fallen. However, this never happened. We quaked, knowing how close we came to being trampled and mauled by the raging bull.

After a while, the bull grew tired of pacing and stomping beneath the tree. Casting us one last surly glare, the animal lumbered off. We waited in the tree's leafy canopy until we thought it safe to crawl down. Looking over our shoulders, we ran and scrambled through the prickly bramble that grew along the pasture's edge. The barbed wire snagged our shirts as we attempted to slide under it to safety. Trying to untangle my shirt from the sharp barbs of the wire fence, I heard it rip as I pulled myself free. Once on the other side of the fence, we ran home to tell our parents about our narrow escape.

I remember sharing with our father how close Murray and I had come to being seriously injured or killed by the bull. Dad remained somewhat skeptical of what we told him. I think, perhaps, he thought we exaggerated to make a better story. A few weeks later, the bull charged another two of my siblings. They, like Murray and me, narrowly escaped.

After happening twice, Dad could not take any more chances. The bull had to go. He phoned and made the arrangements. The following week, the livestock truck came to our farmyard and backed up to the barn. The truck driver and my father put the loading ramps and walls in place and loaded the bull onto the truck. All of us children lined up and waved good riddance to the angry animal that had threatened us. We could hear the bull stamping and huffing inside the rocking truck as it made its way down our driveway. We heaved a collective sigh of relief as they hauled our archenemy to his just reward.

Moving Cows

Growing up, I always chose to complete indoor chores such as ironing clothes, baking cookies, cleaning the house, and watching my younger brothers and sisters. I despised, and avoided if I could, all the outdoor chores such as picking rocks, hauling bales, gardening, and moving cattle. My sister, Sharon, loved being outside and engaging in strenuous physical labour. One of her favourite jobs was moving cattle.

On our family farm, our father had a herd of cattle that he always kept near the barn during the winter to help shelter them from the harsh prairie temperatures. Keeping them close also allowed them easy access to the hay bales at feeding time. Having an ample supply of water during the winter was also important. Once a day during the winter, Dad called Sharon and Murray to help him steer the animals from the fence behind the barn. Collectively, they drove the cows to the pumphouse where Dad thawed the ice in the trough so the cows could take turns drinking water before returning to the fenced-in corrals.

I watched from inside our warm house as my father, sister, and brother pulled their necks deep down inside their coats and stamped their feet so they could stay warm while they waited for each cow to take a drink from the water trough. For a moment, I felt a twinge of guilt because I could stay in our cozy house and enjoy the heavenly smell of the pork roast cooking in the oven. After each animal had taken their turn at the water trough, Sharon waved her arms to guide the animals back to the fence. Even in the house, I heard the cows bellowing and imagined I could hear the crisp crunch of their hooves on the snow as they trudged back to the corral.

Sharon skirted around the fresh, plopped cow pies on the packed snow, still steaming as the warm waste met with the cold air. After the last cow finished drinking, Sharon had a smile on her face as she slammed the fence gate shut and made her way back to the house. Yearning for something warm in their bellies, my father and brother followed. I hurried to the stove to help my mother serve up the meal.

Each spring, Dad eagerly prepared to move his herd to the lake pasture. This pasture, located approximately one and a half miles southwest of our farm site, had a small body of water bordering our property and that of our neighbours. In this pasture, the cows grazed on the rich green sprouts that pushed their way through the crusty ground. The cows had plenty of room to move around and get their fill of the young green pasturage. The lake provided an excellent source of water. At the end of summer, we brought the cattle back to the farmyard pasture for the winter.

From my perch on our bed, I watched Sharon drag her waist-length auburn hair into a ponytail and heard the snap of the elastic as she tugged her ponytail tight. Unfortunately, this time I had to help move the cattle, too. Sharon hurried from our second-story bedroom as she trotted down the stairs to the front door of the house, calling to the rest of the family to hurry. Dad, already seated in the half-ton truck and eager to get this trek started, repeatedly blew the horn. Mom, my brother, and I made our way outside, not nearly as eager as Sharon.

We gathered at the fence beside the barn, hoping the lead cow would emerge from the bawling cows as they milled around. The one cow always took the lead in the procession to the lake. As the herd's matriarch, she had been through this exercise many times and knew the routine and the route. Like sheep, the rest of the cows followed her.

Dad called, "Come, Boss," and soon our lead cow came forth, taking her place in front of the others. With the cow ready, my father instructed my brother to open the gate. Dad followed in the truck so he could herd them on their journey, chasing down any strays that struck out on their own. Conveniently, I jumped in the truck box to hitch a ride so I wouldn't have to run all the way.

Sharon, already off, could easily keep up with the running cattle as they thundered toward the lake. My sister skimmed along the ground with her auburn ponytail flying out behind her. She made her way through the field, over the hill, and around a slough. Sharon quickly brought the meandering cows back to the herd. She kept them all moving. With her arms waving, my sister let out a whoop as she had them all on track and moving as one symbiotic troupe. This time, like so many others, Sharon ran bare-footed because she found it easier than having to deal with dirt-filled shoes as she sped along through the summer fallow field. She had no time for such annoyances. She once told me she liked the feel of her toes in the freshly cultivated earth and the oneness she felt with nature. I loved to watch her run. She was as swift as a deer.

Sharon noticed a young heifer veering off to the right of the path away from the other cows. Immediately, Sharon pursued her. Dad called to my sister from the truck. He said that he would keep following the herd if she could round up that one cow and get her to the lake. Sharon waved her acknowledgment and hurried after the stray animal. She quickly encircled it and headed the cow off before it got too far. This young cow did not know the route, which made it difficult for Sharon to bring her the rest of the way to the lake pasture. Sharon looked across the field. She saw Murray running across the summer fallow on the other side of the cow, directing the heifer. With my brother and sister flanking both sides of the animal to make sure it didn't get lost, they escorted it to the lake pasture.

Dad waved a greeting as he saw my brother and sister shepherding the stray back into the folds of the herd. From my seat in the truck box, I cheered them on. I hollered for them to join me. Murray jumped on but Sharon declined, preferring to continue running instead.

Nearing our destination, I watched Sharon push some stray hair back from her face as she slowed down from an all-out run to a casual jog. The cows at the gate to the pasture bawled and milled around. Murray jumped off the truck to open the gate. The lead cow led the others inside the fence. Sharon assisted him by chasing the remaining animals into the enclosure.

Because of the efforts of my younger sister and brother, another cattle drive was complete. I sat in the back of the truck cheering and applauding, grateful to have them do these tasks so that I didn't have to.

Whew! I hadn't even broken a sweat this time. I considered myself very fortunate.

More Luck Than Brains

"Those damn fools," Dad exclaimed.

He had just returned from an early Saturday morning trip to Middle Lake and walked into the kitchen to plop two large grocery bags on the kitchen counter.

"What are you talking about?" Mom asked, annoyed that her husband had not elaborated further and forced her to ask the question.

"Everyone in town is talking about what happened last night."

My ears perked up. I stood at the cupboard next to Mom, carefully adding three cups of flour to the big bowl, where I assembled all the ingredients to make jumbo raisin cookies. I feared what more he would say.

Mom also waited for him to continue.

"The Cudworth boys were in town. You won't believe it! Those damn fools raced their cars down the sidewalks."

"The sidewalks?"

"Yup. Backward!" he added for emphasis.

"I don't believe it!"

"Ask anyone. That's all they're talking about this morning."

"But the cars are too big, the sidewalks too narrow. There are gas pumps along the side. Surely, they didn't get their cars on that piece of the sidewalk," Mom stated.

"Surely, they did!"

"Did they hit the gas pumps?"

"Nope. More luck than brains."

At that point, both Mom and Dad turned to look at me. They knew

I had been out with my boyfriend the night before.

Mom said, "I'm glad you and Don went to a movie in Cudworth last night and weren't a part of the shenanigans."

I turned on the mixer, effectively drowning out the chances of continuing the conversation any further or having to respond to my mother's comment.

I looked over my shoulder to see my father eventually leave the kitchen and go outside. The screen door slammed behind him. Mom unpacked the bags, putting cans away in the cupboard. I ran the mixer a little longer until the dough was a nice soft glob and Mom had left the kitchen. I then began dropping one spoonful after another in neat rows on the cookie sheets. After I finished, I placed both cookie sheets in the hot oven. Retreating to the living room, I threw myself onto the brown flowered armchair and turned the chair to gaze out the window. The events of the night before quickly came to mind.

My twenty-two-year-old boyfriend, Don, had pulled into our farmyard around 7:30 the night before. Picking me up, he and I planned to head back to Cudworth to take in the new James Bond movie, The Man with the Golden Gun. We loved Roger Moore's portrayal of the fictional spy and had seen nearly all the previous James Bond movies. We looked forward to seeing his newest film.

Don, in his brown bell-bottom plaid pants and his chocolate-coloured shirt, held the driver's door for me. He brushed his dark blonde hair out of his eyes as I slid into the middle of the front seat of his 1969 Ford LTD. Don sat next to me in the driver's seat. His arm went around my shoulders, cradling me, as he looked to back his car up. Gravel spitting, we spun out of the yard and down the driveway. At only sixteen, I felt so grown up going out with a man in his twenties who owned his car. Most of the boys in school still had to borrow their father's car.

"I kinda thought maybe we wouldn't go to Cudworth tonight," Don began.

"Oh. Don't you want to see the movie?"

"Yeah, I do. But we could go next weekend instead."

"OK. What should we do then?"

"Well, everyone's coming to Middle Lake tonight. We could hang out with them."

Don had a big circle of friends. Many of the guys he knew dated girls from my hometown. Middle Lake was only a twenty-minute drive along a gravel road east of Cudworth. Often, Don came to pick me up for a date accompanied by a friend's car as they barrelled into my yard, horns blasting and music blaring. Shrieks of laughter and friendly banter added to the hullabaloo.

Six to eight people crowded in each car, sometimes more, with the girls sitting on the boys' laps. Wearing seat belts was not yet law and the older cars we travelled in didn't have them, so we couldn't wear them even if we wanted to. Everyone looked forward to an evening out.

Never short of liquor, we popped one bottle of beer after another and passed them around. Of course, the more beer we consumed, the louder we got and the more erratic the driving became. In 1974, most people accepted drinking and driving as the norm. Everyone drank and drove. If the police pulled you over, you got a slap on the wrist, your liquor confiscated, and a fifty-two dollar fine. We always solemnly promised not to drink anymore, but as soon as the police officer drove off, we headed straight to the bar to purchase more beer and resumed drinking and partying.

I considered Don's suggestion.

"OK. Sounds like fun," I conceded.

Any time the Cudworth gang got together, we always had fun. At the intersection of two grid roads just north of where I lived, Don signalled. We turned right and headed to Middle Lake where a wide main street ran the entire length of the town. At the east end, the elevators stood guard. The west end of Main Street bordered Lucien Lake.

We got to Middle Lake and cruised up and down the streets, waiting for the others to arrive. One by one, carloads of kids began converging on Main Street. The men bought cases of beer at the hotel. Once the entire gang arrived, we headed east of town to an abandoned farmyard. We parked behind the falling-down buildings, hidden from the road where we could drink and carouse. The night wore on. The drinking intensified. Boasts about whose car was faster and more powerful heated the night. The evening grew louder with electric energy. I wished Don would take me home. A gnawing feeling in my stomach would not go away.

Before I knew what was happening, everyone discarded their empty beer bottles. People rushed to their cars. I crawled into the car beside Don, glad that we were heading home. We sped back to Middle Lake, but instead of going to my parents' farm, we parked on Main Street. Confused and tired, I wanted this evening to end. I wanted to go home.

"Don, it's two in the morning. Please take me home," I pleaded.

"Sure. We have this one thing to do, and then I promise we'll go back to your place."

Don got out and walked to the rear of his car where a group of his friends gathered. I remained in his car. I could hear them talking but I could not understand what they were saying. It took a long time. I drifted off to sleep, stirring when the car door slammed and felt Don beside me once more. I wafted in and out of sleep, unaware Don backed his car onto the east side of the sidewalk. Had I been fully awake, I would have noticed that his friend, Lyle, had backed his green 1968 Mercury Marauder onto the sidewalk directly across the street. I also didn't see that someone had ripped up a white t-shirt and had it twisted around a stick to signal the start of the race.

I became fully awake when the engines revved, and we careened down the sidewalk backward. I turned around in my seat. Watching in horror, I saw the local hardware store, the pool hall, and the hotel flash by in a blur of yellow car lights reflecting in the dark store windows. The gas pumps stood like beacons on the corner of our side of the street. I held my breath. As we bore down on them, I closed my eyes and opened my mouth in a silent scream.

I don't know how, but somehow, we cleared the pumps and won the race. Don spun his LTD around in a grand finale before coming to a halt, parked in the middle of Main Street. Lyle pulled his Marauder up beside Don's car. Both men got out of their vehicles and thumped each other on the back, acknowledging a good race. Cheers erupted from the group of young people crowding onto the street in awe of what they had witnessed.

House and yard lights began flicking on. The raucous commotion had awakened the locals. Like ants dispersing from a destroyed anthill, we all fled the scene. Big cars disappeared, fleeing into the night. The homeowners, with probing eyes, wanted to know what was going on and who was involved. The following morning, these same residents could not wait to talk about the exploits that unfolded on their very streets.

Driving back to my home, Don's enthusiasm and elation in maneuvering his car between the building and the gas pumps, with only inches to spare, had him smiling. I joined in and celebrated his achievement, as crazy as it was. When we arrived at the farm, he got out of the car, and I followed. He grabbed me in a big hug and kiss and spun me around, so pleased with himself.

I thought about it now as I sat in the armchair. I smiled a secret smile. Maybe Dad was right. We probably had more luck than brains, but the high that came after doing something like that was immeasurable. I felt a rush of excitement just thinking about it. Hugging a pillow, I held my secret just as close and got up to remove the cookies from the oven.

Thankfully, no one said anymore on the matter. As far as I know, Dad never learned that I had been in a car racing down the sidewalk. Years later, after he passed away, Mom learned of our exploits. She shook her head and laughed. I know her reaction would have been much different had she heard about it the morning after. Time has a way of mellowing out the effects of even the foolhardiest stunts.

A Chance Encounter

Always the girl who went to mass every Sunday, I sang in the church choir and carried a rosary in my pocket. I never ate meat on Fridays. During Lent, leading up to Easter, I did my penance. I did everything a good Roman Catholic should do.

I loved Jesus.

After I graduated from high school, it seemed fitting that I attend St. Peter's College in Muenster, Saskatchewan. Besides being a monastery for the Benedictine order of monks, St. Peter's College provided students with the opportunity to take their first year of university. The year I attended St. Peter's College, they also offered a secretarial course sponsored by the Saskatchewan Institute of Applied Science and Technology from Moose Jaw. This ideal arrangement allowed me to live with my grandmother in Humboldt, a town only a ten-minute drive away. My grandfather had passed away the previous year. With my grandmother's failing health, my presence helped, especially at night.

Since I didn't own a car, I caught a ride with my friend, Donna, who travelled from Humboldt to Muenster each day, attending the same classes as me. One day after school, I realized I had forgotten my English textbook in my locker and asked Donna to drive me back to the school to get it. I promised I'd only be a minute as I ran across the school parking lot.

Inside the school, the darkness amazed me. With the teachers and students gone, the building had a reverent quiet to it. I climbed the broad staircase to the second floor with my hand sliding along the wall to guide me and then hurried along the hallway to my locker. My body tingled with a creepy feeling as I listened to the old building's creaks and groans. The halls were empty and long shadows cast through the narrow windows from the fast-approaching dusk on this late October afternoon. I found my locker and fumbled through it, searching for my book. I had to hold it up to the window to be sure it was the right one. After locking my compartment, I hurried along so as not to keep my friend waiting.

As I moved down the hallway, I heard stifled voices and heavy breathing. I slowed my steps. I looked around to determine from where these sounds were coming. St. Peter's College has several hallway alcoves. These recesses lead to the classrooms. It was in one of these nooks that I came upon two individuals wrapped in an impassioned embrace. The man's body pressed the woman's body firmly against the wall as his hands moved over her breasts and then up under her long brown skirt.

I gazed in utter disbelief, trying to take it all in, unable to accept it. In the fading light of the day and the darkened hallways of this holy school, my religious beliefs slammed into the wall. The two people caught up in this passionate embrace were a priest and a nun I knew well. She taught me catechism a few years ago during the summer and helped me prepare for my Confirmation. He, a pillar of the religious community, was a spokesperson for the college and Roman Catholicism in St. Peter's Abbacy. Celibacy was a fundamental belief and expectation for anyone leading a religious life. Witnessing this pair succumb to human frailties had my schoolgirl religious ideologies crushed and stomped into the ground like the butt of a cigarette. I felt lied to and betrayed.

Turning in the direction from which I had come, I chose to take a back stairway so as not to be seen. The encounter shook me to my very core. Astounded by what I had witnessed, they desecrated my entire belief system. Everything they had taught me about religion and all I believed in suddenly seemed to be obliterated. Celibacy for those who chose a religious life was central to the Roman Catholic faith. These two individuals had forsaken the most sacred of vows. I ran down the stairs, suddenly feeling like I could not breathe. At the base of the stairs, I searched for the door. When I found it, I threw it open to the brisk autumn air and to Donna, who waited for me in her car.

"You OK?" she asked when I climbed in. "You look like you've seen a ghost."

"No. No ghosts today," I quipped.

I did not tell Donna what I had seen, because not being Catholic, in fact, not being religious at all, I knew she would not understand why I felt so devastated by what I witnessed. I knew she would make light of it. Besides, I just could not talk about it. Not yet. Not now.

Donna backed the car out of the parking stall. We left the schoolyard.

This encounter has never left my mind. I think about it all the time and what it did to shatter my girlhood beliefs in religion, faith, vows, and, most of all, my feelings toward the church. The two people involved never knew I had seen them. They never knew how deeply their actions had affected me, how I felt I had to carry their dirty secret for all these years. Observing this simple lustful act by two people in the church left me questioning everything I held dear. Over the years, I attended church less and less. Pretty soon I stopped going altogether. What I witnessed at St. Peter's College was not the only reason I no longer went to mass, but it was one of them.

The Big Lie

Thinking back, I remembered that the music stopped. It was as though the people in the hall parted to make a path for him. He walked toward me, never taking his eyes off mine. Handsome, with curly light brown hair, blue eyes, and the biggest smile I had ever seen, he made his way across the dance hall. I fidgeted, adjusting my baby blue skirt and running my sweaty hands over my hair. That first time I laid eyes on him, I knew I would marry him. I was so convinced of this that I told my mother later that evening. I also wrote it in my journal.

He held out his hand as an invitation for me to join him in a dance. I put my hand in his and he manoeuvred us onto the floor. As we danced to the old-time waltz, he struck up a conversation by introducing himself as "Cool." I cocked my head to one side, puzzled. He laughed and said that's what his friends called him. His real name was Don. I told him mine.

We talked a bit more before Don casually asked me my age. I panicked. Only fifteen years old, I knew him to be older. I liked him a lot and suspected if I told him I was only fifteen, he would drop me like a hot coal. In that split instant, I spoke the biggest lie of my life.

"Seventeen," I heard the word fall out of my mouth.

"Mmmm," he said. "Jailbait."

"My birthday is next month," I went on quickly.

"Oh, that's better. So, then you will be eighteen?"

I nodded and looked down, mortified I had let that lie slip from my mouth so easily.

After that first night at the dance, Don and I planned to meet the next day at the July 1st Sports Day in Middle Lake. I waited and watched for him all day at the sports ground. He did not come. My knotted stomach added to the hurt in my heart, and I wondered how I could think that I would marry him someday.

Days wore on into weeks and weeks into months. I kept thinking about this man I had met at the dance but did not understand why I had not heard from him. A year later, on my parents' urgings, I attended another wedding dance with them. Wearing a flowered dress that my mother had sewn for me and brown platform-heeled shoes, I felt uncomfortable and out of place. Hanging around at the back of the hall, I wished I could be anywhere else.

I felt a tap on my shoulder and turned to find Don standing behind me with the same disarming smile he had the first time we met. Even though my heart melted into a puddle at my feet, I purposely acted aloof. He grabbed my hand and led me out of the hall so we could talk without having to shout above the music.

I stood before him with my arms crossed, waiting for him to speak.

"You're mad."

"You said that you'd come to the sports day, but you never showed up. You didn't call."

"I know. At the last minute, I had to work. I couldn't get out of it."

"I waited all day for you. You should have called."

"I didn't have your phone number. I did not even know your last name. I couldn't go to your house because I didn't know where you lived. You went home with your parents."

I uncrossed my arms and clasped my hands together in front of me, realizing what he said made sense. We had not gotten each other's last names or phone numbers. He had no way of contacting me to tell me he couldn't come. I looked at him while his eyes pleaded for understanding. I momentarily closed mine, knowing what he said to be true. When I opened them, I smiled, and he reached for my hand. We had a truce.

That evening after the wedding dance, he drove me home. He now had my first and last name and my phone number and he knew where I lived. We began dating.

Unexpectedly one evening, Don said he had arranged for us to meet up with some of his friends at the bar. Alarm bells went off in my head. I almost blurted out that I could not go because of my age before I remembered the lie that I told him on that very first night. Oh, Gawd! What do I do now? I remained calm and pretended I was of legal bar age. Hopefully, they would not ask me to show my identification. Luckily, they didn't. This scenario happened frequently as we went with our friends to bars and cabarets. I never once got asked how old I was.

We dated for a year, and my high school graduation loomed in May. My mother sewed a beautiful long coral-coloured gown for me to wear. Everyone assumed I would ask Don to be my escort, and, of course, I did. Thankfully, he didn't ask why I was graduating so late. After all, by this time, he thought me to be nineteen years old.

* * *

"Can you give me your wallet?"

My fiancé made this strange request of me as we parked alongside the road the night before our wedding on a muggy evening in July. Don and I had left the church after our wedding rehearsal and were headed back to my parents' farm. Dark clouds low in the western sky banged together to see if they could knock some rain out of each other. A few fat raindrops splat on the windshield as I gave him an inquiring look.

"Do you need some money? I only have about twenty dollars. You can have it."

"No, it's not that. Just give me your wallet."

I dug into my purse and handed it to him.

He opened it and clumsily began rifling through it.

"What are you looking for?" I demanded, upset at his strange behaviour.

"Your driver's license. You have a driver's license, don't you? You are old enough?"

I did not care for his tone as I reached to grab my wallet from his hands. I produced my driver's license and thrust it at him. He studied it for a moment before he returned it to me.

"What was that all about?"

"Just double-checking," he said as he winked at me before starting up his car. "I wanted to make sure you were of legal age."

I understood now. Don had not forgotten the lie I told on our very first date. Even though I confessed my correct age to him two months earlier during our marriage preparation courses, he still had a question in his mind. Three years after meeting him, on the eve of our marriage, I regretted lying to him.

And yet, I didn't.

Crop Circles

Most times, while driving our two-door 1972 brown and gold Ford Meteor, I'd have the radio cranked up and would sing along at the top of my lungs to songs like the Bay City Roller's "Saturday Night" or The Sweet's "Fox on the Run." But not this time.

Late and lost, I glanced at the September sky, where the once hazy shades of pink and lavender had long melted into the horizon, making way for the dark blanket of night that now cloaked the countryside. I gnawed on my lip, grasping the steering wheel as I bounced over the uneven field. Driving between swaths, I was careful not to disturb the uncombined grain. The car's yellow headlights searched for something familiar like a ravine, a clump of trees, an approach, anything to help me identify my location in the field.

The neighbours' combines spewed chaff dust into the air as they clambered through the endless rows of swaths in the fields southwest of Wakaw, SK. The musty smell permeated my vehicle, seeping through the air vents. Inhaling it, I found it difficult to breathe.

My heart pounded. Was I in the correct field? I had no clue. Was it possible I was in the wrong field? Oh, sure, anything was possible. At the tender age of nineteen, I had been married for two months, had secured a full-time position at the town's bank, managed a household, and adjusted to life as a married woman. If you could call a girl of nineteen a married woman. I had accomplished all those things, but I could not find my way through the field to where my husband and his father and brother waited for supper.

The lid on the pot shifted from bouncing through the field, allowing the savoury aroma of beef stew to escape and waft through the car, reminding me I was hungry. Earlier, I raced home from work and hastily tossed the cut-up beef, carrots, potatoes, and onions into the cooker. While the meal cooked on the stove, I packed plates, utensils, cups, and buns in a box to take out to the field to serve the hungry men. They combined a field thirty minutes away from where we lived. New to the area and unfamiliar with the landscape, I hoped I turned off the highway at the right intersection. Endless quarters of farmland stretched around me, one quarter of land looking just like the other with no discernible characteristics or features to identify them. I had difficulty identifying our land in daylight, but now in the darkness, I found it nearly impossible.

I glanced at the clock on the dashboard and realized I'd meandered through the field for fifty minutes. I peered through the windshield and tried my best to find a landmark or anything that might help me identify my location. Careful not to hit the rocks jutting from the ground like icebergs that were almost impossible to see in the field until it was too late, I inched along in the darkness. Hitting one of those large rocks could severely damage a tire or the undercarriage of the car, making for a difficult explanation to my new husband. As I groped along, I realized I could no longer see a combine or a grain truck, confirming my belief I might be in the wrong field. But how would I get back to the road?

Another thought nagged at me. I checked the fuel gauge and saw the needle pointing at empty. My hungry stomach clenched, and my heart pounded with an increased sense of apprehension. I cursed myself for being so reckless and not filling the car before I headed out. I hadn't wanted to be late delivering supper to the men and was proud of how delicious the stew had turned out; I eagerly sought my husband's approval. Now, the tasty meal would be cold by the time I found them and before they could eat it.

An orange, eery light flickered in the distance, rattling me further. I strained to see the cause of the strange glimmering light but could not make it out. Don recently commiserated about the number of break-ins and thefts he and his neighbours experienced on their land this year. I immediately worried this light probably guided the crooks as they looked for further items to steal. They probably would not think too kindly of a young woman interrupting their foray. Thoughts of burglars and vandalism filled my mind as I turned the car in the opposite direction and thumped over the rough field, trying to put as much distance between myself and the intruders as quickly as possible.

But how would I get out of this darned field? Why couldn't I find the driveway to take me back to the main road? I groped through the field, looking for an approach and finding none. A vehicle coming up behind me had its lights shining in my mirror. I pressed my foot to the gas pedal, no longer concerned about disturbing the swaths in the field. I had to escape. What would the pilferers do if they caught me? My heart pounded in my chest, trying to get out, and my mouth turned dry. My clammy hands clutched the steering wheel as I leaned forward in my car seat, endeavouring to see into the darkness in front of me as I made a run for it.

The pot filled with stew and the dishes and cutlery clanged around in the box that nearly slid off the car's front seat as I raced to get away. I plowed directly into some standing wheat, heedless of the damage I caused the ripe brittle stocks. I had to get away and hide. Before I kicked that plan into action, I felt the car plunge over a small elevation in the land and came to rest on something. Stuck. I glanced over my shoulder, looking for my pursuer. Where was he? Had I managed to lose him? I could not see him. Suddenly, a face appeared in the window directly beside me. I screamed until I couldn't anymore. The car door opened. I grabbed the pot of stew, my only defence.

I raised the pot to swing toward the open door when I heard a familiar voice.

"Put the pot down before you spill it," Don said matter-of-factly.

I lowered the pot back into the cardboard box. In one quick movement, I jumped out of the car and collapsed into my husband's chest, sobbing. Don held me for a moment and then asked why I drove away from him when he came searching for me. I babbled something about robbers but, even to my ears, it sounded ridiculous. After they saw me driving around in circles in the field, my husband started a fire, the scary orange light, hoping to guide me to where they parked.

Don tied a rope to my car's back bumper and gently coaxed the car out of the shallow ravine into which I had driven. He got my car turned around and asked me to follow him across the field to where his father and brother impatiently waited for their meal. Climbing out of the car, my head down, I dished up the stew and handed the plates to them. Neither of them said a word, but I'm sure I saw a smirk on my brother-in-law's grimy face as he mopped up the gravy on his plate with his bun.

When he finished, he handed me the empty plate and, with an expectant look on his face, asked, "What's for dessert?"

My shoulders slumped. The apple crisp I placed in the oven to warm while the stew cooked still sat in the oven at home. I tried explaining what happened. The men stood and moved to resume harvesting. At that moment, I felt inadequate, like a total failure. And to top it all off, I still did not know how to get out of that darned field. I swallowed my pride and asked Don. In response, he pointed the direction I should drive.

"Can you take me back to the road? I don't want to get lost again," I pleaded with him. I did not want to tell him the needle on the gas gauge pointed solidly to "E".

Don climbed into his truck, the one that had chased me earlier, and led me to the approach that took me back to the main road. Before he left to go back to combining, he climbed out of his truck and came back to my car. With tears of frustration brimming over, I rolled down the window to see what he wanted. A goofy grin lit up his face as he leaned inside to kiss me. The taste of dirt and sweat lingered on my mouth long after he turned and left to go back to the combine. But my heart no longer pounded to break free of my chest. Instead, it beat with a nice steady rhythm.

I turned onto the main road, happy to be on my way home to where the apple crisp waited. The car slowly sputtered to a stop. Out of gas.

My heart sank as I lowered my head to the steering wheel and cried.

In our family, crop circles took on a whole new meaning. Years later, this experience still evokes chuckles from my husband and brother-in-law, eager to share this story with the next generation. Some things you just can never live down.

Our First Home

Our first home, a 72-foot trailer, clung to the outskirts of town, sitting on the edge of a field. The Town of Cudworth officials had purchased this farmland to subdivide into town lots. Our yard, not much to look at, required landscaping with a lawn seeded, flowers and trees planted, and a garden area established.

Don installed plywood skirting around the base of our mobile home and insulated it to keep it as warm as possible. My job involved applying three coats of brown paint to the skirting. Don also built two sets of stairs with railings for both the back door and the front door, which I painted the same chocolate brown as the skirting. Don planned how he would build an addition onto the back of the trailer to serve as a porch and to provide space for a freezer, a closet, and some additional shelving. Running out of time before winter, he knew that would be a project for the following summer.

Inside our home, mahogany walls haunted every single room of our residence with brown vertical wall panelling so boring and nondescript. So ugly. As hideous as the walls were, the floors looked just as bad with worn gold-coloured shag carpet extending from the living room at the front of the trailer to the master bedroom at the far end and everything in between, except for a tiny space that accommodated our kitchen and dining room. The spare bedroom in the centre of the trailer had our water heater tucked away in its closet. A few short months after we moved in, the water heater quit working and needed replacing. Water soaked the carpet in the bedroom and the hallway, and we brought in fans to dry everything out.

The tiny bathroom next to our bedroom also housed our washer spin dryer, a tiny washing machine and dryer combo unit with the drums so small I could only wash one pair of jeans at a time. Doing laundry became quite a tedious and lengthy process.

Our mobile home came with a sofa, an armchair, and a chrome table with four chocolate-brown chairs. It also boasted white lace curtains that hung over the single-sliding windows with slats that you turned with a knob. Even with the windows open, the trailer became suffocatingly hot in the summer. We had no air conditioning. The trailer had a metal roof that absorbed the heat, and this same metal roof thumped and clanged whenever the wind got a little stronger. Sometimes during a storm, the noise sounded like the entire roof would rip off and blow away.

The plywood skirting that Don had painstakingly built around the trailer became a haven for animals seeking shelter. On two separate occasions, a skunk waddled under our home looking to take up permanent residency. Both times my husband crawled under our home after the intruder, inching along on his stomach. As a farmer and outdoorsman, he knew his only chance to avoid being sprayed was to sneak up on it and shoot it in the back of the head. He had success each time, making our little home safe once more.

Our mobile home, manufactured in one of the southern states, perhaps Arizona or Texas, could not withstand a Saskatchewan winter. The astonishing lack of insulation in the walls, floor, and, most noticeably, around the water pipes in the walls and under the trailer spelled trouble. As soon as the temperature dipped to around −15°C, our water pipes froze. Don plugged in an electric space heater under our home to thaw the pipes. Often, the water pipes burst, and he wrestled with having to replace them, lying on the freezing ground beneath our trailer, cursing the day he ever bought this house on wheels.

The mouse invasion presented the biggest challenge and my worst nightmare. Over winter, they looked for a warm place. They chewed their way through the low-grade underfloor and came up around the holes for the pipes. They crept in, occupied our home, and took over our lives. Raised on a farm, I believed that a house was no place for animals; therefore, we did not have a cat. However, as the mouse infestation grew worse with each autumn day, I certainly considered it.

Cowering in bed, I pulled the blankets up to my chin, listening to Don's slow, steady breathing. I heard one other thing. The rattling sound of the two clasps of my jewellery box as the mice ran along it, brushing the clasps with their backs and making the sound. My only saving grace is that if I could hear them across the room, they were not in bed with me. Or, at least, that is what I hoped. I heard stories of mice running through a woman's curlers in her hair at night while she slept, and I shuddered to think what I would do if that happened to me.

At night, when I got up to use the bathroom, I turned on the light just in time to see them scuttle along the wall down the hallway. Often, I tip-toed my way to the kitchen for a drink of water. As I reached for the tap, I saw one run behind the faucet and across the counter, disappearing into the night. I held in the terrified scream so as not to awaken Don. In the evening, with the house quiet, we heard the mice at play. I stored my frying pan with its lid lying inverted inside. The mice liked to get into the lid and run around, making a pivoting motion and sound. Many nights I sat in the living room glued to my seat listening to them at play, too frightened to move and too terrified not to.

We had a gas stove, and several times I turned it on, not realizing a mouse hid inside. I cooked the intruder, and the nauseating smell permeated the entire trailer. Cleaning up the charred mouse remains took all the fortitude I could muster. The same thing happened when my husband set out traps to catch the varmints. Sometimes he did not remember where he placed them, and it was only by the horrific smell weeks later that we could trace back our steps, discover its location, and clean up the remains. One time I grabbed something hard in my drawer of rags. Puzzled, I looked a little closer, only to find a nest of baby mice that had died and hardened. We must have trapped their mother, and they could not survive on their own. I scrubbed my hands raw with soap and water, trying to remove the sensation of touching the dead rodents.

Try as we might, we could not catch all the mice. They infested our mobile home, but, more significantly, they infiltrated my mind. When I think of our first home, it is the mice that I think of first. The mouse incursion seared into my psyche a horrible repulsion of these creatures. I feared and loathed them, and just the sight of a mouse had me trembling with dread. I carried this fear for over sixty years, and I think it will go with me to the grave. We lived in that mouse-infested home for four long miserable years until we purchased a house on an acreage three miles east of town. Relieved, we bid farewell to that horror on wheels and moved into a beautiful, bright house, rodent-free.

Bear Encounter

A fishing trip during the last week of June 1980 took Don and me to Big Sandy Lake on Hanson Lake Road, some 450 kilometres northeast of our home in Cudworth. To get there, we went north of Prince Albert and thundered over 350 kilometres of gravel road in our blue and silver 1979 GMC Crew Cab before reaching our destination.

When we arrived at the camp, I discovered our cabin was little more than a small granary-like building with four walls and a small window on three of its walls. The lodge had no electricity; therefore, no lights and no fridge. All our food had to remain in our cooler for the duration of our visit. A hot plate with two burners offered the only means on which to cook. The cabin did not have running water, so we could not bathe or shower. In the evening, when the sun went down, so did we. The dark cabin remained stuffy with little air circulation, and the mosquitoes already collected inside. They came through the torn screen on the cabin door, looking for a place to land on us and feast. I grimaced and shook my head, already dubious about what this trip would entail.

Nine months pregnant with the nearest hospital 350 kilometres away in the City of Prince Albert, I cringed, thinking about what could go wrong. To make things more interesting, the fishing resort did not have a phone. Because of the lodge's remoteness, an unreliable two-way radio presented the only form of communication with the outside world. I thought back to the worried looks on my parent's faces as we dropped off our two-year-old daughter before venturing out on this expedition, and now I felt the same level of concern. Why had I agreed to make this trip in my condition? It had been hard enough during the journey, bouncing around in the cab of our truck, but staying in these surroundings would be a genuine test of my endurance.

I helped Don unload the truck and make our new home as comfortable as possible. For supper, we roasted wieners over the fire my husband made, and later we snuggled in for a good night's rest. Even the droning mosquitoes with their inch-long stingers could not keep us awake. There is something about the fresh air that makes a person tired. We slept well that first night.

Early the following morning, Don and I sped away from shore in our rented boat. We found a suitable spot and soon had our fishing rods poking in the lake for our first big catch of the day. We brought in several nice pickerels. The sun's hot rays beat down on us, and I could not find a comfortable way to sit on the narrow wooden bench in the tiny aluminum boat. Besides, Mother Nature kept calling, and finally, Don agreed to bring me back to shore. He dropped me off at the dock and then turned the boat and headed back out onto the lake. Don did not want to waste one valuable minute of fishing time.

I lumbered through the deep white sand of the lake's shore and waved to two older men sitting in front of their cabin right next to ours. Both men wore denim overalls with straw hats perched on their heads. Red hankies poured out of their pockets. Good-naturedly, they chuckled as they watched me make my way past their cabin to ours, my back aching and my legs stiff from being cramped in the small boat for several hours. I plodded the short distance to the camp's outdoor toilet. Opening the door, the stench and the steady buzz of flies in the summer heat did not make for an appealing scenario; however, desperation overrode any of the unpleasantries.

That task completed, I went back to our cabin and looked around for a magazine to read before realizing I'd forgotten it in the truck the night before. I found Don's keys hanging on a nail inside the cabin and unlocked our vehicle. I searched the cab for a few items and sat with the truck turned on and air blowing from the vents. It felt so good. Reluctant to leave this one piece of luxury in a place so rustic, I eventually climbed out of the truck and pushed the door shut behind me.

The slamming door heralded a fresh problem. Our only set of truck keys dangled in the ignition. I closed my eyes and counted to ten. I walked around the crew cab, trying all four doors, hoping to find one unlocked. Nope. All were tightly in place. Doesn't that just figure? Knowing Don would be upset with me, I studied the truck to see what my best plan of attack should be. Kicking a tire, I cursed when my toe buckled in my shoe. I cried out in pain.

"Okay. Be calm," I thought to myself. "You can figure this out."

I walked around the truck again and noticed the back-sliding window was partially ajar.

"Aha!" I cried. "My way in."

A good thought, but executing it proved to be an entirely different story. I tried stepping on the bumper and hauling my immense weight up into the truck box but couldn't manage it, no matter how hard I tried. Next, I trudged back to the cabin and found a wooden crate that I brought to the back of the truck and used it to step onto the bumper and then into the truck box. Prying the sliding windows apart, the glass panes moved until they stood open. Great, making progress.

I studied the window opening in the back of the cab and then looked down at my protruding belly.

"Oh, brother," I thought to myself. "What a tight squeeze."

I leaned in the window and felt my stomach brushing up against it. Now, not so sure this plan would work, I stood up and surveyed the situation again.

It had to work!

I had no choice!

My other option, wait for Don to return. I could not bear admitting that I had done something so foolish. I tried sucking in my stomach. Of course, that did not work.

By now, the pair of Old McDonald farmers from the cabin next door ambled over to survey the situation. Both men, larger than I in my impregnated state, would not fit through the window. After sizing up the situation, the men agreed they could not help me and headed back to sit in front of their cabin, entertained by my goings-on.

The sun's direct rays heated the metal of the truck as I considered what to do. With one act of pure determination, I pushed my way through the small window, falling unceremoniously into the back seat of the crew cab. The bachelor brothers hooted and hollered, clapping their hands when they saw I had made it inside the cab. I lay there from exhaustion for a minute, rubbing my stomach, before I crawled over the front seat and grasped the keys from the ignition.

When Don returned from fishing, he found me calmly standing at the stove frying fish for lunch. He never heard about the morning's escapade until years later, when we had a good laugh over it.

After lunch, Don asked if I wanted to go fishing with him. I told him no because I wanted to lie down and have a nap. He agreed and left the cabin, heading for the lake once again. I tell you; this man loves fishing. I tidied up the cabin and swept the floor before lying down on the bed to rest. During that period of drowsiness when a person is not awake but not quite asleep, I heard a snoofing sound. I drifted into a deeper slumber when a louder snort had me fully awake.

I peered through the semi-darkness of the cabin toward the door. With only a screen door separating us, I saw the black bear. The smell of fried fish brought him to our door, and he stood, sniffing the air. I lay on the bed feeling extremely vulnerable, not knowing what to do. I knew I could not just bounce out of bed because in my state rolling over and getting out of bed had become a laborious task. The colossal bear continued to sniff the air. Standing on his hind legs, he seemed to be twelve feet high when he probably only stood half that height. I could not lay there praying he would go away. This bear seemed to have other intentions. He wanted food.

I remembered that Don had brought a rifle with him. I could use that to protect myself! There was one problem. It was eight feet away, leaning against the wall behind the door, the same door that separated me from the bear. Even if I ran right up to the bear and grabbed the rifle, I had no guarantee it held ammunition. If not, what would I do? Use the rifle to beat the bear? I didn't like the odds. Grunting and becoming increasingly agitated, the bear began striking at the door frame. I hollered at it. He dropped to all four legs and walked away. Within seconds, he came back. I continued to yell at him, hoping to scare him off.

My heart pounded as I struggled to get my feet to the floor. My baby inside me, sensing something wrong, kicked and moved, so my hand instinctively went to my abdomen. I pushed myself to a sitting position and stared directly into the face of the bear.

Gunshots exploded.

I jumped.

The confused black bear scrambled into the trees behind our cabin. I heard a commotion outside. The two brothers from the neighbouring lodge ran up to our cabin's door and peered through the screen at me.

"Don't worry, little Missy. We scared that bear away. He won't hurt you," one of them called.

"Are you okay?" the other asked as he peered into the dimly lit cabin.

"Yes. Thank you," I called out. Relief flooded through me. With the immediate threat gone, I began crying. The two men stood outside our cabin, shuffling their feet, uncertain of what to do or say. They shrugged and said they would be next door if I needed them.

Hours later, Don returned from fishing, excited because he had found a good spot miles away on the lake. When I relayed the entire story of the afternoon's events, Don looked incredulous and worried about how close the bear had come to me. He immediately checked his rifle for ammunition and then placed it on the floor beside the bed.

True to form, immediately after supper, Don announced he wanted to go out fishing once again and thought it best that I come with him. He promised we would only go out on the lake for an hour. I reluctantly agreed to accompany him because the thought of staying alone in the cabin did not appeal to me. I worried the bear might return.

Out on the lake, we had just cast our lines when we heard a gunshot ring out from the camp, followed by another and yet another. We reeled in our fish lines, and Don steered our boat for the shore. Reaching the shore's edge, he helped me out of the small boat, and we hurried back to our cabin. Well, he sprinted, and I trundled my way.

As I got closer, I could not believe my eyes. On the ground beside our cabin lay a dead black bear. The bachelor brothers excitedly told my husband how the bear had returned after we left. This time, the black animal stood on his hind legs and raked his claws over our cabin roof, shredding the rolled roofing that covered it, his actions becoming more aggressive. For safety's sake, the brothers decided they had to put him down.

Don helped the men skin the huge male bear. When they finished, he returned to our cabin to find me, wide-eyed and trembling, perched on the bed in our darkening room. Sitting down and putting his arm around me, he assured me I did not have to worry about that bear. All I could think of was that if I had stayed behind and not gone fishing with him, the bear would have had me trapped in the cabin a second time. Maybe this time, I would not have been so lucky.

Within a week and a half of returning home from this eventful fishing trip, our baby arrived.

Our son, now a father to two boys, loves nature and enjoys hunting. He shares a remarkable affinity with bears along with a deep respect for these noble creatures. Perhaps it is because of his first bear encounter before he was born.

Life On The Farm

"Mommy," my two-year-old toddler, Sara, called to me. "Bugs," she proudly proclaimed, holding out two writhing garden snakes, one in each of her pudgy hands. Her blonde curly hair blew in the wind and her blue eyes lit up with excitement.

"Sara," I screeched at her. "Drop them. Now!"

Startled, my daughter cried as she dropped the brown-striped snakes and watched them slither away in the grass. Uncertain if her sobs came from my raised voice or because her "bugs" had disappeared in the grass, I consoled my little girl, taking her into the house to scrub her hands clean with hot water and soap. Having just moved to the acreage in the spring of 1980, this became our first introduction to the ongoing and ever-persistent snake issues.

Our yard, beautiful and huge, spanned four acres just a few kilometres east of Cudworth. Five rows of trees, including spruce, poplar, maple, green ash, and caragana, encircled the entire yard. South of the house, a row of eight lilac trees separated the garden from the main yard. In spring they bloomed all variations of purple and white. A string of wooden granaries, a machine shed, and a grove of fruit trees and shrubs hemmed in the west side. The house nestled into the original bush that protected the yard from the cold northern winds that blew in winter. The driveway climbed up the hill past an old barn and small shed into this lovely yard that we meticulously maintained. During the summer, the large yard took almost an entire week to cut the lawn using a riding lawnmower. Once finished, it was time to begin again. In summer, the lush greenery and the contrast of the lilacs and fruit trees in bloom provided a picturesque landscape. In fall, the vibrant colours of the changing deciduous leaves against the backdrop of the dark evergreens framed by an autumn azure sky created an idyllic image.

Our large house, built by Don's Uncle Walter, spanned nearly 2500 square feet of living area in a four-level split home. In contrast to the small and dark mobile home where we lived for the first four years of our marriage, this house presented a bright ambiance with plenty of room to grow. The huge U-shaped country-style kitchen with attractive walnut cupboards sat next to a large, open dining room. Past the dining room, the L-shaped living room at the west side of the house with the large windows looked out to the south, soaking up the beauty of the lush yard. A main floor laundry, bathroom, and one bedroom completed the main living space with two more bedrooms and a sitting or sewing room on the floor that extended over the garage. The main entrance level stretched the entire width of the house next to the garage. We later developed the basement to hold two more bedrooms, a family room, a cold storage room, and, of course, the cistern, since we did not have a well or a suitable source of water.

Settling into country life, we came to understand the extent the slithering reptiles played in our lives. At first, we noticed them as a branch lying across the road that suddenly moved as our vehicle approached them. Next, I noticed Don strapping on his gun holster every time he cut the grass. He rode around on the lawnmower, pulling out his revolver, aiming it at the ground, and firing it. He disposed of many snakes in this manner. When I questioned him about the need for such actions, he just smiled and tried to downplay the significance of it all. He knew how I felt about snakes.

Our St. Bernard dog, Butch, developed a taste for snakes over the years, and we often saw him slurping up a snake as though eating spaghetti and then licking his chops to savour the last morsel.

One autumn day, I sent our children to the orchard to pick apples.

They balked at doing the task. Later, when they came into the house with their pails half full, I asked them about it. They told me the snakes in the fruit trees fell on them when they shook the branches and tried to pick the apples. I shuddered. As a result, most of the apples remained on the trees that year.

Another summer, I once again sent the kids to pick apples. Glancing out the window, I saw my young son, Adam, dancing around in a panic, hopping from one foot to the other. Later, when they came into the house, I discovered he wore old sneakers with a hole in the toe. An enterprising snake tried to work its way through the hole in Adam's shoe. My son jumped around, trying to get the snake out of his shoe without having to grab it with his hands and pull it out.

What frightened me the most was our house's proximity to where we found the snakes. Occasionally, someone left the front door open. Several times coming down the steps from the kitchen to the entranceway, I noticed a snake coiled on the floor. The feeling of panic that gripped my heart in those instances remains with me today. Each time, I grabbed a pail and set it upside down on the reptile before it slinked away into oblivion. Don always carried it back outside. I feared snakes coming into the house through cracks in our basement's block foundation. I threatened to leave if I ever found a snake in our house. Luckily, except for the odd snake that came in through the front door, I never found one. My husband liked to comfort me by telling me the more snakes around, the fewer mice we'd have. Small comfort.

Don's brother, Dale, loved to torment me about all things concerning mice and snakes. One morning, he caught a garter snake with his bare hands. To prove its harmlessness, he held it up with the snake's head between his thumb and forefinger and looked it in the eyes. The snake did not like being handled and spit a foul-smelling fluid into Dale's face. My brother-in-law cried out in disgust as he dropped the animal to the ground, and it slipped away into the grass.

Springtime always brought a new batch of baby snakes with hatchlings about the thickness of a pencil and four or five inches long. If I stumbled across their nest, the writhing conglomeration of moving disgust repulsed me in every way. I learned we had an old well on the farm that seemed to attract the snakes and held most of the nests. One year, we hauled and stacked bricks near the house, intending to construct a patio. The snakes burrowed beneath this pile of bricks, making it their home before we could build our deck. We soon abandoned the idea of building the patio. I did not want these reptiles taking up permanent residency right beside our house. No, thank you.

We lived an untroubled existence. The snakes never took over our lives the way the mice had in our previous home. The snakes sunbathed on our front step, and we learned to walk around them. They climbed in the trees, and we learned not to pick the fruit then. Their babies hatched and grew, and we accepted there would be more of them that year, content to let them be so long as they did not invade my home.

Deer Hunting

"Sure. I'll go hunting with you. Why not?" I tried to convince myself that I could do this, that I wanted to do it.

A week later, having made that concession, I now helped Don load the same GMC Crew Cab with hunting supplies. After dropping off our two small children at my parents' farm near Middle Lake, we headed for the town of Carievale, in the far southeast corner of Saskatchewan. My Uncle Peter and Aunt Shirley lived just north and a little west of this town in an area where whitetails abounded.

"This will be an adventure. It'll be fun," I tried to reassure myself as we started our seven-hour journey from Cudworth to Carievale in November 1980. My inner voice cried out, "Why are you doing this? You hate hunting. This is NOT your idea of a holiday."

I huddled on my side of the truck, wishing I could sleep as one kilometre after another slipped by. I stared out the passenger window at the snow-covered landscape and ahead to the highway, where the snow had already melted and left the road wet and sullen. The long boring drive took most of Sunday to get there. I loved the smile on Don's face as he glanced at me, excited to be going on this hunting trip and happy that I agreed to go along. I smiled back at him. Feeling chilly, I adjusted the heat, turned the radio up, and settled against the door. I closed my eyes.

"Wake up, sleepyhead."

I lifted my head from where it had bounced against the window. My hand went up to massage the stiffness out of my neck, and I glanced around.

"Where are we?"

"Redvers. I had to stop for gas. Do you need anything?"

"Just a washroom," I said as I reached to open the truck door.

Don provided instructions to the attendant before he followed me into the gas station. We scanned the inside of the building and found a single bathroom at the back of the business. Inside the room, layers of dirt covered the floor, swiped over with a hasty mop, leaving buildup along the edges of the walls. The yellow grime in the solitary sink with the equally disgusting broken faucets proved they had not received any more attention than the floors. A small, discoloured mirror about twelve inches square clung to the wall over the sink with its spidery effect that made it almost impossible to see my reflection.

Both men and women used this bathroom, the toilet seat up, revealing splatters of feces from previous users. Orange traces of dried urine, interspersed with hair strands, covered the porcelain. A dead fly floated in the scum-caked toilet bowl.

I backed out of the bathroom and whispered to my husband, who waited for me just outside the door, "We can't use this. It's disgusting."

"This might be the last bathroom until we get to Pete and Shirley's."

"But Don, look at it." I held the door open with my elbow, not wanting to touch it with my hand.

"Yup, I've seen better. I'm going to use it if you aren't."

"Yeah, but you can stand. I will have to sit in that."

Don shrugged his shoulders and entered the bathroom, closing the door behind him.

I roamed the aisles, casually looking at the chips and bars and the refreshments on display in the stand-up coolers. I wandered around, the need to pee growing stronger. Soon, Don came up beside me.

"Did you want anything? I'm going to pay for the gas."

I shook my head no and turned my gaze back to the bathroom.

"It could be the last one for miles," Don said. He gathered a few items in his hands before making his way to the cashier.

I knew Don was right. I walked to the bathroom in the back corner of the store and decided that I could do this. Not touching the doorknob more than necessary, I pushed into the small room and closed the door. I noticed Don had lowered the toilet seat and I silently thanked him. I took some paper towels, ran them under the tap, and wiped off the seat. Slowly, I lowered myself to it and felt immediate relief. When I finished, I got up, adjusted my clothes, and turned the tap on to wash my hands. Looking around, I could not find soap anywhere. Of course not! Why would I think a place like this would have soap in its bathroom? I let the water run, waiting for it to get hot so I could scour my hands. Nope. No heat. If anything, the water only got colder. I scrubbed my hands and reached for the paper towels to dry them. Too late, I realized the dispenser was empty, having used the last ones to wipe the toilet seat. I sighed as I waved my hands in the air to dry and then rubbed them against my pant legs.

I left the bathroom and went out to the truck where Don sat waiting for me.

"All done?"

I nodded, slamming the truck door behind me. I settled in my seat.

We drove the remaining sixty kilometres to my uncle's farm, pulling into his yard a little after five o'clock. Pete and Shirley bounded out of their grey ranch-style farmhouse, eager to greet us. They hurried us out of the cold and into their warm house, where the aroma of roast beef tickled our senses and stirred up a hunger we did not know existed.

We enjoyed the meal Shirley had prepared and we laughed over recollections of our last visit to their farm a few years earlier. As newly-weds, Don and I had previously stayed at their place because Don went hunting with my two uncles, Pete and Dan, and Pete's brother-in-law, Blaine.

During the first night of that visit, Don and I made our way to the bedroom that Shirley and Dan's wife, Kathy, had prepared for us. Once inside the bedroom with the door closed, I sat on the bed and reached to remove my socks. I heard bells ringing.

"Did you hear that?"

"What?" Don asked.

Neither of us moved. We listened. Nothing.

I removed my socks.

"There it is again. Did you hear it?"

"This time I did."

"What do you suppose it is?" I asked, bouncing lightly on the bed. The sound became more insistent. "It is bells ringing," I said, shifting slightly on the bed.

Don got on his hands and knees and peered under the bed.

"I see what it is." He gazed up at me and grinned. "They've strung bells."

Don crawled under the bed to disconnect the bells. We had only been married four months, and this was my aunts' idea of having a little fun.

That happened four years and two children ago. Tonight, we went to bed shortly after nine with no bells. We slept soundly on the comfortable bed.

The following morning, Don and I wanted an early start. We dressed in our bright orange coveralls and donned our orange caps. After checking the truck to ensure we had our rifles, ammunition, and our hunting licenses, we trudged out to the truck. Shirley handed me a cooler filled with the lunch she and I had prepared the night before. Pete and Shirley had to work but they waved us off before carrying on with their day.

The morning sun awakened and stretched her rosy-coloured arms across the sky as Don and I set out to find our first deer. Pete permitted us to hunt on his property and gave Don directions on where the best spots might be, the places where Pete knew the deer liked to feed. Don turned off the main road and we headed down a dirt trail. We bounced along one field road after another, seeing tons of deer, but all in locations where we could not shoot at them. Either they were on posted land, near cattle, or firing at them would have meant we shot toward a farm. We could not take that chance.

In short order, the excitement of the impending hunt wore off. The truck's heater pushed out the warmth that enveloped me and made me sleepy. We drove around one bluff of trees after another. Soon, they all looked the same.

"Well, you missed that excitement."

Aroused from sleep, I turned to look at Don.

"What do you mean?"

"You slept right through the game wardens' visit. They checked to make sure we weren't breaking any rules."

"Really? The wardens stopped us?"

"Yup."

"What did they want?"

"Just the usual things. They wanted to see our hunting licenses and make sure our rifles weren't loaded. They checked the truck box to see if we had shot a deer. That sort of thing."

"I didn't hear a thing."

"They even checked inside the truck cab. You slept through it all."

"I must have been more tired than I realized."

In all honesty, exhaustion plagued me. Caring for our toddler, Sara, two and half years old, and our baby, Adam, not even five months old, while working full time left me with little energy these days. I had returned to work only six short weeks after Adam arrived and had no time for sleepless nights.

"Are you hungry?"

I nodded.

"We'll find a secluded spot to have lunch."

We drove around a little longer until Don found a grassy area where he parked, and we got out, lugging the cooler behind us. We opened the end gate on the back of the truck and placed the cooler in the truck box. The sandwiches, made of leftover roast beef from the night before, tasted delicious as we munched our way through them and then onto the heavily frosted chocolate cake Shirley had placed in plastic containers sealed with lids. Red grapes completed the meal as we sat together on the back of the truck, scanning the horizon. Peaceful, with autumn's icy fingers running through our hair and sliding down our backs, the briskness in the air reminded us to keep moving.

We packed everything up and climbed back into the cab. Don started the truck, and we rocked back and forth, bouncing over another uneven dirt road. Bored, I began fidgeting with the radio dial, trying to find a station with better reception.

I turned to look at Don and studied my husband's profile. His light brown curly hair framed his roundish face. His glasses settled neatly on the bridge of his nose, and his lips parted slightly. He stared through the windshield at the field in front of him. He turned to look at me, and a smile slowly spread across his face. Don loves the outdoors, where he can breathe in the freshness of a clear day and watch the animals and birds, even the insects, in their natural habitat. As a hunter, Don always did so with the utmost respect, as part of the food chain. Sometimes, an animal had to die for us to survive. He did not shoot anything we wouldn't eat.

"What?" he asked under my intense gaze.

"Nothing."

"Why are you looking at me like that?"

"Just taking in the scenery." I smiled at him.

"Look," Don said, excitement in his voice. He pointed across a slough brimming with yellow reeds and grasses. "Do you see them?"

"Where?" I looked in the direction his finger pointed.

"There," he said again. "There must be eight or ten whitetails."

I stared hard. Eventually, I could make out the small caramel-coloured animals grazing along the water's edge in what appeared to be a hayfield. They blended in so naturally with the shades of the slough and the field that it was difficult to spot them.

"Get out of the truck. Take your rifle with you. Don't slam the door."

I did as Don instructed. We stood side by side. He lifted his forefinger to his lips in a show that I should be quiet. With hand motions, he signalled for me to lever the round into the chamber of my .44 Magnum, preparing it for fire. The sudden sound alerted the deer. They raised their heads and most of them bounded off. All of them except one.

My heart pounded. I lifted the rifle stock to my shoulder, looked through the scope, and took a bearing on the remaining one. She was in my sight. She calmly fed on the hay in the field. My finger trembled on the trigger, my nerves quivered with adrenalin, and my hand shook with excitement. I tried to steady it. The deer continued to feed, unaware of the rifle trained on her. I pulled the trigger; the rifle kicked, and a cracking sound split the air. I stared at the doe in horror, watching her stumble and fall. She got up and tried to run, but her injured leg impeded her. Watching her struggle, I felt sick. How could I have shot her?

"Come on," Don yelled for me to follow him as he took off, running in the direction the doe had limped.

We circled the slough, the going made difficult by the half-frozen mud and reeds. We slipped and floundered until we got to the area where the doe had stood. Looking around, I saw splashes of bright red on the snow. The blood proved that my bullet had found its mark. Don studied the ground.

"She went this way." He pointed and motioned for me to follow him.

I scrambled behind him. The weight of my rifle seemed too heavy to bear. My feet felt like lead. My heart outweighed them both. We tracked the blood droplets in the snow and found the young doe lying in the grass behind a stack of bales.

"There you are," Don whispered to her.

The young doe raised her head. Large, oval-shaped eyes stared at us. She struggled to get up, but the wound I inflicted on her would not let her. I could see that I had hit her in the shoulder, which immobilized her left front leg. Bile rose in my throat and my stomach pitched. Tears trickled down my cheeks as I watched her thrash about in the dead yellow grass.

"Oh, Don. Look what I've done to her," I sobbed.

Don turned to face me.

"Go back to the truck," he commanded.

"But …" I stammered.

"Go," he said, more firmly this time.

I turned and trudged back the way we had come. Halfway around the slough on my way back to the truck, I heard that last echoing shot, the one that finished her life, the one I will forever remember.

I returned to the truck and never went hunting again.

Reflection

"Are you leaving again?"

"I'll be back in about two hours," Don said as the door slammed behind him.

It was December 1980, and I stood at the kitchen window, looking out. My troubled reflection gazed back at me from the darkness outside. I watched my husband back his green and white Ford half-ton truck away from the house. With the yellow headlights pointing the way, his truck headed down the driveway.

Every evening for the past month, I saw the same thing happen. Don had supper with me and our children Sara, almost three years old, and Adam, six months old. He devoured a hasty meal, had his after-dinner cigarette, and then, without explanation, got up, put on his coat and boots, and walked out of the house, leaving me alone with the children night after night.

Rampant thoughts darted furtively in my mind, questioning and dreading what he might be up to. One moment, I thought he was having an affair. In the next moment, I dismissed that thought completely. I knew Don to be faithful. So, if not an affair, what took him away from home night after night? If it weren't for my two small children and their need to go to bed early, I would have followed him to see where he went every evening. Instead, I wondered and worried about what he was doing and why he felt he could not talk to me about it.

The December evening wore on. Eight o'clock, then nine o'clock. Where could he be? By ten o'clock, worry had me pacing the kitchen, occasionally glancing out the window hoping to see headlights coming down our road. It was dark. Several times I picked up the phone to call someone, but who? I had no clue where to look. I heard the icy wind howling outside. Studying the yard light, I saw snow falling and blowing around in the brisk winter air. Five rows of trees encircled our yard, protecting it from the harsh winds. Outside the shelter of the trees, I knew the wind skipped across the open fields, twirling snow around and around in a square dance all its own.

I turned from the window. The baby stirred as he cooed in his crib. I waited to see if he would go back to sleep. Soon his soft gurgles turned into whimpers, and before long, he erupted in full-blown sobs, fully awake. I sighed as I went to change his diaper. That job completed, I carried Adam into the kitchen, grabbing a baby bottle off the kitchen counter on my way through to the darkened living room. I sat down on the brown flowered armchair, cradling and whispering to him as his big blue eyes watched me while he sucked on the bottle's nipple. Long after he had fallen back to sleep, I continued to hold him, deriving what comfort I could from his small, warm body.

"Heh, wake up," someone shook my shoulder.

I felt confused. I struggled to wakefulness. Don stood beside me, reaching to lift Adam from my arms.

"You're home?"

"Yup. Sorry, I'm late."

"Where were you? I was worried."

"No need to be," he said calmly.

"But the storm."

"Not so bad. I'm home now. Let's go to bed."

He carried Adam back to his crib with me trailing behind and checking that Adam was asleep and properly covered before crawling into bed beside my husband. Don rolled over, instantly asleep. His snores were deep and rhythmic. I lay in bed, tormented. I could not imagine what kept him away from us every evening. For me, sleep would not come.

I loved Christmas. Every year, I could not wait to put up the tree, decorate the house, bake cookies, and wrap gifts. This year felt different. I could not shake the unsettled feeling that mercilessly gripped me. Since Don would not provide any answers, I wanted to talk to someone about it but didn't know whom I could trust to bring up such a private matter, so I said nothing.

Putting on an excited face for the children and faking enthusiasm, I went with Don, taking the kids to visit Santa in the centre of Cudworth's Main Street. Sara held back at first, but with some gentle coaxing, she climbed onto Santa's lap to tell him what she wanted for Christmas. Sara received her treat bag and posed so I could take a picture. Adam screamed his discontent, squirming in his snowsuit. He wanted nothing to do with Santa.

On the way home, we promised the children that Santa was coming to our house in a few more sleeps, and that he would be bringing presents. I got less and less sleep as Don spent more time away from home. I decided that if he didn't tell me by Christmas what was going on, I would have to leave him. I could not continue in our marriage if he didn't trust me to share what he did those many nights away from us. I found it difficult to sleep or eat, and I was becoming a physical and mental wreck. I found myself angry as well. How dare he keep this secret from me? How dare he?

My anger bubbled over on Christmas Eve when, once again, he told me he had to leave.

"WHAT? On Christmas Eve?" I cried out. "Don, this has to stop."

"It's nearly over," Don replied as he once more donned his coat and boots.

"I mean it, Don. I cannot take it anymore."

Don turned and walked out. I slammed the door behind him. Furious beyond words, I stomped into the kitchen where Sara, in her pyjamas, stood watching with big sad eyes. I rushed to her and bent to hug and reassure her that everything was all right. Sitting down in the familiar armchair, I lifted her onto my lap. I pulled out The Night Before Christmas and began reading to her while Adam slept in his crib. When the story ended, I took Sara by the hand and led her to her bedroom, tucked her in, and kissed her goodnight.

I decided tonight I would not wait up for Don to return. If he couldn't be home with us on Christmas Eve, then he could come home to a dark house, one where everyone was sound asleep when he returned. It would serve him right. I hazily recalled him undressing and crawling into bed, reaching for me and me pushing his hands away and edging further out of his reach.

"Mommy, Mommy, get up." Sara bounced on my bed.

I opened my eyes and reached to hug my little daughter. I noticed Don standing beside the bed holding Adam in his arms.

"Mornin' sleepyhead," he said with a smile.

"Did Santa come?" I asked my little girl.

"Yes, come see, Mommy. He brought lots of presents and candy."

"Sara let's wait for Mommy to see for herself," my husband interrupted her.

"Come on, Mommy. Get up."

"Okay, I'm coming. I'm coming."

I threw back the covers and crawled out of bed. After putting on my housecoat and slippers, I followed my husband and children down the stairs and into the living room. There, I saw the Christmas tree with all the presents I had put under it the night before.

"Look, Mommy. Santa ate the cookies we put out. They're all gone." Sara's eyes shone with excitement. "And he drank the milk. It's gone too."

"He must have been hungry from making his rounds last night."

Sara nodded, pulling on my hand, and taking me closer to the tree.

I saw it then, a bold and beautiful full-length oak cheval mirror. Stunned, I admired the exquisite piece of handiwork in my living room.

The elegant wooden arms reached up from the base to cradle the mirror that pivoted in its grasp. The mirror shone, and the oak gleamed. It was truly a magnificent creation.

Speechless, I turned to my husband, who still held our son in his arms.

"Merry Christmas," Don said with a huge smile on his face.

"But …"

"That's what I've been working on every night for the past two months."

"But …"

"After the reaming you gave me last Christmas over my poor selection of gifts, I thought I had to do better this Christmas or I'd invoke your wrath once more," he chuckled.

Smiling feebly, I recalled last Christmas eagerly opening my husband's gifts, only to find a roaster in one and a cutting board in the other. Disappointed beyond words, I had nearly thrown the two presents at him. He explained that he had waited too long, and on the day before Christmas, those two items were all that remained in the local hardware store for him to purchase and give to me for Christmas. Angry and hurt, I had let him know.

"Do you like it?" he asked, shifting my attention back to the mirror.

"I love it. It's so beautiful." I cried. "Thank you so much."

"So, I'm not in the doghouse?"

"No, you're not. This is incredible, Don. Thank you."

"The mirror came disassembled. The wooden pieces were so rough. It took hours and hours of sanding to get them the way I wanted them. I had to give it three coats of stain. Then, I had to assemble it. Of course, none of the pieces went together the way they were supposed to. It ended up taking much longer to build this mirror for you than I had originally planned."

"This is the most beautiful thing anyone has ever given me. I love it.

Where did you work on this mirror?"

He grinned again. "At Mom and Dad's. All those nights you worried about me being out in the storms, I was less than a mile away at their place, working on this in their basement."

I shook my head in disbelief, thinking about the evenings I spent at home without him, outraged and hurt, not knowing where Don had gone or what he was doing. I couldn't believe I had considered leaving him. The whole time, less than a mile away, he worked on my present.

My heart hummed.

So, You Think You Can Dance

It wasn't a secret. We could not dance. Well, he couldn't. When I saw a newspaper ad offering dance lessons, primarily learning the old-time waltz, I immediately signed up Don and myself. Knowing he would disapprove of the idea, I carefully planned how I could use my powers of persuasion to convince him this would be fun. I told him this presented an opportunity for us to get out of the house and spend some time together. Don said we could go to a movie. I told him the exercise would be good for us. He said we could go bowling instead. I told him I had never learned how to waltz. Don said he had.

"Come on. It will be fun," I implored.

"Not my definition of fun."

"This is something I'd like to do. Can't you do this for me?"

Don took a deep breath and exhaled, his shoulders beginning to sag a little.

That is a good sign. He's giving in.

"Please, Don," I snuggled up to him. "It's only for six weeks."

"SIX WEEKS!"

"It'll fly by in no time." I quickly tried to redress the situation. "We're always looking for things we can do together. This can be one of those things."

I watched Don consider it and gave him a little time.

Finally, he said, "If you want to do this that badly, I guess I can go with you."

"Thank you! It will be fun. You'll see."

Growing up as a child of the '70s when rock 'n' roll reigned supreme,

I resisted my parents' encouragement to learn how to waltz. With the impatience of youth, I shrugged off my father's offers to teach me how to dance. I vividly recalled our wedding night and how, as a newly married couple, Don and I awkwardly stumbled through the first dance, clinging to each other, hoping to make our attempts at dance seem effortless. Who were we kidding?

Anticipating the dance lessons, I imagined Don and I locked in each other's arms, sailing across the floor in a single, beautiful, and fluid motion as if floating on a cloud. My visions of splendour and magnificence came to a screeching halt when we descended the stairs into the church hall for the dance lessons and met our teachers.

The instructor, a colossal man, had his belt straining under a protruding belly, the sleeves of his white shirt rolled up to his elbows, and sweat running in rivulets down both sides of his face. He mopped away the perspiration with a yellow-stained hankey. His partner looked gaunt. Her blonde-dyed hair was carelessly piled on top of her head with bobby pins sticking out like on a pincushion. She had creases around her mouth as though she had sucked on too many cigarettes over the years. Her twig-like body seemed insubstantial enough to hang her clothes on while her pants threatened to slide right off her narrow hips. Together, the pair did not invoke a picture of grace and fluency.

Coming from a small town, we knew the other five couples that attended the class and, after some quick introductions for the teachers' sake and a few simple directions, the teacher, I cannot remember her name, went to the record player and put the needle down on a classic – "Jean, Jean" by Oliver. Not waltz music in my opinion, but that is what she played.

Don and I moved, he in one direction and I in the other. He quickly pulled me back toward him and we endeavoured again, me trying to be patient with him. After all, this is where we would learn to move as one and glide smoothly across the floor. We watched the other couples as they seemed to have already mastered the steps and could even talk as they danced and twirled around the church hall. We stood a foot apart, staring down at our feet, trying to count out the steps that would make us champions of the waltz.

The instructor came over to us and showed Don where to place his hands and how to guide me across the floor. I smiled encouragingly at my husband as he tried to do as the instructor asked. We managed a few steps until his shoe came down on my sandalled toe. I cried out, certain my toenail would turn black and fall off.

I dreaded the following two weeks' classes. Frustrated by the number of times the instructors came to offer their advice, I tried to make the best of it. At one point, the male instructor danced with me while the female instructor danced with Don, showing us the right way to waltz.

"Hold the frame," the instructor commanded of Don. "Hold the frame."

And, to me, the male teacher admonished, "You must not lead. Let the man lead."

How embarrassing to have the instructors dancing with Don and me! They had not done that with any of the other couples. When the male instructor finally released me back to my husband, I felt annoyed that they had singled us out and I blamed Don for his awkwardness on the floor. No Fred Astaire and Ginger Rogers here.

Toward the end of the third class, I went into the hallway for a drink of water. When I returned, I noticed the two instructors having what appeared to be a serious conversation with Don.

The teachers had their backs to me as I approached. Within earshot, I overheard one of them say, "Your wife has no sense of rhythm. Worse yet, she refuses to follow your lead. We do not see any point in the two of you continuing the classes. It would be a waste of time."

Don solemnly nodded and stared past them, looking into my eyes as I stood behind them, listening to every word they said.

"We felt you should be the one to tell Marilyn. Here's your money back."

"That's OK," I interrupted, my cheeks burning with humiliation and anger. "We were about to leave."

I snatched the money out of the instructor's hand, grabbed Don's arm, and marched him across the hall and up the steps. Once outside, I noticed my husband shaking. I glanced at him, only to see him desperately trying to keep from laughing.

"It's not funny," I told him.

"Oh, but it is," he argued. "If you could have seen your face …"

"You're just happy you don't have three more weeks of dance lessons," I chastised him, to which he nodded, a big grin sweeping across his face.

"Well, maybe I'll find some new dance lessons where the instructors know how to teach."

"Okay," my husband conceded.

We got into our car and slammed the doors shut, knowing that would never happen.

Walking The Dog

Our Doberman-German Shepherd arrived inside a cardboard box. We had rubbed the puppy's mother down with a towel in the hopes her smell would comfort him before we took him away. This little dog, completely black except for his brown eyebrows and knees, squirmed and stood on his hind legs, his pig-like tail wagging, looking for hands to pet him and hold him as he peered over the edge of the carton. After much debate, we called him Rocky.

Our two children, five-year-old Sara and three-year-old Adam gazed into the container at the writhing little dog now on his back with his tummy exposed, waiting for a rub. He playfully nipped at their fingers, and they giggled, delighted with their new pet. Right from the start, Adam loved this wiggling, playful pup, giggling as Rocky jumped to lick his face. Immediately he and the dog took to each other. Our son had never shown much interest in any of our previous pets but this one was different. Early on, the two of them ran around the farmyard, the black puppy bounding behind the child, biting at the boy's boots.

In the past, Adam contentedly watched the farm pets from afar and never made much of an effort to hold them or pet them. He cuddled this newest family member in his arms and laughed as the pup squirmed to lick his face. The puppy had long gangly legs and became quite an armful for our young son to hold.

As Adam grew, so did Rocky. By the following summer, the adult dog still insisted on acting like a pup. Over the winter, Rocky befriended our barn cat as they slept together in the shed. On chilly nights, the dog allowed the cat to sleep on top of him, so its body did not lay directly on the freezing floor.

This dog was not without the odd quirk or two. For instance, Rocky had a real aversion to pork and beans. Eating table scraps, the dog wolfed down all the food, but the beans remained untouched at the bottom of his dish. Once we knew the dog did not like beans, we made a game of it to see if we could hide a bean in his food and trick him into eating it. One time, the kids slit open a wiener, placed a single bean inside, and then closed the meat before plopping the bowl down in front of the dog. Returning a few minutes later to inspect the dish, the kids noticed the wiener was gone but one bean remained in his bowl. All the time we had Rocky, he never ate beans.

One fascinating feat that never ceased to amaze us involved Adam taking the dog for a walk. It was quite the performance. It started with Adam sitting on the floor to pull on his rubber boots. He insisted on wearing them because he wanted to be like his father, who always wore cowboy boots. Adam called these rubber boots his cowboy boots. Next, he fought his way into his red nylon jacket with a hood and a soft flannel lining. Our child had not yet mastered the zipper and needed help with it. Once dressed for outdoors, he made his way outside to find his puppy.

The strangest spectacle that played out before our eyes came when Adam took his dog for a walk. First off, Adam placed his arm inside the dog's mouth up to his elbow because he held on to the dog's tongue and used it as a leash. The first time I witnessed this, I ran up to them, scolding the dog and yanking Adam's arm away from the dog's mouth because I thought the dog was biting my son's arm. Adam led the procession, the child with his arm in the dog's mouth, the dog complacently following wherever the child led him, and the cat riding on the dog's back, claws grasping at the dog's short hair for balance. Round and round the farmyard they walked. Boy, dog, and cat.

This performance happened often that summer, and now, looking back after all these years, my biggest regret is not capturing it on film. I do not have a single photo to prove this happened. Memories, nestled deep, are the only proof I have.

Just In Time

I waited in an examining room at the Wakaw Union Hospital while Don sat in the waiting room. While at work, I received a call from my daycare provider telling me that our four-year-old son, Adam, was not well. I called Don who picked me up from work, and we rushed to get our sick little boy. We had now been at the hospital for twenty minutes. The doctor asked a series of questions, and I relayed what information I had. He examined Adam before whisking him away to I don't know where. My stomach knotted and my hands chilled, I perched on a stool staring through the open examination room door, looking up and down the sterile hospital hallways for some clue as to where the doctor had taken our son and why.

My ears perked up when I heard a child's muffled sobs down the hall. I knew it was Adam. What was happening? What were they doing to my little boy? I had to find him. I grabbed my purse and jacket and prepared to leave the room but stopped. I could hear the doctor in the next room speaking to someone, like a phone conversation. He used medical terms I did not comprehend, but I understood the words "urgent" and "I will notify the parents that you'll be waiting for them." I plopped back down on the stool, panic-induced bile bubbling up inside me from my stomach to my throat. I waited, sitting still with my back straight, listening and straining to hear more.

Footsteps approached the room where I sat. The doctor entered. From the solemn look on his face, I grasped the seriousness of Adam's situation.

"I've asked your husband to join us," the doctor began as I saw Don come through the door and stand beside me. I glanced from one man to the other, looking for clues, anything.

"We have a very sick little boy," the doctor stated. "Your son has Acute Glomerulonephritis. It's an inflammation of the kidneys. I have spoken with a nephrologist at St. Paul's Hospital, Dr. Bleicher, who is waiting for you. You need to drive Adam to St. Paul's Emergency as fast as you can. Our ambulance is out on a call, and it will take too long if we wait for it to return."

WHAT? How could this be? How could Adam be so sick? I thought about him running around and playing just a few hours before. The doctor must be mistaken.

Out loud I asked, "Will he be all right?"

"You need to act fast," the doctor replied, instilling an even greater sense of urgency. In a gentler, more reassuring manner, he added, "You can be thankful your babysitter caught it when she did. Now, please, you need to get to St. Paul's."

A nurse appeared in the doorway with Adam, placing the sobbing, frightened child in my lap. I kissed his tear-stained face, rocking him to calm him down. The doctor smiled and ruffled Adam's hair and once again told us we should be on our way, promising he would stay in touch with the specialist and with us.

Unblinking and in a daze, I carried Adam. Don ran ahead, first to open the hospital doors and then the car doors for us. Once inside the car, my husband pulled out of our parking spot. He made a U-turn in the middle of the street before careening toward the highway. The one-hour drive seemed to take forever, even though Don's foot pressing the gas pedal had us winging along at break-neck speed. Several times I cautioned him to slow down so we could get there in one piece, but that only seemed to anger him as he stared ahead, passing any vehicle that got in front of him, weaving in and out, and manoeuvring curves along the way.

I cradled Adam in my lap and saw that he had fallen asleep, his childish breathing still interrupted by the occasional sob in his sleep. He looked peaceful, with his eyelashes fanning his cheeks and a little bubble protruding from his mouth. I did not understand how our child could be so sick. He seemed healthy, like any other four-year-old, this morning when I dropped him off at the babysitter. How had his kidneys become inflamed? Kidneys are vital organs. What would they do if they no longer functioned properly?

I stared ahead through the windshield and found myself plea-bargaining with God to help make my child well again. I made unrealistic promises if he helped me with this one thing, to keep my son healthy and alive. Tears welled up and spilled down my cheeks as I turned to look out the side window, impatiently brushing them away with one hand. I needed to be strong. And I would be.

After what seemed like hours, we reached Saskatoon's city limits. My husband raced toward the city's core, stopping just long enough at red lights before accelerating once the light turned green. Approaching St. Paul's Emergency doors, we noticed a man in a white jacket with a nurse standing outside the door. My husband pulled up to him and lowered his window. We confirmed each other's identity, and the doctor instructed me to bring Adam and follow him while a nurse waited for my husband to park the car before joining us.

The nurse in the hospital asked me to remove Adam's clothes in favour of a hospital gown. Once changed and settled in his bed, the nurses administered tests. They took his blood pressure, collected a urine sample, and took his blood. They also set up an intravenous line. Adam screamed his discomfort as first one needle took his blood and the next searched his vein for the IV. He howled and clung to me as he tried to ward off the strangers with the needles. I tried to calm him down, reassuring him. Little did I know they required blood samples every hour on the hour for the next week or more.

Once the nurses finished all the preliminary examinations and tests, the nephrologist said he would like a word with Don and me. Dr. Bleicher asked us to confirm that Adam had strep throat a week or two before and we did. We had taken Adam to the Wakaw Union Hospital because of his high fever and throat infection which is how the Wakaw doctor knew that Adam had had strep throat.

The nephrologist explained it is rare but sometimes strep throat can lodge in the kidneys and cause inflammation such as the one our son had. This type of infection quickly develops, and we should be grateful our babysitter noticed the dark brown syrup colour of Adam's urine and called us as quickly as she did. Nephritis is what he called it, which can be very dangerous and even deadly because it leads to reduced kidney function and sometimes complete kidney failure.

The doctor believed we caught it early enough, but for the next few critical days, every bit of fluid intake and output had to be tracked and monitored. Dr. Bleicher explained that one of us had to be with Adam 24/7 to ensure he drank enough fluids and that the tracking occurred. In addition, he advised they had to do blood tests hourly because Adam had protein in his blood, which should not be there. They needed to ensure the steroids and antibiotics they started him on would be effective.

So began the week's stay in the hospital. I sat with Adam all day, every day, for eight days and nights. I encouraged him to drink, measuring every drop he consumed. When he had to pee, I tracked every drop of urine, keeping accurate records, which the nurses reviewed each hour. Also, every hour, like clockwork, the nurses advanced on my son to do another blood test. He screamed his discontent and fought as hard as he could to ward off the inevitable agony. Sometimes it took three of us to hold down my little boy and the fourth to take the blood sample. My son howled and sobbed. I feared he hated and mistrusted me. I think he felt me to be one of his adversaries. We had to have the blood samples to ensure he was getting better. But how do you explain this to a little four-year-old boy?

The days dragged on, but the nights were longer still. The every-hour ritual continued non-stop day and night. I did not have a bed to sleep in, only a hard chair in the corner beside Adam's bed. Exhausted, my nerves frayed, I longed to take Adam home and for him to be healthy like he had been before all this started. Our six-year-old daughter, Sara, stayed at home with Don. I wanted our old life back, our life without a sick child, our life together as a family. I tried to brush these thoughts aside. Right now, the most important thing was for Adam to be well again.

The day came when the doctor gave Adam a clean bill of health. We could take him home. I saw Don smiling and walking down the hospital corridor, holding Sara's hand as they made their way toward us. Adam, dressed, had all his belongings packed in his little backpack. As we waited for the nurse with the final discharge information, our son proudly showed Sara everything to see in his hospital room before we finally headed home.

This harrowing experience is a reminder to us all, how different it could have turned out had our daycare provider not called us just in time. Dr. Bleicher instructed us to bring Adam back for monthly testing. When that went well, we only had to return every three months, then every six months, and then once a year. After several years of this follow-up, the nephrologist pronounced Adam healthy and with no side effects. Relieved beyond all measure, we got to watch our son, now in great shape, take on the world exactly as he wanted.

Black Day In July

"We're almost there. You can have a snack when we get home," I said over my shoulder to my two children in the back seat of the car.

On a searing hot day in July 1984, I closed my eyes momentarily and wished I could have twenty minutes of complete silence to decompress after the long, sweltering day at the bank where I worked. The air conditioner in the office had not been functioning and the intense heat permeated the entire building, making it almost impossible to breathe. The sealed windows meant we could not get any breeze, and I felt exhausted. After picking up the kids from the sitter and on our way home to our acreage east of Cudworth, I just wanted to be home.

"Mommy, can we have an ice cream treat?" my four-year-old son, Adam, asked hopefully.

Darn. I meant to stop and buy some ice cream at the store before I picked up the kids.

"I'm sorry, Adam. We're all out of ice cream treats."

"But I want an ice cream treat," he whined.

"I'm sorry. I don't have any to give you."

"Can we go back and get some?" my six-year-old daughter Sara asked.

"No. I must get home and make supper. Soon your dad will be home from picking stones in the field and we will have supper then."

"But Mom."

"I'll find something just as good to eat when we get home," I promised and turned the car radio on, trying to drown out the complaining from the back seat.

A few minutes later, I turned into our driveway and climbed the hill to where our house sat behind a wall of trees. There, I saw my husband's old green half-ton lurched halfway into the caragana hedge, the driver's door standing open. That's strange. I had not expected Don to be home for another hour or two. Why was the truck door open? And why was his truck in the trees?

I stopped the car and let the kids out of the back seat, calling Don's name. No answer. The kids ran to the truck, me right behind them. I peered inside the vehicle. He wasn't there. Puzzled, I called again, thinking he was in the yard or, perhaps, in the shop. Still no reply. Where was he?

I took the children inside the house, calling as I went. The house was silent except for a water tap running. Relieved, I hurried to the bathroom, expecting to find my husband there. The room was empty. I turned the tap off and left the bathroom.

The kids were again asking for a snack. I dug into the cupboard and came up with a cookie for each of them. They complained about not getting an ice cream treat, but I placed them each at the table and instructed them to eat. It was a cookie or nothing. Sullenly, they both sat there staring at the Oreo in their hands.

I made my way through the house, searching for Don. He wasn't in the living room. Baffled about where he might be, I climbed the stairs to our bedroom to change from my work clothes to my home clothes. There, I found him lying on our bed as though sound asleep. I received no response when I uttered his name. Walking over to wake him, I became alarmed at the heat that seemed to radiate from his skin. Don's forehead and cheeks were flaming hot. I tried to rouse him. No response. I shook him harder. His eyes fluttered a little before rolling back in his head. Uncertain of what I could do to help him, I dashed downstairs to fill a bowl with cold water and grabbed a facecloth. I ran back up the stairs and began bathing his face. The instant cold on his face startled him. His hand came up to swipe at the cloth that I had laid across his forehead.

I spoke to Don again, but he seemed oblivious. I washed his skin, wringing out the rag as it instantly heated from his feverish face. I continued reapplying it, all the while talking to him, calling his name. After what seemed an eternity, his eyes flickered open momentarily. I leaned across him and could feel his heart racing. Something was seriously wrong.

"I'm taking you to the hospital."

Don became agitated, murmuring under his breath as he struggled to sit up. I told him to keep the rag on his face.

I ran downstairs and phoned my mother-in-law to ask if I could drop the kids off at her place in town while I drove Don to the hospital. I told the kids to get back in the car. They must have known this wasn't the time to whine or argue because they followed my instructions without complaint. I hurried back up the stairs to where my husband seemed to have lapsed back into unconsciousness. I fervently shook him, trying to swing his legs to the floor. I hadn't thought this through. How would I get this semi-comatose man down a full flight of stairs and out of the house into a car? Struggle as I might, I could not do it by myself.

Frustrated and desperate, I ran down the stairs to call my in-laws once again to ask if my father-in-law could come to help me. He said he'd be there in five minutes. I heard the kids hollering from outside as they waited in the hot car and fought amongst themselves. I ran outside.

"Hey, guess what?" I tried to sound excited. "Grandpa's coming over."

"He is? Why?"

"He's going to help me with Daddy."

"Oh."

"Can you guys play outside until he comes?"

They nodded as I fled back into the house and up the stairs to our bedroom. Once again, I tried waking Don. All the while, I kept applying the cold cloth to his forehead. I did not know what else to do. Panic set in. Yet again, no response from Don. It seemed like an eternity before

I heard a vehicle's tires crunching on the gravel and then a truck door slam. The kids laughed and called out to their grandfather, eager to show him the tricks they could do on their swing. Through our open bedroom window, I heard my father-in-law tell my children he needed to go inside to help their mom, but when he finished, they could come home with him. They could see Grandma and have supper at their place. The children eagerly agreed to wait outside, excited at the prospect of this new adventure.

When Don's father stepped inside the house, I called to let him know we were in the bedroom. As he plodded up the stairs to our room, I tried telling Don that his father was here to help me get him to the car.

Shocked by his son's unresponsiveness, my father-in-law asked, "What happened?"

"I don't know. I came home and found him this way."

"He drove his truck in the trees."

"I know. I think it's a miracle he got home without being in an accident."

Together, we swung my thirty-three-year-old husband's legs off the bed and struggled to hold his dead weight and get him to an upright position.

Somehow, we got Don down the stairs and into the car. Sara and Adam watched; their mouths gaped open.

"What's wrong with Daddy?" Sara asked.

"We aren't sure, Sweetie."

"How come he won't wake up?" Adam looked puzzled.

"Mommy's going to take Daddy to the hospital so the doctor can check him out," I told them. "You guys can go with Grandpa. OK?"

The children looked worried.

"Daddy's OK. I promise. I just want the doctor to look at him."

I hugged each of my children, crawled into the car, and backed it out of the driveway. With a brave face and a cheery wave, I was off, leaving behind my father-in-law, my daughter and my son standing in the middle of the yard.

I sped along the highway travelling the fifteen minutes from our Cudworth acreage to Wakaw, hoping and praying Don would be all right. I cast a sideways glance at him. He slumped in the passenger seat with his head leaning against the window. My heart pounded and my hands gripped the steering wheel tighter as my foot pressed the gas pedal down. Even though we were flying along, it seemed one of the longest rides of my life. The verdant countryside flashed by, but I hardly noticed. I needed to get some help for Don.

After what seemed an eternity, I pulled up in front of the Wakaw Union Hospital. I hurried out of the car and ran inside to the hospital's admitting desk. No one was around so I hammered on the little bell at the front desk. Finally, a nurse walked toward me. I ran to her, quickly explaining what happened and asking if she could bring a wheelchair and help me get my husband out of the car. She called for another nurse to assist us, and, with great effort, we got Don into the hospital. They told me the doctor, still at the medical clinic, had been called and would be right over. They wheeled my husband away. The nurses asked me a few questions, got me to fill out some forms, and then asked me to have a seat in the waiting room, promising to call me as soon as the doctor had seen him.

I watched the big hand on the wall clock tick one minute off after another. The few people that had been in the waiting room when I arrived had all left. I sat there alone, staring at the clock, listening to the repetitive *tick, tick, tick* as one minute after another fell away. Nothing made sense. I prayed for Don to be all right.

I fidgeted with my wedding rings as I heard the clamour of the patients' supper trays on a cart being rolled down the hallway and delivered to each room, surprised at how good the hospital food smelled as I sat there, not even hungry. With nothing else to do, I got up to use the bathroom across the hall.

When I came out, a nurse peeking into the waiting room, said, "Oh, there you are. The doctor will see you now."

Numbly, I followed her to a little room where Don lay on the examining table. He appeared awake. Or, at least, his eyes were open. I went to his side and clasped his hand.

"Are you alright?" I asked.

He tried a feeble smile, but then the doctor walked in.

"We need to run some tests," the doctor informed me. "For this reason, we'll keep your husband in the hospital for a day or two." He gave a nod to the nurses who immediately began helping Don back into a wheelchair before whisking him away to be settled in a hospital room.

"Come to my office." The doctor motioned for me to follow, leading the way down the hall to a room. He pointed for me to have a chair as he positioned himself behind his desk.

He leaned forward and said, "Your husband will be fine. You did the right thing by using cold water to cool him off. It probably saved his life. You could have been very close to becoming a widow had you not acted as quickly as you did to bring down his temperature."

I sat up straight in my chair.

"You mean he could have died?" I asked faintly.

"Yes, in extreme cases, he might have," the doctor confirmed. "Don suffered severe heatstroke, which accounts for the confusion, the dry, hot skin, the racing heartbeat, and his unconsciousness."

I thought about the many days my husband hauled the rock picker behind his cab-less tractor up and down the summer fallow fields, picking stones in the blistering heat. He probably did not drink enough water, and in the intense heat, it would not take long to become dehydrated. Lost in my thoughts, I tried to focus on the doctor's words.

"His body reacted, and his temperature soared to 104 °F. His loss of consciousness could also mean there is damage to some of his internal organs. For that reason, we need to run some tests."

I sat there, stunned.

"I believe you got to him in time. The cold cloth helped bring down his temperature. I expect your husband will fully recover. The tests will show if there is any internal damage."

The elderly doctor reached across the desk and patted my hand.

He continued, "Your husband has suffered severe trauma. He will have a long recovery time. He won't have to remain in the hospital for his recuperation, but it will be slow. He probably won't be able to work for a year or two, maybe longer."

The doctor stopped speaking, allowing me time to absorb the impact of what he had just said. At that point in the conversation, I tried to grasp everything the doctor told me. It hit me like a bombshell when the doctor said that Don wouldn't be able to work for a year or two. What would we do? I tried to brush off the feeling of desperation clanging around in my chest like cymbals crashing against one another. Never mind, I told myself. There was time to worry about that later. For now, I needed to know he was all right.

"Can I see him?"

The doctor stood up and walked me to the room where the nurses busily settled in my husband. I heard them laughing and joking about his uncleanliness with field dirt streaked across his hands and face and his hair all askew from the wet cloths I had applied.

One nurse was busy setting up an intravenous line and the other sauntered over to me and casually thrust a bag with Don's grimy work jeans and shirt in it and said with a smirk, "These are for you."

The good-spirited nurses fussed over Don, making him comfortable and promising to return later to bathe him.

After the nurses left, I stood there, staring at Don lying in bed, propped up by pillows.

"What were you trying to do?" I asked after they left.

"Get out of working," he said, grinning sheepishly at me.

I smiled back at him, relieved he still had his sense of humour.

At that moment, I knew we would be OK.

Teacher's Call

Don and I walked down the school's tiled hallway with student lockers saluting us on both sides as we made our way to our five-year-old son's kindergarten class. The school day was over, and most of the rural children raced to climb on their school buses. The town kids hurried through the crisp fallen leaves on their way home to play.

I received a call from Adam's kindergarten teacher that morning asking both Don and me to come in for a meeting with her. On the phone, the teacher spoke quietly and sounded concerned. Puzzled, I hung up the phone at work and called my husband so we could go to the school together.

I wondered what happened. How much trouble could one little boy be in? Why had the teacher sounded so uncomfortable when she made her request? I told her we would come right after school. She specifically asked that Don come too.

My husband and I poked our heads into the kindergarten room and saw the teacher.

"Come in. Come in," Mrs. Krimpki said. The middle-aged teacher rose from her desk, her navy suit impeccable with a blue-flowered blouse peeking out, softening the effect of her dark attire. She gave us a rueful smile as we hesitated in the doorway, signalling with her hand for us to enter as she closed a book in which she had been writing.

Together, Don and I made our way into the classroom scattered with primary-coloured desks and chairs. I stared at the bright posters with the alphabet letters and pictures of cartoon-like animals hanging on the walls. Small coat hooks, with baskets beneath for the children to store their belongings, lined the back wall. The side wall of the room boasted a broad expanse of windows that welcomed the sun's late afternoon rays. It looked like a happy place with its ambiance exuding a safe environment for young minds to learn and grow.

"Have a seat," the teacher said almost apologetically as she motioned to the dwarf-size chairs.

Hoping they could hold our weight, Don and I carefully lowered ourselves onto the miniature chairs. Sitting there, uncomfortable not only because of the tiny chairs but because we still did not know the reason for our summoning, we gazed expectantly up at the teacher as she seated herself once more at her desk.

"Ummm," Mrs. Krimpki cleared her throat. She squirmed with discomfort, looking like she wanted to be anywhere but here in the classroom. "I know you're wondering why I called you both in," she began hesitatingly.

Don and I waited.

"There's a lot of stress in farming these days," the teacher began, "what with the drought and the high interest rates …"

Mrs. Krimpki stopped. She was, of course, speaking about the decade of drought and the unprecedentedly high interest rates. My husband and I could only nod in agreement.

"People handle stress in different ways …"

Once again, we nodded.

"There may be stress at home too …" She left the sentence hanging, almost begging us to volunteer something.

"Every family has things they're dealing with," I agreed, intrigued by her approach, yet trying to grasp what she wanted to say.

"As a coping mechanism, some might turn to alcohol." She looked painfully at Don and then at me, almost imploring us to make this easier for her.

I frowned and said, "I suppose they do. What does any of this have to do with us?"

The teacher turned to face my husband.

"Don, you and I have known each other for a long time." She smiled. "I remember teaching you in elementary school when I had just graduated from teacher's college."

Don smiled his affirmation.

Mrs. Krimpki took a big breath as if preparing herself for the deep plunge into the murky waters of the unknown.

"Do you have a drinking problem?" she blurted out.

"What?" Don exclaimed. "No."

"I have to say, I've never seen you drinking in public, but …"

"I don't drink," my husband repeated. "What's this about?"

I could tell the teacher's question and the implied accusation upset Don.

Mrs. Krimpki, visibly uncomfortable, persisted in her questioning.

"Some people don't drink in public. They only drink in the privacy of their homes."

"I DON'T DRINK!"

Mrs. Krimpki gave me an imploring look, almost begging me to weigh in and make the conversation easier for her.

Instead, I said, "I don't know what you're getting at, but please understand that Don doesn't drink. He might have the odd beer on a hot day, but that's it. Never anything more than that."

Mrs. Krimpki looked uncertainly at both of us.

"I'm sorry about all of this, and I'm sorry about your leg," she replied.

"What about my leg?" my husband demanded.

"Aren't you having it removed?" the teacher asked.

"Do you mean amputated?" my husband almost bellowed.

Adam's teacher nodded, a painful look in her eyes.

"For Chrissake," Don cried out. Normally a quiet and patient man, my husband was now agitated. "What's this all about? Where have you gotten these ideas?"

"From Adam."

"From Adam?" I repeated. "What do you mean?" I asked in utter disbelief.

Mrs. Krimpki sighed. "In kindergarten, we have show and tell every morning. This morning it was Adam's turn. He told the class about Don's drinking problem and that he had to have his leg taken off."

"I don't have a drinking problem," Don growled.

Mrs. Krimpki grasped her hands on the desk in front of her and stared at us.

Don and I, more confused than ever, wondered where our son had gotten the notion that his father drank and that he needed his leg amputated. Was he making up such extreme stories for attention? What would have motivated him to fabricate such a tale? And to tell a class full of five-year-olds?

Mrs. Krimpki looked relieved. "So, none of this is true?"

"Absolutely not!" my husband and I vehemently denied in unison.

The teacher gave an uncertain laugh as she pushed her chair back from the desk and stood up. We took this to mean the meeting was over.

"I'm sorry about all of this, but you can understand my concern ..."

Once again, Don and I nodded, still in shock at the conversation.

We said goodbye, promising to speak to Adam about this, and left the school to make our way to daycare to pick up Adam and his sister. When we got there, Glenda, our sitter, pointed to the kids playing in the backyard.

Because I still felt incredulous over Mrs. Krimpki's comments and assumptions, I launched into the story of the meeting we had with her. Recounting the details of our parent-teacher session, I noticed a change come over Glenda's face. She went from looking interested in what I was saying to one of shock and then dismay in less than a minute.

"Oh, my Gawd!" she said, covering her face with her hands.

"What?" I asked. "What's wrong?"

"Marilyn, I know where Adam got all that from."

"Where?"

"From me."

Glenda began her tale of what had taken place the day before. Since Adam only had kindergarten every second day, on alternating days, he was at daycare. Because Glenda had only Adam to watch, she called up her friend, Susie, Don's aunt, to see if she would like to go for coffee. They agreed to meet at a café downtown. Both Glenda and Susie, married to alcoholics, had become friends because of their husband's dependencies. They helped each other as they struggled to deal with their husbands' addictions. Glenda wanted to meet with Susie yesterday because she knew Susie's husband would have his leg amputated in a few days. She wanted to support her friend.

Watching Adam sitting at the restaurant table quietly playing with his toy truck, Glenda did not realize the little boy soaked up all this newfound knowledge. Somehow, our young son transferred all these ailments from Don's uncle to Don himself. My heart broke. Our poor little son carried this information inside of him for a full day. He thought his father was a drinker and one that had to have his leg removed.

"I am so sorry, Marilyn," Glenda apologized profusely. "I didn't think Adam was listening to us."

"It's OK. Now that I know where all of this is coming from, I can deal with it."

Glenda opened her back door and called the kids to come inside. The children clambered into the house, noisily gathering their backpacks, and cried out their goodbyes as they ran to the car where their father waited.

I hurried after them, climbing into the passenger seat as Don started the car.

"Boy, have I got something to tell you," I announced as we drove off.

"Later, when we get home."

Hospital Visit

I said no. Don begged. Still, I resisted.

Yet, hours later, I walked down the hospital corridor with Don, the inside of my nostrils scrubbed clean by the smell of disinfectant. I hugged my secret close within. Even though I had not had a doctor confirm it yet, I knew I carried our third child. I wanted to tell Don today, imagining a happy day full of smiles and hugs. Instead, we roamed the hallways of the Royal University Hospital, looking for Don's Uncle Henry's room.

Admitted to the hospital days earlier, Henry had his leg amputated. Don insisted we go to visit him, perhaps out of a sense of duty but most likely a morbid curiosity.

The hospital's stuffy, unrelenting heat from the water boilers belching and wheezing hot air through the old building had me removing my jacket by the time we found Uncle Henry's room.

Don stuck his head through the hospital door and looked around.

"Come in, young feller," Uncle Henry called out from his bed beside the door.

Don greeted his uncle with a smile and signalled that I should follow him into the room.

I stood at the foot of the bed holding my jacket, my purse strap sliding off my shoulder. I said hello to Henry as he sat up in his bed, propped up by pillows. All I could think about was how hot it was in the small hospital room. I wondered if the window opened.

From my position at the foot of the bed, I scanned its expanse. I could see Henry's entire leg lying under the white sheet, but his other leg only reached halfway down. My world began spinning as I stared at the sight of his missing leg. I felt the colour draining from my face, my ears humming. My hand flew to cover my mouth, and I knew I had to get out of there.

Fleeing down the corridor, distracted by the ringing in my ears, the lack of fresh air to breathe, and the bile rising in my throat, I found myself lost in the endless maze of hallways with no escape, no reprieve. Not able to go any further, I found a window with a thick ledge and sat on it, pressing my face against the cool pane of glass, trying to breathe.

Don and his Uncle Henry found me perched on the windowsill. Ironically, Don and I had come to visit our disabled uncle, but the one-legged man needed to take care of me. He had pulled himself from his bed into a wheelchair and wheeled himself down the hallway after his nephew searching for me. When they discovered me sitting on the windowsill, they made sure I felt better. Don located the ladies' bathroom where I could splash some cold water on my face.

We did not stay at the hospital long. Don got me outside and into the brisk fresh air where I could once again breathe.

My secret out, I explained to Don the reason I got sick and reacted the way I did. He smiled and hugged me. This was not at all the way I planned to share my great news.

Size Matters

He grew to almost 200 pounds. Butch, our first St. Bernard, standing on his hind legs reached taller than my husband. Our dog had a massive square head with doleful eyes curtained by flagging eyelids that gave him a mournful look. His mammoth drooping jowls flanked both sides of his brown nose and splayed drool in every direction when he shook his head. His sloppy tongue, giving an affectionate lick, imitated being hit by a wet mop and always evoked a "UGHHH ..." from those on the receiving end. Butch, a handsome dog, had light brown ears that framed a white face. He had a tan-coloured torso with long, thick, white legs culminating in four colossal white paws. He resembled a gentle giant, always affectionate. Unfortunately, Butch did not recognize his size or his strength.

He loved cavorting with the children, romping playfully amongst them. Often, he ran alongside them, bumping into them and sending the children flying because a light tap from him felt like a brusque push from anyone else. The children loved climbing on his back so they could ride him pony-style. Butch amicably went along with their antics.

Butch never hurt a soul, but not everyone knew this. Living on an acreage, we wanted to keep it that way. One day, I returned home to find a car in our yard. As I drove around the trees, I saw Butch standing on his hind legs with his paws up against the house. I did not right away detect the man between the dog's gigantic paws, one on each side of the man's head. The man stood there with equal amounts of nervous sweat pouring off him as there was drool dripping from the playful St. Bernard.

As I approached, I immediately called off the dog.

In a trembling voice, the small Asian man said, "Yo dog no like Chinese?" It was more a statement than a question.

Even though I tried explaining Butch's gentle nature, the salesperson wasted no time. He ran and jumped in his car, making a hasty retreat. I could not help but chuckle to myself at the poor man's expense. I had to wonder what would have happened had I not come home when I did. How long would Butch have kept the man trapped, licking him to death?

Being so playful, Butch was bound to find trouble. Or trouble was bound to find him. One evening, Don came into the house and announced we had a situation. Butch had tangled with a porcupine. I closed my eyes and shook my head at the inevitable when living on a farm. We could not afford an unexpected vet bill, so my husband took matters into his own hands. Don brought Butch into the entrance of our house where he braced himself against the herculean dog, and, with pliers in hand, attempted to pull the quills out. Butch, in pain, wanted none of it. In one easy manoeuvre, the dog broke free and ran to the other side of the room, staring warily at my husband. Repeatedly, Don and I tried to wrestle the panic-stricken dog so we could extract the quills. We had no success.

Don had an idea. We had an entire cupboard full of old liquor. He asked me to pour some of it together in a cocktail for Butch. I started with two cups and offered it to our dog. Without hesitation, he lapped it up. We waited patiently. The liquor did not affect him, so I fed him more. Still, nothing happened. Finally, my husband told me to give it all to him. I placed the ice cream pail full of the liquor blend in front of him. Our dog drank it and tried to walk away when he finished. Butch staggered and swayed. He spread his four legs as if to brace himself and shook his head. He tottered from side to side as he edged himself closer to the wall so he could lean against it. My husband and I recognized this as our chance. We advanced on him, pinning him against the wall as one by one, Don plucked each sharp barb out of our pet's nose and paws. After an hour or more, we finished. We took him to the garage where we found some old blankets to make a bed for him so he could sleep it off. Deep into the night, we could hear our dog snoring. By morning, the effects of the alcohol had worn off, but Butch seemed to have an insatiable thirst. We fed him bowls of water to help alleviate his dryness. His nose and mouth were still tender. It took a while before he could handle food.

Once healed, Butch loved to terrorize our cats. He thought he was playing with them, but they thought he was out to eat them. One clear sunny day, standing at my kitchen window looking out into the yard, I saw Butch galumphing along after a cat. The cat fled across the yard and dashed under our blue 1979 Ford Pinto hatchback parked in front of our house. I expected Butch to come to a halt at the side of the car. I was wrong. Instead, the dog dove under the car past his shoulders. I waited for him to realize his predicament and squirm out from under the vehicle. Oh no, instead, this good-natured dog tried to stand up. Suddenly, I could see our enormous dog lifting the car on two wheels as he tried to break free. I called my husband as I held my breath and watched in horror and amazement as our small hatchback balanced on the two passenger-side wheels.

What ran through my mind was making an insurance claim. How would I explain to them that our dog had rolled our car?

As I watched, Butch lowered himself to the ground with the driver's side of the car still cradled on his shoulders, and then slowly wiggled his way out from under the Pinto. He did not roll the car. No insurance claim was necessary after all.

We enjoyed the company of this monstrosity of a dog for almost a decade until he developed cancer. We truly admired his playful and affectionate nature, always amazed at how this creature never really came to terms with his size. I am sure in Butch's mind he thought of himself as a pup just wanting to play.

Fear Lives Here

Clutching my purse, I hurried from the house to our three-door Pinto hatchback parked in the driveway. I had to rush. I could not be late for work. Throwing open the door to the car, I cast a precursory glance around the interior. My husband announced the night before that we had a mouse in the car. Searching for evidence, my gaze came to a screeching halt as I noticed one solitary mouse dropping on the dash. It was all the proof I needed that the encroacher still lived in my car.

Panic wrapped its arms around me so tightly I could scarcely breathe. I stood outside my car considering my options. Since Don had already left that morning, I decided I could call our neighbour and ask if he could drive me to work. I thought about it some more. No, too much of an imposition. Living on an acreage, the problem then would be how to get home after work. Maybe I could call in sick. Not a solution either. My strong work ethic would not allow me to skip a day of work because of a mouse. Perhaps I could find one of our outdoor cats and bring her with me to be my guard, but then realized if she spotted the mouse while I was driving, the chaos that ensued could cause me to roll my little car. Besides, what would I do with the cat all day? I could not leave her in the hot car.

I deliberated a few more minutes before realizing I had no choice but to get in the car and drive to work. First, I needed to take some precautions. I dashed back into the house and came out with two rubber jar rings. I took off one shoe and pulled my foot through the rubber ring, tucking in my pant leg. Before stepping back into my shoes, I did the same thing with my other pant leg. If that mouse had any notion of running up my leg, he would have to get by the rubber rings first.

I searched inside the car, hesitating, afraid of what I might see but even more afraid of what I wouldn't. I checked the mouse traps my husband had set out the night before, one on the floor on the passenger side, one under my car seat, and one on the floor in the back seat. They were all empty. I didn't know how I felt. Relief because now I did not have to deal with a dead or, worse yet, an injured mouse. But this meant the rodent still lived.

Hiding.

In the car.

With me.

I gulped and carefully stepped into my vehicle, positioning myself bolt upright in the seat, ready to make a quick exit if need be. I slammed the car door and cast a glance around to see if my actions had stirred the creature. Nope. No sign of him.

I started the vehicle and again scanned the car's interior before backing out of the driveway. My heart pounded in my chest as I held my breath and put the car in gear. I saw my purse lying open on the passenger seat and reached to zip it shut. I did not want to give that mouse anywhere to hide, certainly not inside my purse.

Glancing in the rear-view mirror, I remembered a friend telling me how a mouse had fallen from the sun visor onto her shoulder. I wanted to make sure none sat on my shoulder now. I also checked to see if anything moved in the back of the car. Nothing. A good sign. I relaxed and loosened my tight-fisted grip on the steering wheel. Now on the main road, I picked up speed.

My imagination took over when I thought I could feel something moving on the car seat behind my hips. I tried to laugh away my uneasiness and decided some music would be a pleasant distraction. I reached for the radio dial. At that precise moment, a mouse ran from under the passenger seat, across the floor, and up under the dash. I screamed and yanked the steering wheel so hard my little Pinto now headed for the ditch quicker than I could manage. I turned the wheel to avoid the steep decline. The tires caught the gravel ridge on the side of the road and sent me swerving back to the other side. It felt like the two wheels had lifted on the right side of the car. For one terrifying moment, I thought it would roll. Miraculously keeping the vehicle on all four wheels, I slowed down, pulled the car off to the side of the road and climbed out. I stood, immobile, my heart racing, and my head screaming. Tears of frustration welled up and threatened to spill as I noticed dirt kicked up by an approaching vehicle. I watched as he slowed down, hopeful he might help me.

"Mornin," he called through the open truck window. "Everythin' OK?"

"Th-there's a mouse in my car," I struggled to speak.

"Oh, yeah," he said congenially, glancing at my legs, "I thought maybe you wus havin' car trouble."

"No, but there's a mouse …" I said and watched as he slammed his truck into gear on his way into town.

I stomped my foot. I am not sure what I expected him to do. Upset that he left me on the side of the road, I realized my rubber ring-wrapped pants legs had caught his attention. I felt foolish for letting this tiny four-legged beast frighten me, but I did not want to get back in my little hatchback with him again. I walked around the car, studying it, hating it. That stupid car. How could it let that mouse get inside? Was it not tighter or better built than that? I might have to write a strongly worded letter to the Ford company about their second-rate vehicles.

I checked my watch and gasped. It was nearly time to start work. Defeated, I opened the car door and reluctantly crawled back inside. I knew my fear of mice to be silly but knowing it did not help me overcome it. I went through the steps of checking everywhere in the car once more. Tears sliding down my cheeks, I drove the remaining way into town, my heart racing, hardly breathing.

The mouse never appeared again during that trip.

Driving to work a week or two later, I noticed smoke coming from under the car's hood. Pulling to the side of the road, I jumped out of the car. Unsure of what to do, I felt relieved when an approaching vehicle stopped. Grabbing a blanket from his truck, our neighbour ran to my car, opened the hood, and smothered the fire. He searched under the hood for clues about why the fire had started.

"Right, here's your problem. You got yourself a mouse. She made her nest right next to the manifold," he said, reaching in to pull the grey nest out and throwing it on the ground. "The mouse probably chewed through the wires. That coulda started your fire."

I shook my head, angry at the destruction the little creature had caused. I hoped I never had to get back into that mousetrap of a vehicle again. My wishes came true. Too badly damaged to repair or drive again, the salvage yard claimed my little car. Never again would I have to step foot inside. What a relief!

Tough Lesson

Tut-tut-tut-tut-tut. Tut-tut-tut-tut-tut. Noise exploded from the toy gun.

I closed my eyes and sighed as I pushed my sweat-drenched hair back from my forehead. During the summer of 1989, Don, our three children, and I travelled for hours through the Rocky Mountains in a vehicle with no air conditioning. We had the windows down, trying to capture any possible cool breeze as we wound down yet one more mountain on our way home. Our children all settled in the back seat, not confined by seat belts because our older vehicle was not equipped with them.

Tut-tut-tut-tut-tut. Tut-tut-tut-tut-tut.

"Adam, will you please put that gun away," I implored our nine-year-old son. Several weeks earlier, Adam begged for a toy machine gun for his birthday. My husband and I happily obliged. On his birthday, Adam eagerly pulled away the gift wrap to find the much-wanted gun. Don and I soon regretted this purchase because we did not realize the loudness of the gun and how much our son loved to run around firing it.

Tut-tut-tut-tut-tut. Tut-tut-tut-tut-tut.

I turned around in my passenger seat to give my son a warning glance, letting him know I meant business. He looked innocently at me and lowered his gun. Soon the kids in the back seat began whining that one touched the other and that the other had looked at him and he did not want her looking at him. And how much further? One had to go to the bathroom. Yes, again. Because they hadn't had to go the last time we stopped. And, no, they couldn't go in the ditch. They wanted a real bathroom, to which I responded they had to wait because I could not find a real bathroom for a long way. We knew no towns existed for at least the next hour. At that point, our daughter became upset, sobbing loudly. The loud cries woke our toddler, who had miraculously been sleeping.

Tut-tut-tut-tut-tut. Tut-tut-tut-tut-tut.

"ADAM!" Don and I shouted in unison.

What had we been thinking? It seemed like a great idea at the time to take our three children, aged three to eleven years old, on a vacation. We wanted to show them the mountains. And so far, our trip had been great. We created memories that would last a lifetime. Our journey home, though, proved to be quite aggravating. Cramped in a hot car with three restless children, we still had hours and hours of travelling ahead of us before reaching our home.

Tut-tut-tut-tut-tut. Tut-tut-tut-tut-tut.

"Adam, I am warning you to put that gun away or else," I let it hang there, unfinished, hoping he would take my threat seriously. Don glanced at me with a frown, and I instinctively knew he had one nerve left and our son had nearly reached it. Big time.

Tut-tut-tut-tut-tut. Tut-tut-tut-tut-tut.

Now my husband's turn to admonish our son, he threatened, "Adam, if you fire that gun once more, I'm going to throw it out the window."

Adam sat quietly for a moment as if considering the odds of whether his father would carry out the threat. It seemed he had to find out.

Tut-tut. Tut-tut.

In one fell swoop, Don's arm reached to the back seat, grabbed the offensive toy, and hurled it out the open window.

I could not believe he had done that. Adam had only had the expensive toy gun for a few short weeks. I turned to look at our son, whose huge, disbelieving eyes brimmed with tears. Adam scrambled up on the back seat to look out the rear window where his gun lay in a heap of scattered, broken plastic on the highway as our car continued to speed away.

"My gun!" he cried.

"I warned you," my husband said.

Adam slumped in his seat, fighting to hold back tears. The other children, still in shock at what had just happened, sat beside him, hardly daring to make a sound. From the corner of my eye, I saw Sara reach to hold her brother's hand. And that is how they sat for the rest of the trip, considerably quieter.

Devil Lake

The mid-afternoon sun was as warm as a brooding hen on my upturned face; the light breeze like a hen's feathers tickled my cheeks. My outstretched hand floated on the coolness of the lake as our boat bobbed in the water like a gull enjoying the day. I closed my eyes, taking in the sounds of nothingness. Absolute silence except for the occasional call of some unknown bird or the whirring of Don's fishing reel as he cast his line over and over in his attempts to snag a walleye.

Mother Nature showcased her finest for a perfect day on the boat. I thankfully relaxed and breathed it in. This fishing trip in 1989 had not started that way. Having left our three children with my parents, we made our way north of Prince Albert, escaping to go fishing. After over two hours of travelling from Prince Albert, we passed through the small community of LaRonge and then spent the last hour and a half bouncing over a sandy grid road walled in by jack pines and spruce trees. We had driven through the settlement of Missinipe, which meant "big waters" in Cree, and continued our way to Otter Rapids. A metal bridge spanned this fast-flowing portion of the Churchill River. Dark green craggy jackpines leaned against the aquamarine sky, creating a landscape of raw beauty. Don stopped the truck and got out to wander across the metal-grated bridge.

"Come here. You've got to see this."

I climbed out of the truck and moved toward the bridge to see where he pointed. I stopped dead in my tracks. Through the open lattice of the bridge, I could see the rushing, churning water below. Having a terrible fear of heights, I could not bring myself to go any further. Don continued to call out to me to join him where he stood so he could show me something that had caught his eye. I could not move. He came back across the bridge and took my hand. I cautiously ventured out behind him, not daring to look down as he led me across.

Once we made it across the bridge, we gazed in wonder at the sheer beauty of the surrounding scenery. The contrast of the green-variegated forest with the azure sky and the thundering grey water below left us breathless. The beauty and symmetry grasped my heart. I wished I had grabbed my camera before I left the truck. Don offered to get it for me. Once he returned to the truck, I realized I stood alone on the far side of the bridge. The river foamed and tossed below me as I heard an approaching semi-trailer. I called for Don to get me, but inside the truck searching for my camera, he could not hear me above the roar of the water below.

The semi-trailer bore down on the bridge, the truck coming toward me. Eyes closed, I stood there. I tried pulling myself up against the bridge's railing, all the time glancing over my shoulder at the long drop below me. I didn't know what to do but cling to the metal bridge, praying for the truck to pass. But he didn't. Instead, he slowed right down, eventually bringing all eighteen wheels to a rumbling halt and a whooshing sound as the air brakes caught.

I stood there paralyzed, staring through the dusty windshield at the semi-driver behind the glass. He motioned with his hand for me to cross. I gasped and shook my head. He signalled again. Once more, I shook my head. My hands clung to the bridge's railing. I knew I could not remain there. My fear of heights had me frozen at the thought of crossing the bridge. The truck driver, becoming more emphatic with his gestures, once again beckoned for me to move across the bridge. I tried to step forward. I could not do it. The thought of crossing the bridge where I could see the rushing water below had my anxiety at an all-time high. By this time, Don had crawled out of the truck and waved for me to come toward him. I begged him to help me. By this time, laughing so hard he could barely stand up, Don had the truck driver smirking as well.

When I realized that I would have to do this alone, I trembled, not so much from the fear but the anger that enveloped me. I dropped to my hands and knees. With the semi-truck driver laughing on one side of the bridge and my husband nearly rolling in the dirt on the other side, I crawled across the bridge on all fours, staring down at the churning water below me. My stomach pitched. When I got safely to the other side, I stood up and gave them both the royal salute before I crawled into our truck and huddled in my seat, too furious and humiliated to say a word. When Don tried to apologize, I gave him a cold disdainful glare. The rest of the trip passed in silence.

Now on this elongated lake, nothing more than a bulge in the Churchill River, I relaxed and put the day's earlier events behind me. The lake, a deep part of the river, had areas where huge rocks jutted just below the surface. Don cautiously made his way down the lake in search of a better fishing spot where the plentiful walleye practically begged to be caught.

We felt a jolt. The boat motor died. Don pulled on the cord to restart the motor. Nothing happened. Repeatedly he tried with no success. My husband hauled the motor up out of the water and, after close examination, discovered why the motor had stopped.

"A broken shear pin," he said, grabbing his tackle box and rummaging through it in search of a new one. He came up empty-handed.

I gazed out over the broad expanse of the lake as we rocked in our little aluminum boat, with no other boat around as far as the eye could see.

Almost too afraid to ask, I finally blurted, "So, what do we do now?"

"We row," Don said grabbing the two oars, one in each hand, dipping them into the water.

"What do I do?"

"You sit there."

Don, upset with himself for hitting the rock that caused the shear pin to break and for not having a spare shear pin with him, continued to row. I thought it might be best if I said nothing. We sat together in the boat. He made big circular rowing motions. I cursed silently under my breath. The boat moved ever so gradually. After an eternity, we made our way back to shore. At the boat dock, Don spoke with a local man who told him the location of some excellent fishing spots on the lake. He also had a nail that we substituted for a shear pin. Together, the two men got the boat motor running.

My husband, eager to head out onto the lake again, struck out further than before. If you wanted to find the best fishing spots, the local man said, you had to go further up the lake. The boat droned along further and further across the lake's grey expanse. Nearing our destination, the boat motor sputtered. Then it stopped altogether.

Oh, no!

What now?

After a quick check of the motor, Don looked at me rather sheepishly. I raised an eyebrow questioningly at him.

"We're out of gas."

"WHAT!!!" I cried out, so angry I wanted to stomp away in a huff but could not have that satisfaction since the twelve-foot fishing boat confined me in water eighty feet deep.

Out came the oars. Don began rowing us back to shore. Again. Not one of my finest moments, I chastised my husband for letting this happen. Sitting in the boat, I sullenly watched the sky darken as evening clouds blew in. The breeze rocked the boat, and motion sickness and nausea overtook me. Several times, I hung my head over the side of the boat, sometimes with dry heaves, sometimes not so dry. I felt miserable. The shore remained far away, and darkness shadowed the sky.

I spotted something on the horizon. A boat in the far distance. I told

Don we needed to flag them down so they could help us.

"No, we don't," he said calmly.

"Yes, we do. It's getting dark."

"We're almost there."

"No, we aren't. We have a long way to go yet." I began fidgeting in my seat.

"Stop rocking the boat," my husband warned me. "Now what are you doing?"

"I'm taking off my shirt so I can wave it and get their attention."

Before he could say anything further, I had whipped off my blouse and frantically waved it in the air. My husband howled with laughter, barely keeping the oars from sliding out of his hands into the depths of the lake. I continued flapping my shirt, hoping they would see us and come to our rescue.

The boat got closer. Soon it became apparent that what I thought was a boat turned out to be a canoe. As the canoeists pulled alongside us, they asked if we needed help. By this time, I had put my blouse back on and felt foolish for having bothered these people. We thanked them and continued paddling.

After what seemed a lifetime, the boat rubbed against sand and Don jumped out to pull it onto the shore. My cramped legs begrudgingly allowed me to stand as I scrambled out. Once on dry ground, I dropped to my knees again, for the second time that day, this time grateful for the ground beneath me. Solid earth. I decided this lake, Devil's Lake, had an appropriate name.

The Little Chick And The Fox

The sun shone brightly that August morning in 1989. I stood at the sink in front of the kitchen window facing our beautifully manicured yard finishing up the last of the dishes from the night before. I enjoyed the cloudless aquamarine sky that stretched above the trees as far as I could see. Muffled sounds of my three children frolicking outside in our farmyard floated toward me as they laughed and yelled at each other while they played their make-believe games. I wondered what I should make for supper and if I should try to get the last of the raspberries picked that morning before the sun got too hot.

My reverie was interrupted by a slight movement I saw on the top of one of our round plywood bins. I watched further. My heart stopped in disbelief. I could see the small head of my three-year-old daughter, Brenda, on the other side of the conical roof of the granary. My baby daughter. On the granary roof! No time to figure out how she got up there. I had to get her down.

I rushed from the house and into the yard where my two older children, Sara and Adam, ran toward me frantically, calling and pointing their fingers toward the granary. By now, Brenda stood proudly on the roof like the king of the castle, laughing down at us. Fearless.

Hurrying toward the granary, I saw traces of early morning dew still on the bin's plywood roof, making it slippery. My stomach lurched as my daughter moved along the top of the granary, her bare feet searching for a hold as she tried to steady herself on the precarious incline of the roof.

"Brenda," I called to my toddler. "Stay still. Mommy's coming. I'll get you down."

To my older children running beside me, I asked, "How did she get up there?"

They told me she had climbed the ladder. What ladder? And then I remembered Don had cleaned out the granary the day before, making it ready for the new grain once harvest began in a few weeks. He must have left the ladder leaning against the bin. That would be all my youngster needed to see. I knew she had this inane compulsion to climb things. She had ever since she learned to walk. Anything to climb or scale, Brenda was on it. She climbed into vehicles, up trees, and onto tables and counters. Always climbing. I, terrified of heights, prayed for the courage to climb that fifteen-foot ladder to rescue my little girl.

Standing at the base of the grain bin, I tilted my head backward to call up to Brenda. She stood there as proud as could be, clapping her hands. Prepared to dash around to the back of the granary to get the ladder, I noticed Brenda trying to follow me around the cylindrical roof. I stopped dead in my tracks. I could not risk her moving and falling. If I attempted to move, she tried to mimic my actions.

I instructed Sara and Adam to see if they could carry the ladder to the front of the granary while I stayed and talked to Brenda, trying to prevent her from moving. And falling. Only eleven and nine years old, Sara and Adam were not strong enough to lift and manoeuvre the heavy wooden ladder.

I had no choice. I went around to the ladder, hoping I could clamber up and get to my daughter before she lost her footing and fell.

"Brenda, stand still. Mommy's coming."

"Where are you, Mommy?"

"I am on my way to get you. Stand perfectly still."

"Mommy, I can't see you," my little girl cried out.

"That's because I am the fox."

I made it into a game where she was the chicken, and I was the fox.

As the little chicken, she had to stand completely still so the fox would not see her and come to catch her. That seemed to work as I summoned up all my courage to climb that ladder. My arms trembled, my legs weak, and I climbed higher and higher. I could not bring myself to look down because I knew the ground swam below, making me more unsteady.

At the top of the ladder, I tried to figure out how I would bring my leg over to get onto the granary's roof when my daughter lunged at me. I clung to the ladder with one hand and caught her with my other arm. The force swung the ladder away from the granary and we swayed precariously as I envisioned both of us falling backward with the ladder landing on top of us. Miraculously, I don't know how the ladder steadied itself. I made the descent, clutching my baby in my arms.

Once on the ground, I hugged her and cried into Brenda's shoulder. Her little arms disentangled themselves from around my neck. Pushing me back so she could see my face, her eyes gigantic, she said, "The fox caught me, Mommy. Are you going to eat me?"

"No," I smiled at her, "this fox saved the little chicken, and they became best friends and played happily together for a very long time."

"I like my foxy Mommy."

"And I love my little chick."

Oh, Christmas Tree

"It's time to go," Don called, leaving the house to climb into our car to wait for us to join him.

The serene winter day boasted a sapphire sky that stretched cloudlessly until it met the snow-covered horizon. On this Saturday afternoon, a week before Christmas, our family planned to head to MacDowall, about an hour away, in search of a Christmas tree. Our custom for the past several years, the children delighted in stumbling through the forest looking for the perfect tree to bring home, on which to throw their homemade decorations and make it their own.

Our three children pulled on their boots and mittens and wrapped scarves around their necks, calling out to remind me to bring the hot chocolate. I reassured them I had the thermos with me as I bundled our youngest daughter, Brenda, into her snowsuit and then helped her to her feet. Brenda walked like an abominable snowman, her arms splayed from her side and the thick material prohibiting her from her regular walk.

We all clambered into the car.

"Do you have the axe?" I asked Don, already knowing the answer. "And the ties?"

"Yup."

We settled down for the long ride with the kids in the back jostling for their preferred seat so they could see out the window. Brenda sat in the middle and cried. I let her climb over the car seat so she could sit on my lap and have a better view of things. As one kilometre after another ticked by, the children's eager anticipation and excitement turned to,

"Are we there yet?" and "How much longer?" Their restlessness grew.

"Let's sing some Christmas carols," I said and launched into the familiar "Deck the Halls." The children joined in, singing with youthful gusto even though they did not know all the words. The "Fa-la-la-la" part came out extra loud, and I soon regretted starting with that song.

Kilometre after endless kilometre rolled past as the children pushed to see out the windows. They began talking about past Christmases, and Sara teased Adam about how he always brought his blanket down from his bedroom and curled up under the Christmas tree. He loved the strings of lights twinkling and lighting up the darkened room. Every morning leading up to Christmas, we found him snuggled under the Christmas tree with his blanket sound asleep.

The children began speculating about what Santa might bring them for Christmas this year. Sara, already into adolescence, wanted a specific sweater. Adam had his sights set on an Optimus Prime Transformer, and Brenda only wanted a dolly, one whose eyes opened and closed and came with a baby bottle.

With the children distracted, time passed and soon we neared the area where we previously harvested our trees. The poplars, with their white peeled trunks lifting their branches to the sky, had now given way to the dark green scraggly jack pines and the thick lush spruce trees. The coniferous trees drooped under the shroud of the last snowfall, creating a wondrous sight. Too late, I realized I had not brought my camera. My husband, at long last, turned off the highway near MacDowall. Bouncing down the uneven frozen trail, it felt like our brains risked being shaken loose inside of our heads.

"OK, kids, we're almost there. Start watching for a nice tree," my husband said.

Don stopped the car, and everyone piled out. The brilliance of the day bounced off the snow, and an intense silence fell on us. Briefly, we all stood in wonder at the surrounding beauty until a screaming snowmobile fled past us in the ditch. My husband took the axe out of the car's trunk. We headed south and began stomping through the snow in search of a splendid tree. The two older children ran ahead, laughing and shouting. Our youngest tried following them but the snow was too deep for her to navigate. Frustrated, she threw herself down into a bank of snow and lay there with her arms crossed. Don handed me the axe as he bent to pick up our daughter and swung her up to his shoulders so she could ride there with an ideal bird's-eye view.

"Here's one. Here's one," Adam called from several yards ahead of us.

"We're coming," I shouted to him.

When we reached the tree, we looked up at the entire twenty-five-foot expanse of it. We admired Adam's tree, too tall for us to bring home and set up in our house. In the meantime, Sara begged we bring home a Charlie Brown Christmas tree she found. Sara always wanted to save the underling, whether the runt of a cat's litter or the scrawny puppy. Now she wanted the scraggliest of trees, one almost devoid of needles and already beginning to turn brown. My husband gave her choice a firm no.

We continued to trudge through the deep snow in the ditches and eventually came across another father and his daughter, fortunate enough to have found their tree. We stopped to speak with them before the man pointed us to where they had found theirs, a deeper distance into the forest. At that point, we decided I should take Brenda back to the car and Don and our older two children would continue their venture to find the right tree to bring home and decorate. My husband hauled our daughter down from his shoulders. She and I waved to the other three and then turned to make our way back to the car. Because the snow was so deep and Brenda's legs were so short, I found myself half carrying, half dragging her back to the parked car. We climbed inside, prepared to wait. How long? We didn't know. As long as it took to find the ideal tree.

Brenda and I dallied in the car, and I noticed the thermos with hot cocoa lying in the back seat. In all the excitement, I had forgotten about it. Oh, well, we could drink it at home later. We did not have to sit in the car too long before we heard cheerful voices calling out to us. Don, Sara, and Adam carried the spruce tree between them. As they got closer, I could see big grins on all three faces. Brenda and I crawled out of the car to inspect their jackpot. My husband stood the tree on the ground, brushed the snow off, and turned it to me for approval. I strolled around it, inspecting it from all angles before I smiled and nodded. This perfect tree had the right height, the right depth, and the branches even on all sides with no big gaping holes. I signalled my approval with a smile and a thumbs up. The children cheered and danced around as Don grabbed the ties from the trunk and secured the tree to our car's roof, grunting as he pulled the cords tight.

Everyone back in the car, we headed to our favourite restaurant in the service station just outside the hamlet of MacDowall. Every year, we chopped down a tree in the forest, and every year, we stopped at this same restaurant that made the best homemade hamburgers and French fries. The owners recognized us from previous years and served up the food, along with plenty of hospitality. They threw in some candy for the kids and winked at them from behind the cash register.

With our stomachs filled and the tree on top of the car, we made our way home. Before long, darkness descended. The ride home, much quieter than the ride there, had all three children either nodding off to sleep or sitting and dreaming their little dreams.

When we arrived home, Don carried the tree into the house and set it up in the stand so the branches could thaw and spread out for decorations the following day. The prickly needles of the spruce tree and the small odorous cones clung on for dear life, emitting a sharp, fragrant aroma that filled the room. The children walked around it and studied it, before unanimously nodding their approval.

"It's pretty," Brenda cried out.

"It will look even nicer once all the decorations are on it," Sara told her little sister.

"Can we bring the boxes of decorations up from the basement?" Adam asked.

"Not tonight. It's bedtime now," I replied, followed by a chorus of protests. "Get your pyjamas on."

"Aw, Mom," the children groaned, plodding up the stairs to their bedrooms.

The kids in bed, Don and I shared a cup of hot chocolate, smiling at each other and knowing these to be the best times, the times we would remember many years later after our children had grown and had families of their own.

We sat a little longer and then turned out the lights and made our way to bed as the refreshing smell of the spruce tree wafted through the house, teasing our noses as we slept. We knew once everyone was asleep, Adam would creep from his bedroom and curl up with his blanket under the tree.

Close Call

We arrived at the beautiful lake resort for our three-day holiday. I loved our rented cabin perched on a hill overlooking the lake. The trembling poplar leaves seemed to whisper that here our family could relax in the arms of Mother Nature, lulled in her guardianship.

I examined our temporary two-bedroom home for any evidence of mice. Terrified of those four-legged little rodents, I declared if I found so much as one mouse dropping, I would have the family packed up and headed for home in the blink of an eye. Much to my husband's relief, I didn't find a sign. We were safe.

The kids, eager to explore their new environment, took off running around the campsite and asked if they could look at the lake. Nervous about children near water but wanting them to experience the freedom of the great outdoors, I gave my consent but only if our twelve-year-old daughter, Sara, held the hand of her four-year-old sister, Brenda. Restless after the three-hour drive, the kids promised to stay out of the water and took off running down the slope to where the lake shimmered.

Later that afternoon, Don took Sara and Adam fishing. Brenda wailed at the injustice of it all because she could not go. I stretched out on a lounge chair in front of our cabin with her on my lap, consoling her by reading a story. After a while, her sobbing subsided and her breathing slowed to that of a child sound asleep. I relaxed and closed my sunglasses-shaded eyes and revelled in the campground sounds – the squirrels chattering and the loons calling, distant men's voices as they walked through the camp area, and the sound of a far-off saw buzzing its way through wood they cut for fire. The sooty smell of campfire smoke wafted through the air, as did the smell of barbequed meat.

"She's asleep?" a voice asked, my peaceful slumber interrupted.

I raised my sunglasses and turned my head to see plaid shorts topped off with a flowery blouse. I smiled at the middle-aged woman standing beside me.

"Yes. It's been an exciting day for her."

"How old is she?"

"Four."

The woman scowled as she moved around to stand in front of me. "I have two granddaughters about her age. They live in Grand Prairie. I don't get to see them much."

Changing the subject, she asked, "Did you just get here?"

"Yes. A few hours ago."

Without being invited, she lowered herself into a lawn chair across from me.

"We've been here for a week. Leaving after the weekend."

"Where are you from?" I felt obliged to make small talk but secretly wished she would leave so I could rest.

"Regina."

"That's a fair drive."

"Been coming here for years. Husband likes the fishing. I do, too, but can't sit out on the lake for twelve hours a day like him."

I nodded understandingly.

We chatted for a few minutes before the woman asked, "Will she sleep long?"

I shrugged my shoulders. "Hard to say. Probably not."

"I'll take her picking berries." It seemed a strange thing to say when we had just met. I thought nothing of it and did not comment further.

With that, the stocky woman hauled herself out of the unevenly balanced lawn chair and continued her way down to the lake. From my position on the higher ground, I saw her standing on the dock with one hand on her hip and the other hand over her eyes as she scanned the lake. She stood like that for a long time. I closed my eyes to rest. When I opened them again, the woman no longer stood on the pier.

I drifted off to sleep with Brenda on my lap.

I woke to the sound of children's banter and laughter as my older two children climbed the hill to our cabin. Shaking off sleep, I was puzzled that my youngest daughter no longer lay on my lap.

"Have you seen Brenda?" I called out.

"No. We just got here."

I scrambled off my lounge chair, calling Brenda's name.

Alarmed, I ran inside the cabin and searched the rooms. I could not find her. I charged outside, frantically calling for her. Still no answer. About to run down to the filleting house to tell my husband that our daughter had disappeared, I saw her emerging from the trees, holding the hand of the strange woman from earlier that day. Brenda carried a small pail in her other hand, animatedly talking to her companion. I hurried toward them and grabbed my daughter, all the while searching the woman's face for an explanation. I received none.

"Mommy, we picked berries," my little girl proclaimed, holding the pail up so I could see the red berries rolling around inside.

I nodded, still trying to figure out the situation.

The woman said nothing but grimaced at my daughter. She turned and walked back into the trees. Something did not make sense. Had the woman found Brenda wandering around our campsite while I slept or, and this thought made me shudder, had she lured my little girl from my lap? Uneasy, made worse that my daughter seemed drawn to her, I resolved to discuss this with my husband later.

That evening, our family of five sat around the crackling fire, each with our sticks extended roasting marshmallows. Don told the kids the marshmallows roasted better if they waited for the flames to die down so only the charred logs remained. Of course, they couldn't wait and had the graham wafers and chocolate near at hand to make smores once the marshmallows browned. On a postcard-perfect night, I enjoyed the children's smiles reaching far beyond our inner circle, their faces flushed by the reddish-yellow flames that licked at the logs. I smiled to myself, content with my little family around me, enjoying our escape to nature. So calming. So peaceful.

I roused from my reverie to glimpse Brenda staring past her siblings into the trees behind them. She smiled and held her hand up as she flapped her small fingers in a childish wave. I turned in my chair to see whom she waved at. Startled, I saw the woman I met earlier that day standing just inside the bluff of trees that surrounded our cabin, watching us. Her raised hand acknowledged my little girl before she faded back into the darkness.

"Brenda, I don't want you hanging out with that woman anymore. Do you understand?"

"But Mommy, Birda's my friend."

I realized then I did not know the woman's name and could only assume my little girl had mispronounced her name. Birda probably meant Bertha.

"You can play with your brother and sister."

"But Mommy. They don't play the games I like. Birda said she'll play with me."

I looked at my husband. Don promised to take Brenda for a walk and to the playground the following day. That seemed to appease her for the moment. I relaxed, knowing our little girl would be safe with her dad for part of the day. The balance of the day she would be with me.

The next day, after Don had spent time with Brenda, he handed her back to my care. I cleaned up inside the cabin while my oldest daughter watched her younger sister outside. Sara, carrying an armful of wood to the cabin, tripped over an exposed tree root, falling on top of the firewood, scraping, and cutting her arms and legs. I hurried outside to bring her into the cabin so I could tend to her.

While in the cabin a short time later, we noticed a commotion outside with people yelling and running. Within seconds, three men in their 20s called out to each other as they raced toward the lake. We hurried outside to see what had happened. Looking around, we could not find Brenda. Where had she gone? We called for her. No answer.

Panic seized my heart in a sudden vice-like grip, the way a mother knows when one of her children is in danger. I could not breathe. I began running to the lake, the direction everyone else was headed. As I got closer, I saw the strange woman from the day before standing on the dock. I looked around. No Brenda. The woman seemed calm as I saw her point into the water washing up against the wharf. One of the young men got on his knees to peer into the water and under the dock. Kicking off his shoes, he jumped. The lake engulfed him.

Nearing the water, I watched as the other young men jumped into the deep green lake. When I reached the marina, I asked the woman what had happened.

"She ran on the dock. Her sandal must have caught on a board. She fell in," the woman explained.

My heart lurched as I peered into the black water looking for my daughter. About to jump in, I saw one of the young men resurface from under the dock. He held my little girl, keeping her head above water. Brenda's hair pasted to her face as she sputtered and gasped for air. The other two men held the boats aside so he could raise her to me, her face white, her lips blue, her eyes filled with terror. He lifted her as I knelt to reach for her. Once again, I held my daughter safe in my arms. I tried to comfort her with caresses and words of reassurance. I trembled as hard as her teeth chattered. Her little arms reached around my neck as if to never let go.

The three young men hauled themselves out of the lake onto the pier and told me how they found Brenda beneath the dock, clinging to a rope to keep her face above water. As the moored boats rocked, the waves washed over my daughter, who hung on for dear life. The cold, grey water had nearly become her grave. The reality of how close I had come to losing my little girl sank in. Shaking uncontrollably, I once again turned to ask the woman for an explanation.

    She had vanished.

Elvis

Don and I loaded our three children into the car that Sunday afternoon and headed to a farm near Melfort, only an hour's drive from Cudworth. On this trip, we picked up our second St. Bernard pup. We noticed the owners had five or six fully grown St. Bernards running around inside their house, chewing on their furniture. We should have recognized this as a formidable sign. However, we had all loved this dog's predecessor, Butch, and we expected to get another St. Bernard with the same level of intelligence and affectionate nature he had. We could not have been more wrong.

We brought this cute puppy home when the first Beethoven movie hit the screens. Our children adored this movie and wanted to name their dog after a famous musician as well. They landed on Elvis.

The puppy grew to be enormous, slobbering and drooling his way through adolescence and then into adulthood. As he grew, the children tried to climb onto his back to ride him as they had with Butch. Elvis wanted none of it. He nipped at them and bounded away as he saw them advancing on him. For entertainment instead, Elvis chased the cats and the occasional rabbit, slaughtering them by grasping them in his massive jaws and shaking the life out of them. One time, he even grabbed a skunk and shook it relentlessly, getting himself and my husband sprayed. Not impressed, Don bathed for days in tomato juice trying to rid himself of the horrendous reek. Elvis was merciless in his pursuits, heedless of any discipline.

During the winter, Elvis came up with new pastimes. He loved chewing the plastic windshield and seat of our snowmobile. No matter how many times we replaced the windshield or the snowmobile seat, Elvis destroyed them all over again. Perhaps he thought it was a game.

This unruly dog chewed my car's plug-in cord, frustrating me when I went outside to start my vehicle for work in the morning, only to discover a dead battery. A closer inspection revealed a chewed-off cord, often making me late for work because my car needed a boost to get it going. Amazingly, Elvis did not suffer an electrical shock when his sloppy muzzle and teeth worked their way through the electric wires. If he received a shock, it never deterred him.

In the summer, Elvis relentlessly sought things to chew. He found a piece of loose siding on our house that he ripped off and then continued to eat his way through the surrounding white siding, tearing his way through to the raw wood beneath. We had a beautiful caragana hedge that encircled a portion of our front yard. Elvis soon realized if he chomped down hard on the shrubs, his strength allowed him to rip the entire tree out of the hardened ground. Destroying our yard became his new hobby.

One time, my husband left the shop door open overnight. Elvis wasted no time wreaking havoc on all my husband's tools and shop supplies, mangling and biting everything to pieces. I guess it would have been less infuriating if the dog had the common sense to look repentant, but he appeared pleased with himself as he searched out the next thing to destroy.

That summer, we planned to redo the exterior of our house and hired a contractor who delivered the insulation, siding, shingles, and nails the night before so he could get an early start. Excited for our house to get a facelift, we awoke that morning eager for the work to begin. What we did not realize until we got outside was that Elvis had been busy the night before. He had ripped open the bags of insulation and then chewed his way through the bales, leaving clumps of partially chewed insulation all over the yard. He did not stop there. Oh, no.

He had picked up a 25-pound box of shingle nails in his mouth and proudly trotted around the yard, spreading the flat-topped nails all over the ground. Finding the empty chewed cardboard box, we discovered nails covered the entire yard, making it a walking and driving hazard.

I think our neighbours within a thirty-kilometre radius heard Don's curses that morning as he roared into the house and demanded I keep the children inside, afraid one of them would step on a nail. He went to the back storage room and took out his rifle. This dog's nonsensical act produced the final straw, leaving no way for Elvis to redeem himself. As Don left the house, the clueless dog traipsed along at his side. About fifteen minutes later, my husband returned. Alone.

The Hangings

Thinking back, the first hanging on our acreage was a near catastrophe.

Don and Adam hauled refuse to a trench Don had dug in the field. They tossed the garbage into the earthen pit and then kept a close eye on it as they lit it and watched grey billowy smoke rise out of the hole.

On that overcast day, when the clouds played hide and seek with the sun, my husband and son watched the fire burn itself out before returning to the yard. Adam rode in the truck box of our GMC crew cab along with Butch, our full-grown St. Bernard. Driving through a narrow arch of maples, poplars, and green ash, Don maneuvered the truck between the trees, careful not to scratch the truck's paint. Adam hung out the side of the box with his arms extended, letting the branches slap his hands. Butch panted with his massive mop-like tongue hanging out. Drool slobbered down both sides of his mouth as his jowls wobbled back and forth from the truck's movement.

"STOP THE TRUCK!" Adam yelled.

Sara played in the front yard. I had come outside and was walking across the yard to the garden. We both looked up hearing the alarm in Adam's voice.

"Dad! Stop the truck!" Adam hollered again.

By this time, Sara and I were running across the yard toward them, shouting and pointing to the back of the truck.

Don stopped and jumped out to see what the commotion was about. The three of us stood gaping at the sight before us. Butch, our 200-pound dog, hung by his neck, caught by a branch from one of the maple trees. The maple bough had snagged the chain around Butch's neck and left him dangling from the tree's limb, some five or six feet in the air.

We all rushed forward, knowing we had to hurry to save this dog from being strangled before our eyes. Don and I pulled on the maple tree, lowering the branch closer to the ground to release Butch. By this time, Adam had jumped out of the truck box and, together with Sara, worked to wiggle the chain free from the maple tree's clasp. The dog's head lolled forward as the pressure around his neck and throat cut off his oxygen. We worked as one unit, frantically trying to save our much-loved pet.

Sara and Adam struggled to release Butch and finally, Sara cried out, "He's free!"

Don and I let go of the maple branch as it swung back up through the air, the leaves swooshing.

The colossal dog staggered a little before getting his balance. He looked disoriented as Don administered a close examination, checking for any abrasions or harm done to him.

"He looks fine to me."

Don stepped back, releasing the dog, who trotted up to the kids looking for a pet on the head.

Butch survived that ordeal and came out of it none the worse for wear.

Good fortune did not shine upon us years later when we had a second hanging.

I don't think anyone in our family remembers where we got her, but she delicately stepped into our lives, a slender, black and white cat named Star. Because we lived on an acreage with many animals and pets, I set boundaries allowing no pets in the house. No pets except Star.

We learned she was pregnant when we awoke one morning to the agonizing howls and whimpers of a cat in labour. The kids and I searched the house, following the sounds until we located her on the royal blue carpet under the girls' bed. We found her with three writhing kittens who blindly sought their mother's warmth and milk.

Star, a young mother cat, cared for and fed her little brood until they were big enough to move into the garage. There, she continued to look after them and teach them things that growing kittens needed to know.

Star was an outdoor cat by the time her second litter arrived.

"Mom! Dad! Come quick! Star hung herself!" Sara, fifteen years old, rushed into the house, panic in her voice.

Sitting at the breakfast table, Don jumped up to follow our daughter outside. Sara, tears streaming down her cheeks and horror in her eyes, pointed at the limp cat hanging from the shed's slightly open overhead door. Don turned over a plastic pail to stand on, reached up, and removed the dead cat entangled between the door and the jamb. He shielded the lifeless pet from Sara's view, gently laying the cat in the grass behind the building. He opened the shed door and walked inside with our daughter right behind.

"I think maybe Star slipped on the frost build-up on the door, lost her footing when she tried to sneak back in the shed, and got her neck trapped in the door."

"But I thought cats were nimble and steady on their feet …"

Don put up his hand to silence Sara.

"Listen," he said.

They stood in the shed's semi-darkness, listening closely.

"Hear it?"

Sara shook her head no.

"There it is again. Do you hear it? I think Star is a mom again."

Sara heard it, too, the soft mewling sounds of little kittens. She pulled the cord dangling from the solitary lightbulb on the ceiling and the light came on. Together, she and her dad searched for the litter. Almost immediately, they found them in a makeshift nest of rags in a wood box next to the wood-burning stove inside the shed. Six little black and white bodies squirmed and cried for their mother.

"Oh, boy," Don said. "They will never survive without their mother."

Sara looked down at the helpless kittens.

"Poor Star. I have to take care of her babies."

Skeptical, Don shook his head.

"I don't think so. The kittens are only a few days old."

"I will keep them alive. I want to try. Please, Dad."

"OK," Don conceded, "but they need constant care and attention. It won't be easy."

"I know. I want Star's kittens to live."

Sara phoned the local vet to get a recipe for a formula to feed the kittens. It consisted of 2% milk, eggs, and vegetable oil. The vet assured Sara this concoction would be as close to the cat's milk as she could get. She found a plastic toy baby bottle to use when she fed the little creatures. One by one, Sara held each kitten and forced the tip of the bottle's nipple into their mouths. The milk poured out and ran down the kitten's face. The toy baby bottle wasn't working.

Sara searched for something else and came to me for ideas. After rummaging through the medicine cabinet, I produced an eye dropper and handed it to her. Sara smiled as she grabbed it and skipped down the basement steps to her bedroom, where she nestled the kittens in blankets to keep them warm. The eye dropper worked much better as the kittens' pink tongues slipped out of their mouths, lapping at the milk the eye dropper dispensed.

At night, I snuck downstairs to check on Sara. I found her sitting cross-legged on the basement floor, leaning her head against the wall, almost asleep with the kittens in her hands.

"Sara, you must get some sleep," I reminded her.

"I will, but I feel sorry for these kittens having lost their mother."

"I know but understand that these little things might not make it no matter how hard you try."

"They will. I'll see to it that they live."

"Perhaps but go back to bed now and get some sleep. You have school in the morning."

As the days and nights turned into weeks, the kittens grew stronger. With their eyes open and soft round bellies full of milk, they scampered with their pointy little tails sticking straight up. They romped and play-fought to exert their dominance over their siblings. Sara laughed and played with them, giving each one special attention.

All but one thrived. Sara named this tiny kitten Little Bill. He did not progress as he should have. Sara quickly identified there was something wrong. His head seemed too big for his underdeveloped body. This kitten trembled and quivered. When it tried to move, it was with jerky movements, and sometimes it fell over.

Sara loved this teeny kitten and gave it extra love and care, trying to make it healthy. One day, despite her best efforts, the little wretch disappeared. Sara searched everywhere for the lost kitten but never found him. She didn't know that her father had paid a mercy visit.

By this time, we had moved the kittens to the garage. Here, they had more room to frolic and play. Here, they gained more independence from our daughter, their surrogate mom.

Remarkably, the five remaining kittens grew to adulthood. They became good mousers and lived on our acreage, with Sara keeping an ever-watchful eye over their progress, stepping in to help them when needed.

Christmas Premonition

Each year as the festive season neared, I inevitably thought of past Christmases. As a girl, I celebrated the birth of our Lord by going to Mass on Christmas Eve with my family. We always arrived early since my sister, Sharon, and I sang in the choir. We sang the holy hymns from the choir loft, our voices resounding through the church as we looked down and watched the parishioners filing into their pews.

Our church in Middle Lake was a humble one with four rows of honey-coloured benches, each separated by blue carpet forming three aisles that led to three carpeted steps that rose to the altar. Six plaques mounted on each side of the church symbolized the stations of the cross. Statues of the Blessed Virgin Mary and Jesus adorned the front of the church. White lights twinkled on the spruce trees behind the altar sparsely laid out, waiting for the priest to arrive for Mass.

Part of a predominantly German Catholic community, even though we could not speak German ourselves, we often sang some of the German hymns like "Stille Nacht" and "O Tannenbaum" which translated to "Silent Night" and "Oh Christmas Tree." The people below sat and listened as we serenaded them with Christmas hymns, often smiling and nodding to each other, whispering Merry Christmas, and shaking hands.

The church, filled to capacity on these holiest of nights, seemed to be alive with activity. Ushers placed chairs in the aisles and at the back of the church. Many of the congregation that you did not see at church the rest of the year attended now. Many parishioners had family members home for the holiday season, and they, too, all crowded into the church benches and chairs. Christmas, a great time to see friends and neighbours that had moved away, presented a chance to get re-acquainted.

Each year as Mass ended and the last chord of the organ sounded, I always hoped that when I left the church, I would find fat snowflakes wafting down, snowflakes that kissed my face with a serene, melting caress. Nothing epitomized Christmas Eve more than gently falling snow to blanket the ground and soften everyone's footsteps. That, to me, represented the perfect Christmas Eve.

By 1996, I had a family of my own. After a day at work that seemed to drag, I finally made it home to be with my family. The five of us sat down for supper, but something nagged at me. The uneasiness came from deep within me, difficult to explain. I spoke with Don about it, telling him I had this feeling, this gripping need, to drive the thirty minutes on country roads to see my mother and father. I could not explain it. I did not want to leave my family home alone; however, this pressing need, this voice inside me, insisted that I needed to be with my mom and dad. I HAD to see them. I begged Don to understand, even though it sounded completely irrational, even as I voiced it out loud to him.

"Marilyn, you were at work all day. We're going to be there tomorrow. Isn't that enough?" Don asked.

"I can't explain it. I feel I NEED to be there tonight. If you won't come with me, I'll go myself."

"It's −35° out there. What if you have car trouble?"

"I'll manage," I stubbornly said.

Don shook his head and looked frustrated. I felt horrible having to put him in this position.

"I'll come with you," Don relented. "But the kids stay home. I don't want them out with us on such a freezing night."

I agreed and explained to the children that Dad and I had to go to Grandpa and Grandma's house. My heart broke to see their crestfallen faces, but I promised an exciting morning unwrapping gifts before making our way to Grandpa and Grandma's house the following day. I hated leaving them alone on Christmas Eve, but I needed to do this.

Don and I ventured out into the frigid evening on our way to my parents' house, glad my husband had come with me. Bitingly cold, omnipresent darkness enveloped our car which seemed to groan toiling its way from our acreage toward my hometown of Middle Lake. After twenty-five minutes of driving in arctic conditions, we pulled into my parents' driveway.

My mom opened the door on the second knock, shocked to see us standing there. By the worried look on her face, I knew something was wrong. She told me Dad was not feeling well. We walked into the softly lit kitchen, where Dad sat in his usual chair at the head of the table. Christmas carols played lightly in the background.

Weakly, Dad smiled at us as I went to hug him. Sweat drenched him. I stood back and saw rivulets of perspiration making their way down each side of his face from his temples to his cheeks. He insisted he was fine. I peered at him. He did not seem okay.

"I was just leaving for Christmas Eve Mass," Mom said.

Looking from her to Dad and back to her again, I felt unsure of what to do. I could see that Dad was not feeling well, but Mom hoped he would lie down and rest if we all left. In the end, Don and I joined her.

Christmas Eve Mass conjured up memories of long-ago childhood days – the choir, the hushed excitement, and the feeling of peace and joy. After Mass, we stood outside and briefly chatted with friends I hadn't seen in years. Mom's gaze kept drifting toward her house, wanting to get home and check on Dad. I cut my visits short, and we walked the short distance from the church to her place.

Entering the house, we saw Dad sitting in his chair at the table where we had left him an hour earlier. He looked scared as he hiccupped, and the sweat continued to pour off his face. Dad opened the top buttons of his shirt and said he felt like vomiting. Feeling very apprehensive, I caught Don's eye. I didn't know what to do. On one hand, we had my sick father, who insisted all he had was the flu. Nearly thirty minutes away, we had our three children home alone on Christmas Eve. Torn about what we should do, I could not make this decision. I glanced at Don, my eyes pleading with him to decide for me.

"The kids are home alone," he said. "We need to get going …"

Panic crossed Mom's face, realizing we were leaving, and she would be home alone with her sick husband once again. She asked us not to leave.

Once we made our decision, there was no need to delay our departure any longer. Don went outside to start the car so it could warm up. I walked over to where Dad sat and bent to give him a hug and a kiss.

"Have a good night's sleep, Dad. I'm sure you'll feel better in the morning."

He gave me a dubious look before nodding. I turned to make my way to the door, with Mom trailing behind.

"We'll all be here tomorrow," I assured her. "Try to get some rest."

After hugging my mother, I turned to leave, trying not to look at her beseeching eyes. I hurried out to the car where Don waited. I felt torn between a dutiful daughter and a responsible mother.

The following morning, we opened our gifts early. The kids ripped through bows, ribbons, and wrapping paper to get to the boxes inside. Lots of "Oohs!" and "That's just what I wanted!" and "Thank you!" bounced around the living room as our family shared in this cheerful moment. With the last gift opened, I ushered everyone to their bedrooms to get ready to leave for Grandpa and Grandma's.

Dressing in our upstairs bedroom, I heard the phone ring. I rushed downstairs to answer it. My youngest sister, Cindy, sobbed on the phone and I found it hard to understand what she said.

Finally, after asking her to repeat it a second time, I heard her moan,

"Dad passed away."

I got a few more choked details from her, and we wept on the phone before ending the call. I had to tell my children their grandpa had died. On Christmas Day.

After speeding back to my parents' home, I found out that my mother rose early Christmas Day morning to begin meal preparations for her large family. Before leaving their bedroom, she spoke briefly to Dad where they wished each other Merry Christmas and professed their love one last time. Mom told Dad she would call him for breakfast in an hour or two, but that he should rest after such a sleepless night. Two hours later, when she returned to wake him up, she thought he must be in diabetic shock. Panicked, she called a family friend, a nurse, who came to the house and, after a brief examination, regretfully told her that Dad had passed away. He suffered a heart attack and died in his sleep.

In utter disbelief and shock, I now understood why I had such an unexplainable need to visit my parents the night before. This inherent longing was a premonition of what was to come. Because I acted on the strong feeling, I got to see my father, to hug and kiss him, one last time. May he rest in peace.

Acting On A Dare

This business trip to Winnipeg in 1997 started much the same as all the others. The long wait in the airport, the jamming into economy plane seats, the shared taxi to the indistinguishable hotel room to which I returned after each long, tiring day of meetings. Always the same. Nothing much of notable significance ever happened. Or, at least, that's what I thought.

The taxi dropped me off at the upscale hotel at Portage and Main in downtown Winnipeg. Standing in front of the check-in counter, I noticed people milling about inside the lobby. The clerk behind the desk seemed flustered and continually made mistakes with my check-in, for which he apologized before proceeding to make one more. I shifted from one foot to another, trying to be patient with him. I looked over my shoulder at the growing number of people behind me. The raucous sounds intensified.

With my check-in finally complete, I rolled my suitcase to the perimeter of the mob. I saw the assembly of people now pouring out onto the paved area in front of the hotel and security guards in navy uniforms trying to control the masses. I glanced at my watch and noticed I had plenty of time before I had to meet some colleagues for supper. My curiosity was piqued. When the celebrity arrived, I wanted to be there. I asked people beside me, but they either did not respond or, if they did, I could not hear them. I waited, shifting from one foot to the other, observing the pandemonium.

I lingered for over an hour, pushed and shoved, people falling over my suitcase, me apologizing. When I saw the intensified bedlam, I had enough and was about to leave. The mob outside began to clamour and scream. At that moment, the crowd was electric, almost pulsating. I saw four men ushered into the hotel through the swarm of people. From my distance, I could not distinguish who they were.

After it was all over and the crowds dispersed, I asked someone who it was. The person beside me looked incredulous and said, "It's U2!"

Oh, wow!

Sara was a big fan of this rock band that hailed from Dublin, Ireland. She followed their rise to fame and their international acclaim for their album, The Joshua Tree. I remembered her cranking up the radio volume every time their song, "I Still Haven't Found What I'm Looking For," played. Many times, I saw her closing her eyes as she listened to the haunting melody, "With or Without You." I had to admit that I enjoyed their music as well. Excited, I vowed to tell Sara about it when I called home later that evening.

I made my way up to my room, unpacked, and got ready to meet some of my colleagues in the lobby before heading out for supper. As was customary, I arrived first. I sat on a lobby chair next to a pillar and casually gazed around, watching for one of my friends getting off the elevator. What I saw instead had me holding my breath. It was Michael Evans, aka The Edge. He is the lead guitarist for the band I had seen enter the hotel earlier. The Edge, wearing his familiar toque and deep in conversation with another man who hurried to keep up with The Edge's long casual strides, walked past me and out the hotel doors into the warm summer night's air. I could not believe my good fortune to have seen him up close. Now, I had even more to tell my daughter.

The balance of the evening slid by without incident. We shared an enjoyable meal at a downtown restaurant before returning to the hotel, and each of us went back to our respective rooms for the night.

The following morning, the sun's radiant rays poked its fingers past the light-blocking drapes that hung over the windows in my hotel room. I crawled out of bed, showered, and made ready for the day of meetings. I, along with all the branch managers and district leaders from Saskatchewan and Manitoba, assembled in the conference room and found our seats as the first keynote speaker stood behind the podium. He reviewed our financial results from the previous three months and laid out the agenda for the next three day's meetings. And thus began the procession of talking heads, each presenter thinking his speech more imperative, more inciteful, than the person before.

After four hours of sitting on straight-back uncomfortable hotel chairs, listening to one presentation after another, lunchtime approached. Today was a treat. Instead of a tasteless buffet meal of soup and sandwiches, we had the freedom to take in downtown Winnipeg. Some people went shopping, others for a walk to stretch their legs, and others sought an enjoyable meal. I, along with about eight friends, chose the latter. A friend who lived in Winnipeg suggested we all walk one kilometre from the hotel to The Mondetta World Restaurant at The Forks. This last suggestion sounded like a great idea, so off we headed.

Winnipeg is beautiful in June, and we eagerly soaked up the alluring surroundings, making our way down the promenades to the historic site where the Red River and Assiniboine Rivers meet. Arriving at the restaurant slightly before noon, the hostess seated us outside in the patio area, handing each of us an oversized menu to make our meal selection. The server finished taking our orders and served our drinks when one of my friends noticed two people escorted onto the patio. The man appeared slight in build, wearing baggy pants, a black hoodie with the hood pulled up over his head, and sunglasses. The woman who accompanied him had her long hair tied back in a ponytail, and she had jumbo-sized sunglasses framing her face. The woman seated herself against the restaurant's wall, while the man sat with his back to the rest of the tables on the deck.

"Hey! That's Bono!" my friend exclaimed. Bono is the charismatic frontman for the band U2 whom the mob had besieged in the hotel lobby the day before.

No. No. We were all quick to reject the notion. My friend insisted. I shared my story of the two incidents at the hotel the previous night. I described how I saw U2 arrive and later watched The Edge leaving the hotel. My friend kept studying them as the conversation continued. At last, I agreed with him. I, too, thought that was Bono. Our meals arrived and we casually shifted our conversation to other matters as we ate.

When it was time to settle our bills, the subject of Bono arose again. I mentioned how my daughter was such an avid U2 fan and how much it would mean to her to have his autograph. Before I knew it, my friends dared me, no, they double-dog dared me to go up to him and ask him for his autograph. Never one to ignore a dare, I stood up and, knees shaking, I walked toward the couple. By now, the woman had removed her sunglasses and peered up at me. I cleared my throat as the man continued to stare down at his plate, moving his meal around with his fork.

"I am so sorry to bother you," I murmured, wishing a hole would open in the floor and swallow me up.

The man slowly and deliberately placed his fork on his plate and looked at me. I saw my reflection in his sunglasses. The hood of his sweater still covered his head.

"What can I do for you?" he asked, already reaching for the pen I held in my hand.

"My daughter ... well, she is such a big fan of yours ... if you could please sign ..." I stuttered and could feel my face turning the colour of red wine.

He took the hotel pad of paper and pen I offered. In a flourish of fluid movements, his signature filled the entire page. He added '97 beneath his scrawled name. He smiled as he handed it back to me.

"Thank you so much!" I turned to walk away.

"You have a beautiful city," he commented, his Irish brogue quite pronounced.

"Thank you," I said, not bothering to explain that I was as much a visitor to the city as he was.

"Do you eat here often?"

"No, this is my first time."

"Hope you have a good meal," he smiled and raised his sunglasses as he looked at me.

"You, too."

"God Bless you," he added as I turned to leave.

I did not know how to respond. I smiled and returned to the table where my friends' staring eyes waited for a description of the conversation I just had with the celebrity. After sharing my experience, I grabbed my purse to leave. I saw people swarming around Bono and his wife.

Walking past their table, Bono glanced at me with a wry smile and a slight shrug of his shoulders. What a champ of a man, a true idol. I will always remember him and the grace he displayed. I know that celebrities and idols long for the adoration of their fans but also crave their privacy. Bono, an internationally acclaimed superstar, sought only to have a quiet lunch with his wife while on a stop in Winnipeg. Because of a silly dare, I felt like I had taken away that chance for him. I put my head down and hurried past his table as the throng of people pushed toward him with pens and paper in their hands.

Assaulted

I sped down the highway in our Ford minivan, driving the one hundred kilometres from our Cudworth acreage to Saskatoon. My foot grew heavier and heavier on the gas pedal. I saw the speedometer needle creeping past 140 kilometres per hour. I had to slow down. An hour earlier, I received a phone call from Sara. She said she and her friend Emily were at the Royal University Hospital in Saskatoon. A man had broken into her friend's ground-floor apartment and attacked and raped Emily at knifepoint.

Sara, a school librarian in the town of St. Brieux, had driven the two hours into the city the night before and stayed at Emily's when the break-in and assault occurred. Oh, Gawd! My daughter had been there! She could have been attacked as well. How could this have happened? My stomach quaked.

Sara told me on the phone the doctor had finished examining Emily. The girls planned to leave the hospital shortly and go to the police station to provide video and written statements. After that, they would return to Emily's place. These young girls, nineteen and twenty years old, were about to walk back into the apartment where the assault occurred. I did not want them to deal with this alone. Sara told me they tried calling Emily's mother but could not reach her at work. At a time like this, a girl needed her mother.

On that Saturday morning in May 1999, the rural Saskatchewan highway yawned endlessly in front of me. The drive had never seemed so long the many times I travelled it before. This morning it seemed an eternity. I wound through the curves past Prud'homme and then through the hills near Vonda, resuming higher speed in the areas where the road was flat. I turned the corner at Aberdeen and sped toward Saskatoon. Not wanting a speeding ticket, I thought it best to slow down to 110 kilometres to ensure I got there safely. The atrocity had already taken place. The girls had lived through that. All I could do was be there to listen, comfort, and support them.

I could see the city emerging on the horizon as I sped toward all the uncertainty that awaited. I approached Saskatoon and eventually crossed over the University Bridge, a few blocks away from Emily's apartment. On the phone, Sara sounded exhausted, perhaps in shock. I didn't know. I did not press her. Somehow, I had to remain calm and even though my heart and my head screamed at the injustice of it all, I had to support them and be their strength. Sara provided only a few details. The horror she and Emily had experienced was something I could not imagine.

I pulled up in front of Emily's apartment building on the corner of 26th Street and 4th Ave. Getting out of my vehicle, I hurried around to the back of the suite and descended the outside flight of stairs leading to Emily's kitchen. Sara stood waiting in the open doorway. I grabbed her in a fierce hug. Not one for physical demonstrations of love, this time she did not try to break away. I held her close. I remembered Sara as a newborn baby, how I cradled her for the first time and promised to protect her and keep her safe. I felt like I let her down. Last night, someone had seriously terrorized her and her friend. He could have killed her. Just having my arms around her, I felt like collapsing into tears, but I knew I couldn't. I had to remain strong, be the voice of reason, yet be a source of comfort and reassurance for the girls who had been through so much.

Sara pulled away and stood aside so I could enter the apartment.

"This is the way he got in," she said in a flat tone, pointing to the door we had just walked through. "We are usually careful to bolt the door, but I guess we forgot last night after we went out for a smoke."

"Was Chloe here last night?" I asked, referencing Emily's roommate.

"No, she is in the hospital. That's why I came into the city, to visit her."

Chloe had ongoing health issues and spent considerable time in the hospital. I nodded and waited for my daughter to continue.

Sara pointed to a knife block on the kitchen counter with one empty slot.

"He grabbed a knife," she breathed.

I felt a shiver run through me as the physical evidence made this all too real.

From out of nowhere, Emily materialized. She was a waif of a girl for nineteen, barely five feet tall, with dark hollow eyes that were now more sunken because of the trauma she experienced. I held my arms open to her as she sunk into the motherly comfort they offered. Her mother could not be here right now, so I was her surrogate. I tried consoling her, rubbing her back as I would my daughter. She was like a daughter. The girls were close friends, and I knew Emily well. Many times, when I came to Saskatoon, I went for coffee with them and laughed over their antics, always fond of Sara's friends.

I held Emily at arm's length, trying to look deep into her eyes.

"Are you OK?"

Emily kept her eyes fixed on the floor. She nodded. I grabbed her in a hug once again.

"They caught the guy who did it," Sara blurted out.

"What? How?" I stammered, shocked to hear this.

"He stayed at the halfway house across the street," she said. "The police dogs tracked him. They found him in front of the Blue Cross Insurance building on 2nd Avenue, lying on the sidewalk, unconscious from blood loss."

I closed my eyes, trying to control the anger boiling up inside me. Months after Emily and Chloe had moved into the apartment building, they found out there was a halfway house across the street. Their signed lease held them to the apartment. They noticed men standing in the window of the halfway house watching them through the girls' living room window. For that reason, Emily and Chloe always kept their curtains pulled tightly shut and were careful about securing the deadbolt. Except for last night. They unknowingly left the door unlocked.

That halfway house. The one with the recently released convicts the justice system placed there to reintegrate into society. The house was in the middle of a residential area where many university and college students lived because of its proximity to both educational institutions. Why had the city allowed a halfway house in this part of the city?

Wait. What had Sara said? He was unconscious because of blood loss?

"I cut him with the knife he used on me," Emily said defiantly, the first time she had spoken since I arrived.

"OK. I'm confused," I said, sinking onto a chair at the kitchen table. "You'd better start from the beginning."

Emily began explaining the events of the previous night.

"I was sleeping. Then I woke up. First, he tripped over a box in my room, and then he flicked his lighter so he could get his bearings," she began. "Before I could scream or react, he was on top of me, holding me down, and had his hand over my mouth and nose."

She eased herself onto a chair and wrapped her arms around her legs, which she pulled up to her chest.

"I was so scared," her voice broke. "But I couldn't breathe. I have a cold and I'm congested. His hand on my mouth and nose meant I couldn't breathe."

Emily stopped, her eyes growing big as she recalled that moment. "I pushed his hand aside long enough to tell him that."

"He asked if there was anyone else in the house. I lied and told him no. He said if I promised not to scream, he would take his hand away from my face."

"Of course, I agreed. He held a knife to my throat and told me he'd kill me if I made a sound."

Emily looked at me and, at that moment, her small narrow face was like that of a child. It saddened me to look at her dark, pain-filled eyes.

I reached to put my hand on her knee, encouraging her to go on.

"He kept the knife at my throat. I could feel the sharp point against my neck. I was so scared. I thought he was going to kill me for sure. He tugged at my pyjamas to pull them off. His hands were everywhere as he was on top of me. He was slobbering all over me, kissing and drooling. It was so disgusting. All I could do was lie there and let him do this to me. I wanted him dead."

Emily stopped. I could only imagine how difficult it was for her to talk about it. She had probably told and re-told her story to the police. Now, here I was, asking her to re-tell it once again, revealing so many intimate details a person should never have to recount.

As if to get this over with, she plunged into her story once more.

"He penetrated me."

"I'm sorry, Emily. That isn't how it should be."

"Then he told me to get on top," she whispered before I could say more.

"What?" I asked, not because I hadn't heard her, but because I couldn't believe what she had said. "He told you to get on top," I repeated her words.

She nodded.

"Yes, he seemed to like that part. He even started talking like we were having an ordinary conversation, ordinary sex. It was so weird. I played along with him, answering him. I hoped to gain his trust. He seemed to relax a little, and then I grabbed for the knife."

"You got the knife?" I asked incredulously.

For the first time, she looked pleased with herself. She nodded in affirmation.

"What did you do?"

"I jumped off him and crawled under the bed. He kept trying to reach for me. I grabbed his arms and started sawing at his wrists with the knife. Boy, he was mad!" she declared triumphantly. "I kept cutting him and he kept swearing, calling me a bitch and yelling that he would kill me."

Flabbergasted to hear this girl recount what had happened to her only hours before left me speechless. Yet, I felt incredibly proud of the actions she had taken, the spunk she had mustered, and the courage she had shown.

"How did you get away?"

"I kept sawing at his arms. He got madder and madder, trying to get the knife away from me. He would kill me if he did. I screamed for Sara, hoping she would come."

Sara was a deep sleeper. With her bedroom door closed and her customary fan running, she would not have heard a thing.

I studied Emily, trying to grasp the enormity of the situation and what she had experienced. I glanced at Sara. She stood behind her friend's chair with a grim look on her face. Our eyes met briefly before she looked away.

Sara jumped into the conversation.

"I woke up and heard Emily screaming. I opened my bedroom door and heard shampoo bottles falling into the bathtub. He must have already been trying to crawl out the bathroom window. I didn't know what happened."

"He was gone," Emily chimed in. "He had broken the small window over the tub in the bathroom and climbed out that way."

Puzzled, I asked, "Why didn't he use the back kitchen door, the way he came in?"

"The police think Emily's cutting him and the blood loss caused him to become disoriented. Maybe he thought he was back in prison and that the window was his only way out," Sara responded, shrugging her shoulders, before continuing. "We called 911, at about 4:20 a.m. The police arrived fifteen minutes later. They asked us a few questions, and then one police car took us to the University Hospital, and the other police officers remained here. This guy from the halfway house had missed his curfew. The guard at the house reported it, and the police were already looking for him. They had a police dog track him and found him unconscious. He had lost a lot of blood from Emily cutting him."

"While I sat in the waiting room, they brought the culprit in on a stretcher. I wanted to kill him with my bare hands," Sara growled.

"I asked for a female doctor to do the examination," Emily spoke up, "but they wouldn't call one. Instead, I got this beastly old male doctor with a white, scruffy beard and messy white hair, not gentle at all when he performed the rape kit. He didn't believe me when I told him I was a virgin. I'm glad Sara stayed with me during the whole thing."

Both girls stopped speaking. They looked at me with anguished expressions.

"I'm so sorry this happened to you," I said. "I want you to know this wasn't your fault. It wasn't."

I continued, "You girls did the right things. Both of you. You were incredibly brave. I am so grateful you are alive. Emily, you showed real courage and strength in dealing with this monster. Sara, your level-headed support of Emily went a long way, I'm sure."

To this, Emily nodded her head. She looked over her shoulder at Sara, who still stood behind her chair.

"I couldn't have gotten through this without her," Emily said.

"We won't know for a few weeks if Emily is pregnant or if she contracted AIDS or any other disease from him," Sara added.

My stomach revolted. I felt like I might be sick. These girls, too young to be dealing with this type of brutality, had more to face and worry about. I sat there, not knowing what to do. What can a mother say after something like this? Still trying to process everything, I saw Emily stand up, motioning for me to follow her.

We moved out of the kitchen and down the hallway.

Blood.

His blood.

Shocked and repulsed, I felt my stomach pitch. I had noticed the strong, coppery smell of blood when I first entered the apartment, but now, as we moved through the house, the odour, even stronger, smelled like a combination of copper and browning ground beef, the stench was sickening.

Blood splattered on the walls and on the floor, sticking like oil to the hinges of the bathroom door, shining red in some places, a darkened gummy brown in others. Emily stopped as her bare foot stepped on a sticky drop of blood on the floor. She shuddered. I reached out to touch her arm and felt her tense up as she brushed my hand away. So young, she carried herself like a warrior.

Blood clung to the entire bathroom. His escape route had been through the small window over the bathtub. Blood splattered the mirror and in it, I saw Emily close her eyes as if trying to block out the disgust. Sara stood there, as did I, not knowing what to do or what to say, trying to conceal the repugnance we felt.

"I haven't been back to my room since it happened," Emily mumbled.

"You don't need to go there if you don't want," I told her.

Emily ignored my comment, her bare feet padding down the hall to her bedroom, where the violent assault had occurred. Emily walked ahead, with Sara and me following. It felt almost like a funeral procession. I saw the pools of blood that soaked the carpet and the bed and felt outraged. I saw the bedsheets, yanked and torn in Emily's struggle to escape. His drying blood marked the walls, the mattress, and the bedroom floor.

I watched my daughter and her friend standing inside the bedroom, not saying a word, surveying the scene. I could see the disgust and revulsion etched on their faces, and my heart ached for them. Once again, I marvelled at their strength and solidarity.

I went to the kitchen to get a tub of hot water and disinfectant. The girls followed with tubs of their own. We scrubbed with a vengeance. We scoured the walls and floors until our arms ached. Next, we looked at the blood-covered clothes, sheets, and pillows strewn across the floor. They remained after the police had taken the items they needed for evidence. We gathered everything up, jamming them all into garbage bags. Slowly, we cleaned away all signs of the violence that had occurred in their home, the physical work an outlet for the anger and helplessness we felt. Emily had a strong desire to reclaim her room. I understood that.

Hours later, after all the cleaning and disinfecting, only the blood-soaked mattress remained. We walked across the bedroom and began to tug and pull it from the bed to carry it to the dumpster. Something fell to the floor. Emily bent to pick it up.

"His cap," she whispered. "The police must have missed it."

Emily began crying. Maybe the sight of the cap reignited memories of her harrowing experience. Perhaps the gravity of what she had just lived through had become all too real. Relieved to see Emily finally give in to her emotions, I put my arm around her. She sobbed as Sara and I stood there, unsure of what more we could do.

"I want to see Grandpa and Grandma," Emily wept like a child.

I knew Emily's grandparents lived in Saskatoon and understood her need for her family right now. Emily called her grandfather to pick her up after I offered to drive her. Asking Sara if she wanted to go home with me, I caught the imploring look Emily gave Sara and knew my daughter needed to stay with her friend.

I waited until the girls left with Emily's grandfather before I climbed into my minivan and headed home. Emotionally drained and physically exhausted, I thought about the girls and the long, agonizing stretch ahead of them. I knew Emily would have to tell and re-tell all the details of that night first to her grandparents, then to her mother, then to her lawyer, and then again in court. An investigation followed by a gruelling trial would no doubt place Emily's character and reputation in question. From what I knew of rape trials, it would be as though she was raped and assaulted all over again. I prayed the girls would have the strength they needed to withstand the legal battery when this case went to court.

Jolted from my reverie by the sound of a blaring car horn, I looked down at my speedometer and realized how slowly I had been driving. Through my rear-view mirror, I saw vehicles lined up behind me. I sped up ever so slightly. My trembling hands would not hold still. I once again decreased my speed, signalling as I pulled my vehicle to the side of the road. I parked my van as the tears spilled over. With my head on the steering wheel, I sat alone and cried.

Leaving The Acreage

I searched for romaine lettuce in Cudworth's only grocery store where coolers surrounded four short aisles. Not seeing any, I sighed and dropped a head of iceberg lettuce in my shopping cart. They didn't have what I wanted, so this would have to do.

"Marilyn," the owner-cashier hurried down the aisle toward me. "There's a phone call for you. Says it's urgent."

"Who is it?"

"The woman wouldn't leave her name."

I rushed to the pole-mounted phone and answered as the clerk continued to ring up the other customer's groceries.

"Hello?" I struggled to hear over the chatter and noise of a busy shop toward the end of the day as people rushed in to buy last-minute items before going home after work. Shopping carts clanged, children whined, and impatient shoppers grabbed things wishing they were home.

"Marilyn? Barb Goodridge. Sorry to track you down on a Friday afternoon, but I needed to speak with you. This will only take a minute."

I held my finger in one ear to block out the racket as I strained with the phone pressed to my other ear. Barb was a Community Manager with the financial institution I worked for. Several weeks earlier, the bank, in an unprecedented move, had eliminated all leadership roles and revamped them. The bank's entire organizational structure had changed overnight. As a result, all previous leaders, managers, and those in human resources, as I was, found themselves unemployed. The bank requested each employee to submit a preference document with their top three jobs and location choices. Each of us hoped to be rehired in one of the new roles.

I held my breath, waiting for her to continue, wondering what she would offer.

"Marilyn, are you there?"

"Yes, sorry. I'm listening."

Barb said she would like me in a branch manager role and that she had Meadow Lake and North Battleford open. Both branches were comparable in size and had similar makeup and staffing. She told me a little about what made each location unique and what she felt I should know when considering the two options.

"Marilyn, I know this is a big decision. Regardless of which one you choose; you and your family will be required to move. I wanted to give you the weekend to discuss this with them, but I have little time to fill both roles. Can I have your decision by Monday at 9 a.m.?"

I asked a few more questions, which she answered. We ended the call.

"Good news?" the cashier, in her mid-fifties, turned to me with a smile.

"Yeah, I think so."

I smiled at her as my mind raced.

"Thank you for letting me use your phone," I murmured, stepping away from the check-out counter and steering my shopping cart back to the produce aisle. I plopped down the lettuce and headed out the door, racing to my car through the pouring rain. I turned the key in the ignition, starting my van, and the wipers jumped into motion, slapping at the moisture on my windshield. In mid-October, the rain could turn to snow and make for icy driving conditions. I drove to our acreage where I knew that Don and our thirteen-year-old daughter, Brenda, waited. I burst into the house, calling for them. Don appeared from the kitchen and told me supper was in the oven and would be ready in thirty minutes.

"Where's Brenda?"

"In her room."

I called for her to come join us at the table. She bounded down the steps.

"What's up?"

"Sit down. I need to talk to both of you."

Don and Brenda glanced at each other before seating themselves at the kitchen table.

"I just received a call from Barb Goodridge. She has offered me the branch manager position in either Meadow Lake or North Battleford. I have until Monday morning to decide which, if any, I want to take. What do you guys think? Are we ready to move?"

"I am," Brenda said. "Where's Meadow Lake?"

"It's an hour and a half north of North Battleford."

"Oh. That's a long way."

"Yup. I have never been there before," I acknowledged. "Have you?" I asked, looking at Don.

He shook his head.

"The only way we can decide is to drive there and check it out for ourselves," Don said, pushing his chair back from the table and standing up.

"When? What do you mean?"

"Pack your bags. We'll leave as soon as we eat supper. We can't decide without going to see each town."

"But there's a storm coming. Snow and freezing rain."

"All the more reason to hurry and get going."

Brenda and I dashed to our bedrooms to pack while Don finished making supper. I had planned to do laundry during the weekend, so Brenda and I had to pick through to find our cleanest dirty clothes to take along. There was no time to wash clothes now.

We packed, ate, and left for North Battleford. Don drove as the sleet slopped against the windshield and the wipers desperately tried to keep the window clear. As the temperature outside dropped, the accumulated moisture on the pavement froze to ice. I cautioned Don to slow down as our van swerved. The impenetrable night and the ice on the highway hindered our progress as we inched toward North Battleford. Don clutched the steering wheel, leaning forward to peer out the windshield. Brenda and I stared straight ahead, not saying a word. We did not want to break his concentration. The usual two-and-a-half-hour drive now took three-and-a-half hours. We arrived in North Battleford and stayed at a hotel for the night. We decided continuing further in the dark on these treacherous highways was pointless. After a good night's sleep, we would continue to Meadow Lake in daylight.

We woke up early and had a quick breakfast before venturing onto Highway 4 North, which took us directly to Meadow Lake. The sun's warm rays had melted the ice, making travel considerably easier. We passed through Glaslyn on our journey north. The raw beauty of the northern forests, the muskeg and creeks, and the brilliant azure sky drew us in. I smiled at Don and Brenda, welcoming the serenity and peacefulness, letting the allure of the north reel me in like a fish on a line.

I had called the night before and arranged for a Meadow Lake realtor to show us around town. She met with us and proudly showcased the new high school, new health centre, and relatively new indoor swimming pool. The Town of Meadow Lake and the Flying Dust First Nations Band partnered for government funding. We appreciated the enterprising nature and the progressive thinking the administrations displayed. After the realtor left, we stopped in a restaurant to eat and shamelessly listened in on the local's conversations. The snippets of conversation we overheard confirmed how we felt about the town. We liked what we heard.

We climbed into our minivan, drove south back to North Battleford, and stayed overnight in the same hotel as the night before. The following day was Sunday, and we did not have the benefit of a realtor to take us around North Battleford. We checked out the school, the hospital, the stores, and the houses for sale on our own. We experienced a different vibe to this town, a distinctive feeling. It seemed to lack the positive vibes we had gotten from Meadow Lake. That evening, we enjoyed supper in a Greek restaurant in North Battleford. The three of us discussed both towns, listing off the pros and cons of each and sharing our feelings and impressions. By the time the server presented us with the bill for the meal, we had reached our decision. Unanimously, we chose Meadow Lake.

Driving back to our acreage, we discussed ideas and made plans for how to make this move happen as simply as possible. Thankfully, Don had held a farm auction a few years earlier, where he had sold off all his farm machinery. He now worked for a crop insurance company that allowed him to live anywhere within the province. The first thing we had to do was list our acreage.

My phone rang on Monday morning precisely at 9 a.m. I told Barb our decision. Happy that we had chosen Meadow Lake, she asked me to report to the Branch Manager position the second week in November 1999.

Don and I decided that, for now, he and Brenda would remain on the acreage. We were reluctant to leave our property vacant because we feared someone would vandalize it once word got out that we had moved. I took up residence in a gloomy motel room in Meadow Lake because it was all I could find with a vacancy that could be rented by the month. The brown panelled walls and the heavy light-blocking curtains projected a depressing environment. Two table-top lamps did not throw enough light to brighten the place, which was maybe a good thing since I wouldn't be able to see what might be on the dark worn carpet. Outside, the steps next to my room led to the motel's second floor. All night I heard truck drivers arriving late, stomping up the stairs to fall into bed before stumbling down at first light to hit the road once more. I found it challenging to get a good night's sleep.

It was a lonely existence for me. I missed Don and Brenda and having the stable influence of a home. By this time, Sara and Adam were on their own and living in Alberta. After work on Fridays, I drove four hours to Cudworth, where we made moving arrangements and began packing. I tried to catch up on my husband's and children's lives. The weekends flew by in a blur. I returned to Meadow Lake late Sunday night. Driving in the dark, I strained to see if any wildlife had wandered onto the road. Bored and sometimes threatening to fall asleep, I fumbled for the radio dial, finding only a religious channel spoken in Dene. I made these treks each weekend for six long-drawn months. During this time, we strived to keep Brenda's life as normal as possible as she worked through Grade 8 and Don filled the role of Mr. Mom at home. It was far from ideal.

Our acreage sold in five months. We stored most of our household belongings because we hadn't yet purchased a house in Meadow Lake. There weren't many houses to choose from.

In May 2000, after we packed the remaining items in our van, Don and Brenda waited outside while I did a final walk-through of the house on the acreage. This home had sheltered our three children as they grew and had been there through the hardships and the joys. Now it sat empty with sunlight streaming through the windows waiting for the next family to grace its space. I looked around the empty rooms, noticing every nick in the walls and stains on the carpet. I reflected on the aches and pains our family experienced growing up together over the past twenty years. The house bore the battle wounds.

I clung to the memories.

Sighing, I turned and walked out the door, locking it behind me. I turned to look at the beautifully manicured lawn. For one last time, I inhaled the heavenly aroma of the lilacs and apple trees in bloom before climbing into the van's passenger seat, avoiding Don's gaze. I didn't want him to see the tear that escaped and slipped down my cheek as we backed out of the driveway and drove away, not looking back.

The Train Ride

At the Meadow Lake bus depot, I watched my mother climb down the bus steps before I rushed to hug her.

As we walked to my vehicle, she asked, "Does he know yet?"

"Nope," I grinned wickedly, "And he isn't about to find out just yet."

"I don't see how you'll get him to go if you don't tell him where we're going."

"Oh, I can do it. Never fear. You'll see," I quipped.

I had not told Don that my mother was visiting for the weekend. I knew he'd understand. As a recent widow, visiting us gave her an enjoyable break. That evening, we settled in for a relaxing night at home.

The next day, Don went to work, and Brenda went to school as usual. I had not mentioned to Don that I had taken the day off from work. Some things he did not need to know. I wanted to spend the day with Mom, and I had to prepare for the weekend's events. I drove our Shih Tzu to a country kennel just a few kilometres outside the town of Meadow Lake where he would stay for the three days we would be gone.

I notified our neighbours of our plans and gave them a house key. Next, I began packing. After I finished, I put my suitcase, our daughter's, and my mother's luggage in the back of our minivan.

"He's going to notice the bags in the back," my mom said, "then your gig will be up."

"Always the skeptic," I said, bemused by my mother's lack of confidence in my ability to pull this off.

Brenda returned home from school that afternoon and Don came home from work shortly after. I asked if everyone would like to go out for coffee. My husband, always game, and my daughter, in on the prank, agreed. We all piled into the van, and as I drove toward one of our favourite coffee spots in town, I calmly suggested that we should go to St. Walburg. The drive allowed Mom to take in the beauty of the northern forests west of Meadow Lake. We planned to have coffee in St. Walburg. Don agreed. He settled in the passenger seat for the additional hour's drive. On our way, I glanced in the rear-view mirror at my mom and daughter in the seats behind us. Brenda grinned back at me and gave me a thumbs-up gesture.

Approaching the town of St. Walburg, I made a big show of checking my watch,

"We're only an hour away from Lloydminster. Would anyone mind if we continued so we can go shopping there?" I asked.

Everyone nodded their agreement.

Brenda added, "We could stop for supper before we head home again."

Don consented, and we drove south of St. Walburg and turned right at the intersection, arriving in Lloydminster an hour later. I parked the van in the mall parking lot, and Don got out to stretch his legs and smoke. As he walked around our vehicle, he glanced through the van window and noticed our luggage stored in the back. When he asked about it, I told him an adventure lay ahead. Ask no questions and I'll tell no lies. I told him I had changed my mind and did not feel like shopping, so we all piled back in the van and continued in a westerly direction. We still had a long way to go.

In the passenger seat, Don asked a few questions, and I, as elusive as possible given the circumstances, answered with brief non-committal responses. He guessed Edmonton was our destination. Wrong. I remained close-lipped for the rest of the trip. When we reached Vermillion and turned south, confusion and amusement washed over Don's face. Knowing he wouldn't get any answers, he sat silently. We pulled in at a motel in Wainwright and scrambled out of the van. I asked

Don to bring our suitcases while I registered. After checking in, we went out for supper. Don looked baffled but cooperated. Later, when Mom, Brenda, and I went to the restaurant's bathroom, Mom couldn't believe that we had gotten Don this far in our journey, astonished he hadn't pressed me further to find out what was going on.

"You're going to tell him tonight, aren't you?" she asked.

"Not planning to," I responded.

Mom looked at Brenda and asked, "Don't you think we should tell him?"

"Not a chance!"

We left the ladies' room, paid our restaurant bill, and returned to the motel room.

"You're still not going to tell me?" Don asked before we went to bed.

I grinned and shook my head.

After breakfast the following morning, we drove two hours before pulling into the town of Stettler. Here we had an early lunch before making our way to the train station, where Don looked more confused than ever.

"We're going on a train?" he asked as he stepped off the platform to peer down the railroad track.

"GET BEHIND THIS LINE!" a voice boomed.

Don jumped at the sharp command and immediately stepped back. He turned to face a man dressed as an officer in a period costume.

"Who are you?" Don asked.

The strange man puffed up his chest and stroked his moustache. "I am Louis Riel."

"You don't look like him," Don laughed.

The man huffed and walked away, only to bellow out a command to another unsuspecting visitor.

It was about this time that we heard a wheezing sound and saw people beginning to gather on the train station platform. A vintage passenger steam engine chugged its way down the track before coming to a complete stop. Again, we heard the hissing sound as the enormous bulky train engine gave a loud sigh, and the person inside threw the doors open.

"ALL ABOARD!" the conductor called out in his most official voice.

People lined up, producing their boarding passes. Don looked at me and grinned.

"We're going for a train ride," he commented, "on a real steam engine."

I showed the conductor our tickets, and Don, beaming, glanced back at Mom and Brenda. We all made our way into the rustic passenger car and seated ourselves. Four seats in a cluster had a two-person bench facing another two-person bench. Enormous windows on both sides of the railcar allowed a fantastic countryside view.

The elderly conductor shared with us how he had been a conductor for over forty years. After he retired, he volunteered his time on the Alberta Prairie Railway Excursion to keep busy doing something he loved. He, like my mom, had recently lost his spouse. The old conductor's attention toward my mother amused Don, Brenda, and me. He hovered around our seats, speaking with Mom and asking her questions. The three of us smiled at each other as Mom blushed under his attention.

The trip from Stettler to Big Valley, Alberta, was calming and enjoyable. Big Valley had been the divisional point for the Canadian Northern Railway in the early 1900s. Chugging along, everyone sat back to enjoy the ride. I explained to Don that when we arrived in Big Valley, we could roam around the little heritage town's boardwalk, browsing the authentic period shops. The town's volunteers would then serve an Alberta roast beef buffet supper while we enjoyed a dinner theatre before heading back to Stettler. Don nodded, watching the conductor making his way down the aisle past our seats, glancing over his shoulder at my mom.

A commotion erupted in the back of our car. Four rowdy actors dressed in costumes, each carrying glasses and acting drunk, made their way through our car. As they passed by us, we discovered the premise of their sketch. A well-known haughty opera singer's manager mistakenly booked her to perform at the Grand Ole Opry, thinking it was a grand opera house. One of her sidekicks, Dusty Bottoms, had too much to drink. Four characters entertained the travelling guests with their antics and hilarious plays on words as we neared our destination.

Interrupted by gunshots fired, everyone looked out the windows to see the Reynolds Raiders gang approaching the train on horseback. Their black trench coats billowed out behind them as their horses drew near. The robbers' pistols pointed in the air, firing blank shots.

Two little passenger boys, with their noses pressed against the windowpane, had huge, worried eyes.

"Are we going to get dead?" they solemnly asked their parents. The adults quickly reassured the children they would be OK.

The armed men on horses brought the train to a halt and boarded it. In loud, harsh voices, they declared this was a stickup. The robbers moved from seat to seat with white bags in their hands demanding money. They wanted no jewels. We later found out they donated the "stolen" money to a local charity. Lucky for us, Louis Riel arrived and single-handedly drove the robbers off the train, ultimately saving the day. The passengers clapped and cheered, and the train continued on its way.

Not much later, we pulled into the train station at Big Valley and disembarked. We wandered the sidewalks of the Old West town, popping into the taffy-pulling shop, the cinnamon bun bakery, the blacksmith, and the leather tanning shop. Soon, the announcement came for us to make our way to the community hall for supper. We stood in the buffet lineup. The smell of roast beef teased and tantalized our senses and appetites. With heaping paper plates, we made our way back to our chairs at the long table. No sooner were we seated, when we saw the four actors from the train begin their performance on stage. A comedy, of course. The entire hall shook with laughter.

At the skit's end, the actors ushered everyone back on the train to begin the trip back to Stettler. Once again seated, the elderly conductor showed up with a cinnamon bun for Mom that he had purchased at the bakery in Big Valley. She graciously thanked him as he moved away to tend to his other passengers. Don, Brenda, and I could not contain our amusement any longer and howled with laughter at all the attention the conductor lavished on Mom. Looking uncomfortable but in good humour, Mom admonished us. Stomachs full and faces sore from laughing, we enjoyed the return ride.

In Stettler, we detrained, pleased to see the four actors, Louis Riel, and the conductor on the platform bidding us farewell. I asked if I could take a picture of them with Don and Brenda. Mom hates having her photo taken. The others obliged.

Click.

I captured that moment in time forever.

Answer To A Prayer

My job bored me. After achieving all my objectives and targets, I feared I would become complacent and lose motivation if I did not continue to seek advanced roles with new challenges. What I called the Four-Year-Fidget had gripped me once again, as it had throughout my career. By this time, I had been with the same company for nearly twenty-five years, advancing from an entry-level role through various positions to one where I was now a branch manager with about a dozen employees. Time for a different job, something new.

Management asked me to consider a district leadership role that required me to move my family to a city about three and a half hours away. As part of this job, I also needed to complete a self-study course that I knew to be extremely difficult. Without the course certification, I could not hold the role. I did not know if I could do it. I had not met the person who would be my new supervisor. But I heard he could be demanding. Did I want that?

A competitor headhunted me for a position. One of my former bosses, who had left our company, was looking to recruit me to his new organization. I always enjoyed the autonomy he provided me when I worked for him and felt flattered to receive his call. He asked me to consider a district leadership role with this company, but I would need to learn all their new products and computer systems and adjust to their culture. Like the other job offer, this one also required me to move.

I had to consider if I wanted to remain with the same organization where I felt comfortable and had a proven performance record or venture out to a new environment with new expectations. Both opportunities appealed to me at a point in my career when things felt mundane. Both offers came at the same time. The following day, decision day, I had to make my choice.

During this time, Don travelled for his crop insurance job. Away from home, he phoned, and we chatted that evening about the two offers. I tried soliciting his city preference, but he insisted I had to decide the position right for me. Why couldn't Don tell me which city he wanted to live in? Instead, he left it up to me to decide. My head reeled.

When I got off the phone, I called my mom. Knowing she wouldn't tell me what to do, she always listened as I explained my dilemma. With her, I listed the pros and cons of going either way before ending with a pathetic plea for her help. She empathized with me. What came out of her mouth next surprised me.

"Talk to your dad," she said calmly.

"What?" I asked incredulously. My dad had died seven years earlier. I thought my mother had lost it. I laughed feebly.

"I mean it," she insisted. "Whenever I need to make a hard decision, I talk to your dad through prayer. He always seems to answer me."

We talked a bit more before I ended the call, but still no closer to a decision than before I had called her.

What should I do? Both companies wanted an answer first thing in the morning. How would I decide?

Preparing for bed, I knew it would be a long, sleepless night with this big problem unresolved. True to form, I tossed and turned, searching for a comfortable position. I tried to erase all thoughts from my mind, creating a vacuum. That didn't work. I focused on my breathing so I could approach a meditative state. No luck. I even tried counting forward and backward. Nothing helped. By two in the morning, exhausted from my attempts, crying seemed the only answer. As I mopped the tears, I remembered my mom's advice: "Talk to your dad."

I closed my eyes tight and began my solemn appeal, seeking guidance from him. I must have drifted off to sleep.

"Ballen," a voice said.

Half asleep, I heard it again.

"Ballen," the soft voice called. Who was that? I looked around.

And yet, I knew. Only one person called me by that childhood nickname. My father.

I raised myself halfway off the pillow. At the foot of the bed, my father's face floated. Just as I remembered him, his full round face had a gentle expression, and I relaxed.

"Ballen, why is this so difficult for you?" He continued, "You always make excellent decisions. You need to trust yourself."

With that, his face faded into the night.

Puzzled, I glanced around the room. Alone in the dark, I glimpsed the time. 3:10 in the morning. It gave me an eerie feeling. When he farmed, Dad always came to the house for coffee shortly after three every afternoon, and this was when we children got to see our father. We talked with him about life's problems. It seemed serendipitous that he chose that exact time to appear to me, with his voice as soothing as I remembered.

I laid back down in bed and pulled the covers to my chin. An overwhelming feeling of peacefulness washed over me and bathed me in serene tranquillity. This incredible sensation left me feeling like I didn't have a care in the world, as though I floated on a cloud.

Sleep captured me and rocked me in its arms until my alarm sounded.

I woke feeling refreshed.

I knew what I would do.

The answer had come to me in a prayer.

Friends

It should have been one of the happiest days of my career. I was the Branch Manager at a Meadow Lake bank in 2003. On a conference call early that morning, the District Vice President announced they had awarded me an all-expense-paid trip for two to Puerto Rico. The congratulations poured in all morning. I drifted in a state of euphoric disbelief.

Shortly before noon that day, my cheery demeanour changed to one of apprehension. This feeling moved in like a fog overtaking me and I could not shake it. These unexplained premonitions occurred every so often in my life. When this happened, I knew I had to pay attention. I needed to act. I needed to phone my friend, Nadene. We came to know each other over the years as employees for the same company, even though we never worked under the same roof.

In the late '70s, Nadene and I started our careers as tellers for the bank. We worked our way up, becoming small branch managers and eventually managing much larger branches. We attended the same bank meetings and conferences and sat on similar committees. Over twenty-plus years, our friendship grew.

Nadene and I came from similar upbringings. Both of us were older children of a large family. We grew up on family farms, toiling and labouring, where everyone learned to help each other. Nadene and I started our bank careers in rural branches shortly after high school. We both had strong work ethics and a desire to succeed. Our paths ran parallel since we both exhibited leadership qualities and simultaneously began advancing our positions within the bank.

The next step in the progression of our careers was to become District Leaders. Nadene became the District Leader of Operations, and I became the District Leader of Sales Effectiveness. For these leadership roles, both of us needed to move to Saskatoon. The first to move, Nadene set up her new department, organizing offices, hiring employees, and getting her team ready for their new roles.

That November day, I experienced an unexplainable need to talk to her. I sensed something was wrong. I dialled Nadene's newly installed office phone number. No answer. After leaving her a voice message, I waited for her to call me back. The minutes ticked by, and she did not call. My anxiety mounted. With Nadene in Saskatoon and me three and a half hours away in Meadow Lake, I called random people in the city to see if any of them knew where Nadene might be. No one did. I tracked down her new assistant, Lori's, phone number and called her. Luckily, I reached her as she prepared to leave for lunch. Lori told me how Nadene had appeared upset and preoccupied all morning. She said my friend had received a phone call and then grabbed her coat and dashed out, saying she had to go home. Lori told me that Nadene had recently gotten a new cell phone and she provided me with the number.

I didn't waste any time calling her. Thankfully, Nadene answered. I noticed right away that she did not sound like herself.

"Mare, stay with me. Don't hang up," she said in a whisper.

"What's wrong? Are you OK?"

A long silence.

"Nadene?"

"I'm here. Give me a moment, Mare."

I could hear Nadene speaking to someone, but I couldn't understand the words. I knew something was desperately wrong. I could feel it deep inside me, like a parasite chewing on its host. I waited for what seemed an eternity.

When Nadene returned to the phone, she shocked me as she explained what had happened. She told me the police were at her house and the EMTs had just arrived. I could barely breathe, not knowing what to expect.

Over the past year or two, Nadene shared how her adult son, Darren, found himself in a volatile relationship with a woman who mentally abused him. The two lived together and now had a three-year-old daughter. Nadene told me how her son felt powerless and worried for the safety and well-being of their daughter. He considered leaving his common-law partner but stayed out of concern for his little girl. Darren and his partner's relationship reached a critical point where something had to give. He became more and more withdrawn. His health deteriorated, and he lost significant weight. Nadene tried to intervene to get him the help he needed, but nothing seemed to work.

That morning, Darren's common-law partner contacted the police to tell them Darren might be at risk and that he had gone to Nadene's home. The police phoned Nadene and met her at their recently purchased house in the southeast area of Saskatoon. When Nadene arrived at her residence, the police, already there, led the way into her home and instructed her to remain in the kitchen while they went through her house. It didn't take long for her worst nightmare to come true.

"He's in the basement," Nadene told me softly.

"Who is?"

"Darren."

I waited for her to say more. When she did, it came out in a choked sob. "They'll be bringing up his body soon."

"Oh, Nadene."

"Stay with me, Mare. I need to know you're with me. I can't do this alone."

In short monotone sentences, Nadene began relaying what had transpired. She told me how the police had searched her house, how they found her son hanging from a beam in their unfinished basement, and how she waited all alone in her shiny new kitchen as her world tumbled in on her.

"Mare, I'm so glad you called. How did you know to call me?" she asked.

"I don't know. I just knew I had to. I can't explain it."

Nadene's husband, still three hours away, was travelling to Saskatoon. She and I had to navigate this horror alone. Together, we clung to the phone line that connected us, me trying to console her from a distance and she standing in front of her sink staring out into the snow-covered yard trying to make sense of it all. She said she heard noises on the basement steps as they brought her son's body up on the gurney. She could not bear to look. We kept talking.

Finally, she said, "Mare, I need to go now. My sister is here, and the police want to talk to me."

And with that, the line went dead.

I sat at my office desk listening to the dial tone before slowly replacing the receiver in the cradle. My head swam, and my heart ached for my friend at her sudden, unfathomable loss. I could not believe it! How could a young man feel so desperate and trapped that he had to take his own life? What would happen to their three-year-old daughter? How would his mother, my dear friend, cope with this trauma?

The insurmountable loss my friend experienced spurred me to do something. I had to help her through this most difficult time. The next day, I drove the three-and-a-half hours to Saskatoon to be with her. The cold November winds blew snow that stuck to the highway, creating a slippery surface and making it difficult to see. Hands gripping the steering wheel, I made my way south of Meadow Lake along Highway 4. The drive seemed endless.

Four hours later, I arrived at the northern outskirts of Saskatoon, maneuvered onto Circle Drive East, and headed directly to Nadene's house in the southeast part of the city. Pulling into the cul-de-sac where she now lived, I immediately noticed all the vehicles parked in a semi-circle in front of her house. I sat in the car, closed my eyes, and took a deep breath before getting out to carefully make my way up the icy sidewalk. I rang the doorbell and waited. The door opened, and a matronly-looking woman stared at me.

"Is Nadene home? I'm a friend of hers."

Without a word, the woman turned. I saw Nadene behind her.

She brushed past the woman and grabbed me in a hug. We clung to each other. I could hear the commotion of people in the background, someone banging dishes in the kitchen, another's voice rising above the steady drone of people visiting and children playing.

"Mare, what a surprise. I didn't know you were coming."

"I had to. Let's go somewhere."

"Now?"

"Can you leave now?" I asked.

"You bet." She did not hesitate, even for a moment. Nadene briefly introduced me to the woman who had opened the door as her mother before she reached into the hall closet for her jacket.

We left the stifling atmosphere of the house where well-wishers and family had converged and we escaped into the brisk, grey-clad day.

As Nadene and I slipped and slid down the sidewalk, I asked her where she'd like to go.

"You know, maybe we could go to a dress shop. I need to buy a dress for … Well, you know."

"A dress shop it is," I said with a smile as we climbed into my car and pulled away from the curb.

We drove in silence for part of the way until Nadene began speaking. She wanted it to be like all the times we had gone out together. She didn't want to talk about Darren right now and what had happened. I understood and followed her lead. We shared an enjoyable afternoon filled with shopping, conversation, and even the occasional laugh.

Later, on our way back to her house, Nadene said, "I'm so glad you came. I needed to get out of the house. How did you know?"

I shrugged, "I guess I put myself in your shoes and how I would feel."

"Mare, this is what I needed. Thank you so much for coming all that way to see me."

"I had to, Nadene. You're my best friend. I could not let you go through this alone."

"And I got myself a dress," she proclaimed, holding her shopping bag triumphantly in the air.

"You certainly did!"

That evening, on my way back to Meadow Lake, I thought about Nadene and the events that unfolded in her life. Once again, I wondered how I knew to call her at precisely that time on that specific day, the time she needed me the most, the time she couldn't bear to be alone. I concluded the lasting, unbreakable bond we shared had played a role in it.

I continued driving, peering through the windshield as the snowflakes pierced the glass in funnel format, and I prayed my friend would find comfort and solace. We were two friends, together at the worst of times.

Moving Day

I rubbed my eyes. Something had woken me up. I rolled over to look at the clock beside our bed.

9:00.

Now I heard it. The doorbell ringing. Who could that be on a Sunday morning?

I jumped out of bed, grabbed my robe, and slipped it on as I ran down the short flight of stairs to our front door. I nearly tripped over the bodies sprawled on the living room floor, remnants of our daughter's graduation party the night before. Tying my robe shut, I unlocked the door and peered out.

"Good morning. We're here for your move."

Two young men dressed in royal blue coveralls stood at the door, smiling.

"There must be some mistake. You weren't supposed to be here until tomorrow," I floundered, pushing my unruly hair back, attempting to look more presentable.

The first man checked some papers on his clipboard, looked at me and replied, "Nope, it says here that we should start packing you up on June 27. That's today."

"But it's Sunday. Our daughter's graduation was yesterday. We have about a dozen kids sleeping here. There must be some mistake."

"Afraid not. We drove from Saskatoon this morning to pack you."

"Well, okay," I said as I stepped aside and invited them in.

Both men entered the house and stopped to stare at the kids sleeping on the floor and couches. Some kids slouched on chairs with blankets thrown haphazardly over them. Some had limbs hanging out, and others were missing heads. Blankets and pillows covered parts of their bodies. Backs and stomachs were on display as they slumbered. Most collapsed only hours before, now dead to the world, oblivious that three adults stood amongst them, looking at the tangled heap of bodies and limbs.

Stepping carefully over the sleeping youth, I asked, "Where would you like to start?"

The one man who seemed to be the more senior of the two said, "How about the garage? We could start there so we don't disturb the kids."

"That sounds good to me."

The movers followed me down six steps to the second lowest level of our four-level-split home. I opened the door to the garage to show them where they could begin packing and pressed the garage door opener so they could carry in boxes from their truck.

I turned and ran upstairs to our bedroom to rouse Don, explaining that the movers were here a day early. We dressed in a hurry and Don went to the garage to provide further instructions to the movers and to back our minivan out so they would have more room to work.

A year ago, I accepted a promotion to become a district leader for the bank. One of the offer's conditions was that I work out of an office in Saskatoon. Brenda was in Grade 12 and doing well. The bank granted a concession that I could remain in Meadow Lake until she graduated. Her graduation was yesterday, and the movers showed up today.

"They really took it literally," I chuckled to myself.

Brenda graduated at the top of her class from Carpenter High School. The ceremonies spanned two days. Opting not to attend the large class party, Brenda invited some of her friends over for a private party. The kids celebrated all night and well into the morning. Finally, exhausted and maybe a little drunk, they crashed on our living room floor. We did not want any of them driving in their state. It was safer for them to sleep over. But it was time for them to leave now. I felt sorry for them as we roused them from their deep sleep.

"Mom," Brenda complained. "What's going on? Let us sleep."

"I'm sorry, but the movers are here."

"Okay. I'm tired. Let me sleep."

"Brenda, the movers are here. They are in the garage. Packing."

"What? Today? Now?" Brenda rolled over wide awake.

"I know. There's been some miscommunication, but the movers are here," I explained.

Brenda sat up, rubbed her face, and looked around, getting her bearings. Slowly she got to her feet, still wearing the jeans and shirt from the night before, her makeup smudged and her hair standing every which way. Brenda tramped down the stairs to the garage door and peered through the window. She turned around and fled back up the stairs to where I waited for her, standing in the sea of teenagers' bodies.

"Okay, everyone up!" she yelled. "It's time to get going."

A few moved their arms or legs and grumbled. Brenda hollered again, this time louder.

Some teenagers swore until they opened their eyes and saw me standing over them, then stopped. Brenda nudged them, all the while telling them to get up. When most young people were awake and sitting up, I explained the movers had come a day early. The kids would have to leave now. They moaned and groaned as bodies slowly moved and limbs disentangled themselves. Some called their parents to pick them up, while others who lived in town walked home. I had hoped to feed our guests breakfast, but the unexpected arrival of the movers thwarted my plans.

I watched Brenda say goodbye and hug each of her friends. With our upcoming move, Brenda knew she wouldn't see most of them again. I sensed her excitement and sadness about leaving her home of four years. After our move to Saskatoon, she planned to attend university in the fall. I sighed as I watched my youngest daughter close the door after the last friend left. She turned to me, eyes watering, and I reached for her hand.

A new chapter in our lives was about to begin.

The Door Is Always Open

Thankfully, our bi-level in Saskatoon had five bedrooms. We needed all of them during our four years in the Silversprings community. Moving from Meadow Lake at the end of June 2004, we settled nicely into city life. Brenda had all her university classes selected, learned the bus routes, and bided her time waiting for school to start in the fall. Her best friend, Caitlin from Meadow Lake, moved in at the end of August. She stayed with us for the next three years while she, too, attended university. The girls occupied the two bedrooms on the lower level and had much of that area to themselves, including a bathroom.

Moving and taking on a new district leader role at the bank stressed me, plus planning our oldest daughter's wedding had me tense with worry and exhaustion. A month before their wedding, Sara and her fiancé, Reiss, moved from Fort Saskatchewan, Alberta, to Saskatoon. They had not yet found jobs or a place to stay, so the logical thing was for them to move in with us. They took one of the upstairs bedrooms.

Six adults living in one house could be challenging for most; however, we all found ways to coexist. We shared the household and outdoor chores and gave each other space when we knew they needed it. Our grocery costs and water bill increased exponentially. I sighed each morning as I watched a line form for the shower and listened to the washing machine tremble with activity.

At the beginning of April 2005, Sara and her husband rented a house on 6th Avenue. Reiss had found employment, and Sara prepared to start her new job at a car dealership in June. I watched as our Dodge half-ton loaded with their belongings pulled away from the curb and waved to them as they drove off to start their new life. Climbing the six steps up to the main level of our house, it seemed deserted, almost hollow. I looked down the hallway and saw that their bedroom door was open, knowing that they had emptied the room of all their belongings.

Two years later, Adam and his girlfriend, Christy, back from Alberta, moved in for a month or two. Their stay was brief, waiting for their rented house to become available. They took up the same bedroom Sara and Reiss had vacated less than two years before. Again, it felt great having our son back under our roof and, this time, with our soon-to-be daughter-in-law.

Adam and Christy had just moved out when Nathan, Brenda's boyfriend, joined us. He had stayed with several friends until it made the most sense for him to move in with us. We loved having Nathan around. Brenda was happy about it, too. He stayed for about seven months before he and Brenda struck out on their own, moving into a rented duplex in the Exhibition area of the city.

We had kids and their partners come and go in Saskatoon for four years. We welcomed them all and were sad to see them leave. It fills my heart with joy to know that all our children were comfortable returning home and that each of their partners felt at ease living with us.

Coincidentally, many years later, in 2018, after our house in Rosthern sold quickly, Don and I found ourselves without a place to live. Without thinking twice, all three of our children offered their homes to us. We moved in with Sara and Reiss and lived with them for four months. Again, though not ideal, we made it work.

Isn't that what families are for?

Neighbourhood Watch

At the end of June 2004, we moved to "beige-ville," a name our children had given the cookie-cutter homes in Silversprings. In this Saskatoon neighbourhood, it seemed every house was a shade of beige or light brown with a two-car garage in front, and every yard had one token tree. Ours was no different.

Right from the start, we felt unwelcome in this neighbourhood. The moving truck rumbled up in front of our new house, and the movers carried in and unpacked the boxes. The neighbours showed no interest in our arrival. No one greeted us with a smile or a friendly wave. No one seemed drawn to stop and attempt idle conversation. No one except the older Serbian woman across the street. She immediately took Brenda under her wing, inviting her into her home for cookies when she forgot her house key. This kind woman kept Brenda safe in her house until I came home from work. Several nights later, this neighbourly woman sat up all night, rocking in her chair, guarding our house. We had inadvertently left our overhead garage door open. When she noticed the open door, it was late, and she thought we were in bed. Not wanting to disturb us, she watched over our house all night from the vantage point of her living room window to make sure no one stole anything from us. She was a real gem. Her name was Zorca.

A single dad lived on the corner to the west of us. He had custody of his children every second weekend, where he provided minimal supervision. He allowed his pre-adolescent children outside to thump their basketball against the vinyl siding of our house at one o'clock in the morning. *Thump, thump, thump.* It seemed to go on for hours as we tried to sleep. Vehicles came and went from that house at all hours of the day and night, each staying only for five minutes. Even though he told us he was a landscaper, we never saw him go to work. Four years later, on our moving day, we learnt from other neighbours that he was a drug dealer. Now it all made sense. It explained the top-of-the-line half-ton truck and a large pontoon boat parked in his driveway. These were things an unemployed landscaper could not afford.

The most peculiar of our neighbours were the ones that lived directly behind us, the ones we shared a back fence with since we had no alleyway. We learned the husband worked in computer technology and had an office at home. His wife, with flaming red curly hair springing out from her head in every direction, was a stay-at-home mom whose parents had gifted them the house. I don't know if they didn't like us or didn't like people in general, but from day one, it was as though they set out to make our lives a living hell.

Shortly after we moved to this house, I came home after work and searched for Don. I found him on the back deck barbecuing meat for supper. We stood on the deck talking about our day. I stopped when I thought I heard a bleating sound.

"Don, you're going to think I'm crazy, but I could swear I heard a sheep."

"No, you're not crazy, but they are," Don said, pointing to the neighbours across our back fence. "They have a goat tied up in their backyard."

"A goat?"

"Yup. Someone brought it over a couple of hours ago."

"You're kidding. Is that a new pet?"

"No idea."

The goat remained in the neighbour's yard until shortly before dark. We saw them lead the goat away by a rope around its neck. A little while later, the redhead came out with her house vacuum cleaner and began sucking up the goat's droppings. Don and I could only stare incredulously at her goings-on.

Don noticed our neighbour across the back fence was coming to the front of our property on garbage collection days and rummaging through our garbage. When Don asked him what he was doing, the man acted like he had every right to search our rubbish. He didn't hide the fact that he was doing this. It unnerved us. What on earth was he looking for? Don asked him to stop. He didn't.

Another day, I returned home from work. Some of our kids and their friends were in the backyard. Don called me over and pointed to the neighbour's window.

"They have a video camera. They're filming us."

"What?"

I looked where he had pointed. Sure enough. I saw a video camera poking between the vertical blinds in their house window aimed directly at our backyard. I don't know what they hoped to capture, but it made us uneasy. Violated. They continued videotaping us for the next several months. We felt unsafe and intruded upon in our backyard.

Don and I were watching TV in our living room one evening when the doorbell rang. I opened the door to find the man from across the back standing there. He asked if he could come in. Without waiting for my consent, he brushed past me and went to sit at our kitchen table. Don and I followed suit, apprehensive about what he wanted. With him, we never knew. It couldn't be good.

Not engaging in any preamble, he said, "Yeah, I'm here to talk about your fence."

"What about it?" I asked, puzzled.

"Obviously, you need a new one."

"Yes, we're aware of that. We plan to have a new one built this summer."

"Good. I caught you in time. I wanted to tell you what type of fence we want so that it will match with the rest of our fence."

"We know what type of fence we want."

"Will it be a wooden one the same colour as our existing fence?"

"No, it will be a chain-link fence with white privacy slats."

"That won't do. I want a wooden fence stained the same colour as the rest of my fence."

"Well, if we split the cost, maybe we can work something out."

"I don't see why I should pay for your fence."

"Because it will be your fence, too. We share it."

"I'm not paying a cent for your fence."

"Then we will build the type of fence WE want," I could hear my voice rising out of frustration.

"We'll see what the city has to say about that," he roared as he pushed his chair back, scraping it against our dining room wall. He slammed out of the house.

Don and I stared at each other. What had just happened? How could that man be so unreasonable?

These eccentric neighbours occasionally provided us with some comic relief. Often, Don and I sat in our kitchen and watched them through our French doors. They arranged their patio furniture with significant flair on warm evenings. After admiring it, they sat for two minutes before springing up from their chairs to put everything away. They went through this routine at least once every week during the summer, sometimes more. It defied reason. After making the effort to set out all their patio furniture to their liking, why didn't they relax and enjoy it?

Sara dropped by for a visit and sat out on the deck. Coming into the kitchen, she said, "Mom, you've got to see this."

We watched from the window as the man on the other side of the fence built a playhouse for his little daughters. As he measured things, he held his hands apart for the distance of the measurement and then walked across the yard to the corner where he planned to build the house. This is how he measured things. I shook my head and closed my eyes. Unbelievable.

And then there were the police visits. The redhead constantly berated her husband or screamed at her daughters in a loud, shrill voice. As a result, some of the other neighbours called the police. It was not uncommon to see one or two patrol cars sitting alongside their house. I don't know if she physically abused anyone in their home; however, the cops seemed to be frequent visitors for whatever reason.

The final straw came when Brenda and her boyfriend were at a local restaurant in Saskatoon. Unexpectantly, the redheaded woman approached their table. She yelled at them in public, creating a scene. Brenda could not understand what the woman was screaming and accusing her of, but she was so embarrassed that she and her friend got up and left.

We had had enough. That incident prompted us to search for another house. We found one in Rosthern.

Strangely enough, on our moving day, only four years from when we first moved in, many of our neighbours stopped by to tell us how sorry they were to see us leave. Three of them asked if it was because of the neighbours across our back fence. We told them they were the main reason. We discovered that all the other neighbours felt the same way that we did. Those with young children forbade them to play with the couple's children. Others admitted to calling the police because of the bizarre happenings on that property, things we did not even know about.

Yikes! All this in what we thought was a nice middle-income neighbourhood. We could not get packed and out of there quickly enough. We hoped our new home would be better. It was in a small town. It had to be. Right?

On A Whim

Easter came early in 2008. Don and I lounged in a booth in one of the few restaurants open on Good Friday and glanced out the window at the grey overcast day that threatened more snow. Traffic moved slowly on Central Avenue in Saskatoon, partly because of the snowy streets and partly because people were not in a hurry. Schools and stores were closed for the holiday, as were most offices.

"Look at this!" I exclaimed, turning the Star Phoenix insert, "Homes" for Don to look at. "It's our dream home."

I pointed to the picture of the grey bungalow advertised on the front page of the realtor's magazine. I read the details to Don and looked at him expectantly.

"Doesn't it sound perfect?"

"Yeah, it does. It's the best one we've come across so far," Don agreed.

"Should we go look at it?"

"But it's in Rosthern. It's a private sale."

"So what? It's not that far. Phone them."

"Don, I can't. It's Good Friday. What if they're with their family?"

"Phone them. We won't know if we don't try. Call them."

Don and I had searched for a bungalow in Saskatoon for months, not finding one we liked. The one on the magazine's cover looked ideal. It seemed like it was meant for us.

I opened my purse and dragged my cell phone from its pocket. Pulling the magazine toward me, I dialled the number in the listing. Almost immediately, a woman answered. I explained who I was and why I was calling and asked if it was all right if we came out to look at their house. She agreed to one o'clock that afternoon. I hung up and looked at Don. We both smiled.

We drove forty-five minutes from Saskatoon to Rosthern and arrived at the listed house. A large grey bungalow sat in the middle of the lot, surrounded by banks of snow that had black dirt peeking out. Wood pallets serving as a sidewalk stretched across the ground and snow to the side door where makeshift wooden steps leaned against the house.

A woman stood at the door waving to us as we gingerly tread across the wooden boards to the house. She apologized for the "grand entrance." Don and I entered the house and gaped at the large U-shaped kitchen with trendy maple cabinets. The spacious kitchen held more cabinets than I could ever hope to fill. Next to it, an expansive dining room faced west. It was big enough to seat twenty people. Greek-style pillars graced the entrance to the living room. Here, cathedral-style windows stretched from floor to ceiling, letting in abundant sunlight. I imagined sitting in that room and enjoying the majestic Saskatchewan sunsets. There were three bedrooms with an ensuite off the master and two extra bathrooms on the main floor. The basement was unfinished.

Now, I thought to myself, this is a house!

We eagerly spoke with the woman who owned the house to get more details and discuss the price and terms they would be willing to accept.

Our heads spinning with joy, we drove around Rosthern, examining the businesses to see if it was a place that we could call home. The restaurants and shops were all closed for Good Friday, so we could not go in, but we circled the town, noting the hospital, the RCMP, and the large grocery store.

We had both fallen in love with this house. It was everything we were looking for but could not find in Saskatoon. The lot was huge, fringed along the back by a wall of mature evergreens. Don and I both loved evergreens because both our childhood homes had had them. We knew the lot needed to be brought up to grade to allow for proper drainage.

We needed to landscape, pour a driveway, construct a double-car garage, and add steps for the front and back doors. The basement also required development. The list went on and on, but we loved this house.

Don and I talked about the daily commute I would need to make for my job, and we calculated the cost of gas and the wear and tear on my vehicle. We discussed the two-hour commute and how the time on the road would add to my already long workday. We considered what moving out to the country and away from our kids, who all lived in the city, would involve. We ruminated over it all, weighing and measuring the pros and cons, calculating the costs associated and the time spent. We pondered it all. Neither of us slept that night. We both wanted that house. The next night we slept on it again.

On Easter Sunday, we drafted an Offer to Purchase and presented it to the sellers on Monday. And then we waited. I was in a meeting at work when the phone rang. The owners of the house phoned to tell us they accepted our offer and to check our email. We were ecstatic!

The purchase went through without a hitch. We took possession the second week in May. On the long weekend, all our kids helped us move. Our son and both our sons-in-law leant their backs to lifting, loading, and unloading all our belongings. They stumbled over the pallets, sinking into the mud on their way into our new house. The girls helped me unpack and put everything away in our new home. They marvelled at all the space we had, but they still could not resist asking, "Why Rosthern?"

"Because we fell in love with the house."

We continued to love that house for the next ten years while we lived there. With the arrival of one grandchild after another, we soon realized that we needed to be in Saskatoon, closer to our family.

Another move was on the horizon.

Gone Too Soon

I huddled in my SUV outside my sister Audrey's house on Avenue B, in Saskatoon. It was October 29, 2008. I received a phone call from my brother, Ron, who lived two hours away. He told me our sister needed help. Since I lived an hour closer to Saskatoon than him, I could get to her quicker. Don was working six hours away from home. At about 9:30 p.m., leaving my home in Rosthern, I called Don from my SUV. I told him that even though I felt frightened, I had to check on Audrey to ensure she was all right.

An hour later, I sat cowering inside my vehicle, staring at Audrey's curtained house windows. Fearing the trauma that Phil, her common-law partner, might inflict upon her, I felt too afraid to go in. A few years earlier, Audrey first introduced Phil to our family. A slovenly man, he wore out-of-date, ill-fitting pants and a buttoned-up sweater vest with holes and snags in the wool, his hair unruly, and his hands and nails dirty.

Phil didn't look anyone in the eyes. We wondered if he had something to hide, something he couldn't face. A big talker, he bragged a lot. During this first meeting, we learned Audrey had quit her job one she had held for several years, one she enjoyed, and one that was easily walkable in the city since she did not own a car. Phil convinced her to join him in starting a cleaning business. Audrey proudly produced business cards that showed their new business name. Lacking any direction and motivation, their new enterprise never took flight.

Phil did not hold a regular job. Instead, he did odd jobs for people. Audrey met him when she saw his online ad and called him. She planned to do a few house renovations and found his rates affordable. Not long after, Phil moved in with Audrey.

My family and I began noticing things not typical for our sister. Budget-conscious, Audrey always made sure she paid her mortgage and bills on time. Now, she bought items she could not afford and did not need, purchases she wouldn't have made before meeting Phil. Soon, they owned two large golden lab retrievers, an outside swimming pool, and an indoor jacuzzi tub. Phil knocked out Audrey's bathroom walls and tore up the floor before realizing the jet tub they purchased would not fit in her small bathroom. The tub was not returnable. He never put the room back together. It remained torn apart for years until the house sold.

Phil worked less and less. He could not seem to find a job. Lengthy bus rides, a consequence of Audrey finding alternative employment with extensive hours for very little pay, had Audrey sacrificing even more. She spent many hours at work and on the bus while she supported Phil with his two big dogs and his smoking and drinking habits.

Audrey drifted away from our family. She phoned less frequently, and we noticed her conversations were hesitant and guarded as though someone was monitoring her calls. We learned she no longer stayed in touch with her friends, either. Phil had taken over her life, restricting and limiting contact with those who loved and cared about her. When Audrey called our mother, Phil hovered, listening. In sheer rage one time, he ripped the telephone cord out of the wall while Audrey spoke with her on the phone.

Often, alcohol spurred Phil's irrational behaviour. When Audrey's son, Trevor, graduated from Grade 12, Phil showed up at the graduation party, took an axe from his beat-up truck, and chased some kids with it. Someone called the police, who came and immediately arrested Phil.

An alarming incident, my family and I heaved a collective sigh of relief, knowing that Phil was in custody. Audrey should be safe. Or so we thought. In no time, we discovered Phil had persuaded her to provide the court with a character reference in which she extolled his positive attributes. She must have been convincing because the courts released him. He was once again a free man. Living off Audrey.

I, as well as my mother and siblings, began getting snippets of information from Audrey. She sometimes alluded to Phil dragging her into the basement, where he yelled at her and berated her. He may even have physically assaulted her. Audrey never really said for sure. We could only assume what went on in the rooms below her house.

My mother, sister Cindy, and I appealed to Phil's probation officer. We learned Phil had previously spent time in prison. We wondered what his other offences had been. The probation officer either could not or would not assist us. As our next course of action, we met with a lawyer to see what we could do to free Audrey from the grasp Phil had on her. The physical and mental abuse escalated. We desperately needed to get Audrey out of his clutches and beyond his control.

The meeting with the lawyer proved futile. While he listened with a sympathetic ear, he told us that until Audrey willingly brought charges against Phil, there was nothing we could do. The lawyer stood up and prepared to leave the boardroom.

He turned to face us and said, "Off the record, if she were my sister, I would arrange for two or three large men with baseball bats to meet with him in a back alley somewhere."

With that, he turned and left. My mother, Cindy, and I stared at each other before rising from our chairs and silently leaving the room.

* * *

I jumped, my reminisces interrupted by a man standing outside my vehicle, tapping on the window beside me.

"Are you having car trouble?" he called to me.

"No. No. I'm fine. Thank you."

The man nodded and continued walking his dog down the street.

Halloween decorations in the trees and the yards made me cringe. I peered through the glass but could no longer see the man and the dog in the night shadows. I heard the evil cackling of a witch as a motion sensor, presumably triggered by the man and his dog strolling by, went off. Pulling my coat tighter around me, I shuddered. Two nights before Halloween, I was outside Audrey's house in the dark, summoning the courage to check on her. I watched the white ghosts swaying in the wind from the porch's roof across the street and the illuminated skeleton scaling a neighbour's tree.

I looked out the passenger window at Audrey's house. I studied the curtains for shadows or movement and saw nothing. All seemed quiet, but I cringed to think of what was happening inside her house. Too late. I wished I had grabbed a baseball bat or something to defend my sister and I should Phil attack us. Now, I wished I had asked the man with the dog if he would accompany me into the house. He probably wouldn't have, but I could have asked. I debated phoning the police, but I hadn't spoken with Audrey myself and didn't know the level of concern. Undecided about what to do, I hunched in my car, frightened and trembling.

Extreme fear and cold can either immobilize a person or spur one to action. Resolutely, I grabbed the door handle and opened the car. Swinging my legs out into the frosty night air, I again wished I had brought something to defend myself. I crept up the front sidewalk, listening for any sound coming from her house. Nothing. I looked at the houses on each side of Audrey's house and contemplated going to their doors and asking for help. One of the two houses had lights. Should I go over and knock on the door? I decided against it. If needed, surely Audrey and I could overtake one man.

Breathing deeply, I marched up the outside steps leading to Audrey's front door. I strained, trying to see anything along the edges of the curtain in the window where light filtered through. Again, nothing. I listened, placing my ear against the door. Still nothing. Summoning up courage, I rapped on the door. I called to Audrey. A few moments later, my sister threw open the door. She stood inside, looking at me with enormous eyes.

"What are you doing here?" she asked.

"I thought you were in trouble and needed help."

Audrey laughed nervously.

"Adam and one of his friends came by."

"They did?"

"Don phoned him."

"Is Phil still here?"

"No." Audrey laughed. "He left in a big hurry when Adam got here."

I sighed with relief. I found out later Don had called our twenty-eight-year-old son Adam, who lived in Saskatoon. Adam and a friend had gone to Audrey's house. They told Phil to leave, which he did, fully realizing that these young athletic men could have easily overtaken him.

Audrey's wild look and halting sentences revealed her demeanour. She was a woman who had seen and borne too much. A woman in pain.

"Are you OK?" I asked her.

She nodded before saying with a wince, "It was bad this time."

"Grab some clothes, pack a bag. You're coming with me."

"But why? He's gone now."

"He could come back. I don't want you here alone if he does."

Audrey became almost childlike, giddy at the prospect of a sleepover. I asked her to hurry before Phil returned. We locked the house when we left, a rather pointless exercise. Phil had a key.

With Audrey safely tucked inside my SUV, we headed out of Saskatoon and into the moonless night back to Rosthern. On the ride home, Audrey seemed exhausted. I asked her to promise she would take steps to get Phil out of her house, out of her life for good. She promised. I looked over at her. She stared straight ahead, watching the tiny flakes of snow, like daggers, plummeting the windshield. I closed my eyes momentarily, wishing I could believe her. I prayed she had the fortitude to extricate Phil from her world to rebuild her life again, a life without him. In my heart, I knew this was unlikely to be the case.

I had not spoken to Audrey in months, partly over my frustration and anger that she had let Phil back into her life and wouldn't do anything to help herself, partly because the endless drama tired me. I did not understand the far-reaching effects of domestic violence or how he left my sister feeling powerless and ostracized.

"Hello, Marilyn?"

"Yes. Hi, Audrey. Nice to hear from you."

On Friday, December 18, I picked up the phone and heard Audrey's voice on the other end. We made small talk before she said, "I kicked Phil out. This time it's for good."

The skeptic in me had heard this so many times before. I could not help but be doubtful this would last.

"You did?"

"Yeah, and was he mad!"

"For good this time?"

"Yup. The kids and I are coming home for Christmas! It's been so long, and I can't wait to see everyone. I just called Mom. She will pick us up from the bus in Humboldt. We're going to stay with her for a few days."

I detected something different in Audrey's voice. She sounded excited and energized. Was it possible that this time she meant it? Had she ousted Phil permanently?

I hoped and prayed for this to be the case. I eagerly looked forward to Christmas and the prospect of her and her two children spending the holiday season with our entire family. Her teenage children, Trevor and Kiley, lived with their father, so for Audrey to have them at home for Christmas meant something special.

* * *

I stood at the back of the Canadian Martyr's church in Middle Lake with the rest of my family. Whispers and nods, sympathetic smiles, and tears dabbed away with tissues prevailed as we lingered in the church's vestibule. The funeral attendant informed us the casket would be closed soon. I glanced at Audrey's son and daughter and asked if they would like to go up to the front of the church one last time to say goodbye to their mother. They nodded and asked if I'd take them. With Trevor on one side and Kiley on the other, arms locked, the three of us walked down the church's center aisle that led to the open casket in front of the altar. I glanced at the congregation as they watched my young niece and nephew bid their last farewell to their mother. The church seemed to sigh with an overwhelming sadness and grief that gripped everyone in attendance.

* * *

On Tuesday, December 22, 2009, Phil called Audrey's therapist to tell her that he had not heard from Audrey in a while. Not surprised, it seemed Phil had pushed himself back into the picture. I had expected it. But why had he called Audrey's therapist? His phone call set things in motion. The therapist contacted Mom because Audrey had her listed as an emergency contact, to see if she had heard from Audrey. She had not. Alarmed, Mom phoned the Saskatoon Police. My sister Cindy rushed to Mom's place in Middle Lake to be with her while they waited for a call back from the police.

When the police realized that Cindy was in Middle Lake with Mom, they told her over the phone, rather than driving out. The police said they broke into Audrey's house. They encountered two ravenous dogs, so aggressive, they had to spray to subdue them. After searching the house, they found Audrey dead at the foot of the basement stairs. They believed she had been there since Sunday night. The police also indicated the basement door at the top of the stairs had been closed. Thankfully, the dogs could not get to her.

The police informed us that they did not suspect any foul play. Something about this information did not sit right with my family and me. Call it a gut feeling. We all felt it. Someone had something to do with her fall and untimely death. A person with an uncontrollable rage who needed to exert power over her. Someone who could not wait any longer for her body to be discovered. Someone who had called her therapist.

We will never know for sure the extent of Phil's involvement. We will never prove it in a court of law.

But I know.

My heart knows.

Winter Roads

During the last twenty years of my banking career, first as a District Leader in Sales Effectiveness and then as a District Manager, I spent a significant amount of time travelling the northern half of Saskatchewan. I travelled to the towns and cities that were home to my branches. Often, I left on Monday for a road trip and didn't return until Friday. While always careful to stick to the paved highways, I occasionally ran into fierce, unpredictable weather and wicked driving conditions. In Saskatchewan, the weather can change abruptly, and the roadways can quickly become treacherous.

Such was the case on a particular afternoon in February 2012. I left Maidstone, a town thirty minutes east of Lloydminster, near the Alberta/Saskatchewan border, and headed to Turtleford, a thirty-minute drive north. I decided to leave Maidstone early because I heard the weather reporter predicting freezing rain. The thought of driving on ice struck fear in my heart. The feeling of having no control as my vehicle's four wheels slid across the smooth polished surface filled me with terror.

I struck out as it rained slightly, and I cringed to think what that meant. The precipitation would soon freeze. My windshield wipers slapped happily at the rain droplets, pushing the wetness to the side. After driving for about ten minutes and realizing it had been raining longer in this area, I noticed my wipers no longer cleared the windshield. The glass iced over, and the vent blowing warm air inside didn't help. I pulled over to the side of the road. What was I going to do? I could not see out the windshield.

I stepped outside the car and nearly lost my balance as my

smooth-soled shoes glided on the slippery surface. I cursed myself for not putting on my boots. Instead, I had packed them in my suitcase in the back of my car. I grabbed the door handle, trying to stay upright. I moved along the car's side to the back door and opened it. Inside, I rummaged under the seat and produced a rag. Making my way carefully back to the front of the car, I hung on for dear life as I wiped the windshield with the rag so that I could see.

I scrambled back into the car having solved that issue, but I had a bigger problem. In front of me was the deep V-like coulee that extended deep into the countryside. The road went straight down and came straight up on the other side. It was a narrow country road with no guardrails, nothing but a broad prairie expanse on both sides. At the bottom, a tiny bridge crossing over the creek trickled during the summer. How would I manoeuvre this steep, mountain-like slope on these icy roads? I could not simply inch along because that would not give me enough speed and momentum to get up on the other side. If I didn't go fast enough, I wouldn't be able to climb the steep icy incline on the way up. If I picked up speed too quickly and my car swerved and went out of control, I hated to think what could happen. I could easily roll my vehicle. What a dilemma!

I sat in the car pondering the predicament in which I found myself. Now, I noticed my windshield had iced over again. Once more, I climbed out of my vehicle and crept slowly to the front to wipe the windshield. Slipping and sliding, I made my way back inside the car. I knew what I had to do.

Before I could change my mind, I slipped the car into gear, and with prayers tumbling from my lips, I began my steady decline into the coulee, gripping my hands on the steering wheel. The car went straight as an arrow, never swerving. As I neared the bottom, I carefully stepped on the gas to propel my car forward and give it the thrust I needed to climb to the top. My car ascended slowly but surely. At one point, it seemed to slow down, and I feared it would peter out and slip backward.

Ever so gently, I increased the pressure on the gas pedal. Miraculously, I did not lose control of the car and it took me safely to the top of the hill. I breathed a sigh of relief.

I made my way along the highway and, all too soon, I remembered another coulee I would need to pass through before I reached Turtleford. Buoyed by my newfound confidence of completing the passage through the last one, this smaller coulee did not seem so scary. Once again, I clung to the steering wheel as though my life depended on it. Which it did. I steered my car safely down one side and up to the top on the other. Having mastered the second coulee, I felt jubilant and continued to Turtleford, occasionally stopping to wipe my windshield clean. After an agonizingly slow trip, I reached the small town and noticed the service station still open. I asked them to replace my wipers.

Another time, I headed home to Rosthern from Meadow Lake, which was ordinarily a three-and-a-half-hour drive on a dry highway. On a clear day, it was a beautiful ride filled with forests in the north, graduating to rolling hills and then open fields where crops waved in the summer. Today, a blustery winter day, I made my way south on Highway 4, noticing the road conditions worsening. The gods seemed to have dumped buckets of fluffy snow everywhere. To make matters worse, gusts of wind swept the freshly fallen snow into billowy white clouds, impenetrable to the naked eye. The heavy snowfall left a deep accumulation on the highway and made me grateful for my 4-wheel drive SUV. The foot-deep snow made navigation almost impossible.

The snow kept coming down. It swirled so that I could not tell if I was still on the highway, in the ditch, or, worse yet, on the wrong side of the road. I could not see a thing. The blinding conditions made it nearly impossible to stop because I might be on the wrong side of the road or if in my correct lane, another vehicle might not see me in time and ram into me from the back. The growing accumulation of snow on the highway made it increasingly difficult for me to manage, and I feared that if I stopped, I would be stuck. I had to keep moving.

And then I saw it. A truck advanced toward me in reckless haste. Do you ever wonder about those trucks travelling at breakneck speed in the middle of a storm? I considered my options. If I left my track, I feared it would pull me to the side, unable to move because of the deep snow. Stubbornly, I clung to the wheel and stayed on my track. The driver bowled by, leaving behind him a flurry of snow blinding me once again. I slowed until I could barely keep my vehicle going. I felt positive that if I stopped, I would be stuck. On this long stretch of highway, I guessed the nearest town to be forty-five minutes away. I honestly had no clue how far I had come in the white-out conditions. I inched along. What was typically an hour-and-a-half drive had now turned into a three-hour drive. My arms, neck, and shoulders ached from muscle tension.

Finally, in the late afternoon's fading sun, I saw a few orange lights peeking through the whiteness. I knew I had reached the small village of Cochin, a thirty-minute drive from North Battleford. From there, the storm lessened. The snowplows had been out, clearing the remaining seventy kilometres to North Battleford. Even though I was only a little over an hour from home, I stayed in a hotel. My nerves could not take any more driving.

Another time, on my way home to Rosthern after a day at work in my Saskatoon office, a normal day filled with troubleshooting and coaching my branch managers, I left my seventh-floor office, unaware of how quickly the storm had moved in. With my head down, fighting the cold and wind that pelted my face with the crystalized snow, I fought my way down the city block to where I had parked my car that morning. I removed the four inches of accumulated snow on my vehicle before steering it out onto the street, taking me to the city's outskirts on my way home. Nothing in the city prepared me for the horrific, blinding snowstorm in the country that made it nearly impossible to drive. A total white-out.

Occasionally, I caught sight of the painted line on the highway, validating I remained in the correct lane. Focused on ensuring I stayed on the road and did not venture off into the ditch, I nearly failed to see the three deer that sprang up out of nowhere, bounding across the highway in front of me. Upon seeing them, I had no time to hit the brakes. I narrowly avoided hitting them. I don't know how because, by rights, I should have. A close call. Thanks to Bluetooth in my vehicle, I often called my mom to help pass the time as I drove. Not this time. The near-white-out conditions commanded all my attention. Relieved to pull off the highway and onto the road leading to our house in Rosthern, this white-knuckle drive got me safely home once more.

During my career, I travelled from one end of the province to the other in every kind of season. I drove through many a storm, many a downpour, and on many an icy surface. When the weather or road conditions were too bad, I cancelled my trips, but this didn't happen often.

Lodging in one hotel after another made for a lonely life. Often, I double-checked my hotel room number because they all began to look and feel the same after a while. I ate in one greasy restaurant after another and stared at the same twelve or thirteen channels on TV that held nothing of interest to me. Instead, I called my husband, children, Mom, or siblings. Speaking to them brought home life to my empty hotel rooms with the paper-thin walls and leaky taps with constantly running toilets.

When I had to venture out on the road, I always carried a survival pack in my car. Stashed in the back, it held a warm blanket, an extra pair of boots and socks, a thick scarf, a tin can, a large candle, matches, a flashlight, and a deck of cards. I never wanted to take any unnecessary risk; however, if I found myself stranded somewhere, I felt adequately prepared. No matter how far I travelled or for how long I had been away, I always found my way home safely.

Oh, what a life!

Doggone

We turned into the driveway that was nothing but a dirt trail on that hot July Sunday morning in 2010. Weeds edged in from the ditch on both sides and down the centre of the road. The tall, tufted blades of June grass poked their fingers into the bottom of our Ford Explorer, and the bumpy road made progress slow. Rocking and swaying over the unevenness of the track, we drew closer to the unkempt farmyard that cried out for the attention and whirring comfort of a lawnmower. We were about thirty-five kilometres west of Rosthern, almost to the South Saskatchewan River. I cuddled Bozley, our ten-year-old Shih Tzu, on my lap, stroking his soft wavy ears.

Don guided our SUV to a stop before a tired, slumping mid-century farmhouse. He turned off the ignition and gave me a questioning look.

"I guess we're here," he said. "Not much of a place."

I nodded. "What do you think? Can we leave Bozley here?"

Before Don could respond, four large chocolate-coloured Labrador Retrievers came bounding through the tall grass toward our vehicle with an eruption of barking. Uncertain of what to do, we waited in our vehicle. The dogs encircled our Explorer. We weren't getting out. Bozley jumped up from his slumber and gazed out the window. We watched as a man in his 50s, wearing a plaid shirt and carrying a shotgun, emerged from a dilapidated, unpainted barn about one hundred and fifty meters away. He picked his way through the bramble and weeds, getting closer to where my husband and I waited in our SUV like sitting ducks.

We heard the man with the gun call off his dogs and command them to be quiet as he made his way to the driver's side of our vehicle. My husband lowered his window. Bozley cowered.

"Howdy," the man said. "Have any trouble finding the place?"

"No," Don replied. "Your wife gave us good directions."

"She ain't my wife."

A little taken aback by the man's abruptness, we waited for him to say more, but words seemed to be in short supply.

The man in the plaid shirt had an accent that sounded like a Southern drawl. It seemed as out of place in central Saskatchewan as we felt, sitting in the middle of this tumbledown yard.

"Cummon' in," the man asked us to follow him.

Not a friendly man, he seemed a little put out that we had interrupted his day.

Don and I glanced at each other. Reluctantly, we opened our respective car doors and gingerly stepped out of our vehicle. The man had already turned, making his way to the house. I noticed the bottoms of his loose-fitting dirty jeans pushed into tan-coloured high-top boots. The boots with the undone laces threatened to fall off with every step he took. Two of his dogs followed him while two hung back to sniff at Don and me as we stepped carefully through the grass and weeds. Bozley squirmed uncomfortably in my arms. Don carried Bozley's crate, dog dish, and leash. We looked at the old dwelling before us with the sagging porch that threatened to break free and collapse with a groan onto the grass.

The man disappeared into the house and in his place a woman stood in the doorway, beckoning us. She appeared to be in her 50s and looked much like her house, shabby and messy. She wore dirty clothes that hadn't seen the inside of a washing machine for some time. Her mousey-brown hair begged for a comb to untangle the knots and bring some order.

Don and I followed the woman into the gloomy house filled with clutter everywhere. I wrinkled my nose at the offensive musty odour that crept into my nostrils. The smell was unpleasant. Dust particles or insects floated in the air in the slants of the sun that escaped through the broken window blinds. My skin crawled. I felt itchy.

The woman pointed to two chairs for Don and me. I held back. I did not want to touch anything, let alone have my clothes come into contact with something in the house. She insisted, so Don and I eased ourselves onto the chairs while she pulled another chair from behind the table and seated herself. I could not see the man who had met us in the yard. I could feel Bozley's tense little body on my lap, alert and glancing here and there at the big brown dogs that roamed freely about the kitchen, sniffing at us, and brushing up against our legs.

The woman, Carol, said she hailed from Saskatchewan, and her partner, Lloyd, from Alabama. Carol explained that she and Lloyd trained Labrador Retrievers to hunt pheasants. They had customers all over North America. She bragged about how they expertly trained their dogs and how their American clients relied on the quality of their animals when looking to purchase a hunting dog. She smugly proclaimed they had a highly lucrative business as she sat back in her chair.

I glanced around the dingy kitchen. My first thought was if the business was that profitable, perhaps the couple could consider improving their living conditions, but I said nothing. The retrievers sniffed around Don and me. Bozley writhed in my arms, uneasy, having the big dogs so close.

Abruptly, Carol stood up.

"You need to be on your way," she reached for Bozley.

Carol took our dog from my grasp. I didn't want to leave our pet with this strange woman in this dirty place, but we had run out of options. I had called one dog boarder after another, but at the beginning of July, everyone wanted to get out of the city on vacation. Every dog kennel I called told me they did not have a vacancy. Don and I had to be out of town for work the following week. I had even tried calling dog boarders along the way in the hopes I could find a vacancy. No luck. Someone in Rosthern told us these people sometimes watched dogs. I called and spoke with Carol, and she agreed to take our dog for the few days we'd be gone. It had seemed like the answer to our problem until we drove into the yard and met the people. Now, I felt very apprehensive.

"He's a pampered house dog," I told her. "He sleeps in his crate at night with his blanket. We give him only this brand of dog food to eat." I held up a pail with his dog food inside. "Anything else will upset his stomach. Please wash out his water dish every day because otherwise, he won't drink from it."

"So much fuss," Carol said dismissively.

"He's a house dog. I guess we have spoiled him, but he is our pet."

"We'll take care of him," she promised.

I stood, looking at her uncertainly and scratching my arms and the back of my neck. I felt like mites crawled on me. Maybe they did.

Don and I walked through the dimly lit kitchen to the porch and out into the blazing July sun. I shaded my eyes from the blast of sunlight as we exited her house. When I turned to say goodbye, Carol had already closed the porch door. Don and I stood alone in the yard with no other recourse but to get back into our Explorer and drive away.

After three days and our business trip completed, we returned to the farm to pick up Bozley. Once again, we stopped our vehicle in the tall grass in front of the run-down house.

The man in the customary plaid shirt materialized from an outbuilding.

"Your dog's gone," he snapped.

"What?" I asked.

"Your dog's gone," he repeated.

"What are you talking about?"

"He took off, scared as a rabbit."

By now, Don had come around our vehicle and demanded, "What do you mean he's gone?"

"He took off. We looked everywhere and even got the Hutterites from over there to help search for him." Lloyd pointed to the Hutterite Colony in the distance, with its many shining steel grain bins perched on the cliff's edge leading down to the South Saskatchewan River.

"He's gone."

Carol hurried from the house, wringing her hands.

"We're sorry, but your dog ran away," she said.

"What happened?" I experienced a sinking feeling as I stood in that falling-down yard with knee-high grass everywhere.

"We were outside working with the hunting dogs. Lloyd fired the shotgun. Your dog took off. We looked everywhere, but we couldn't find him." Carol looked somewhat apologetic.

"How did he take off? Didn't you have him on his leash?" I asked, dumbfounded.

"No, we couldn't find it. We didn't think it would be a big deal," Carol replied.

"When did this happen?" Don asked.

"On the second day," Lloyd said. "We done all we can."

With that, Lloyd walked away, leaving Carol standing with us, trying to explain their shortcomings.

"I can't believe this. We trusted you to take care of our dog." I was angry and worried.

"Which way did he go?" Don intervened.

Carol pointed in the southeast direction.

"We saw him a day later, creeping back into the yard to the dog's dish, but we couldn't catch him. As soon as we got close, he took off. He's spooked for sure."

I shook my head in disbelief.

"Is there a road?" Don questioned her. "Any way to get to that field from here?"

The woman nodded, pointing to where a trail led to the field.

"I'll get your stuff," she said as she turned and dashed back into the house, returning shortly with Bozley's kennel and belongings. My heart sank at the sight of his empty crate. I choked back a sob.

Carol handed it to Don. He stashed everything in the back seat of our Explorer. Without another word and without offering to pay her, we climbed into our vehicle. Don started our SUV and shifted into gear, and we drove across the uneven yard to the field road Carol had indicated. Slowly navigating along a grassy field line, calling through the open windows for our dog, we moved slowly, squeaking one of his toys, scanning the horizon for any sight of our beloved pet. We meandered around the summer fallow field, searched the grassy pasture beside it, surveyed the horizon, and called his name. We did not catch even a glimpse of Bozley. After searching for over an hour, our minds decided we could do no more but head home. Our heavy hearts wanted to stay.

I lay in bed later that night, sobbing. A storm rumbled in the distance, increasing in intensity. Soon, an ear-splitting clap of thunder with an accompanying light show brought pounding rain. I thought about our little dog and his fear of thunder. Every time a storm arose, we knew to look for Bozley in our bedroom closet, huddled amongst our shoes, quivering, his sad brown eyes peering up at us. I knew the terror he'd feel all alone in this thunderstorm, cold and wet in the piercing rain. For me, sleep would not come.

Since I had to work in Saskatoon the following days, Don recruited our neighbours, Reg and Dianne, to help in his search for Bozley. They made several daily trips to the area where our dog had gone missing. They drove around the field and walked through the grass, calling his name, squeaking his treasured toy, trying to lure him with delicious-smelling meat. Nothing worked. On Wednesday evening, I overheard Don and Reg talking about how they had found a coyote's den with four pups, fearful that the mother coyote would hunt to feed her babies and find Bozley as easy prey. Horrified, I voiced my concerns to Don, who tried to downplay it so I wouldn't worry. Too late. That night in bed, I prayed Bozley had died, spared the atrocities he would otherwise face.

Each day, Don and our neighbours searched for our dog. They returned home late Thursday afternoon feeling jubilant, having spotted Bozley roaming along a grassy ridge that separated a field from a pasture. At least now they knew his approximate location. Don tried to approach our pet with food in his hand, attempting to lure our small dog close enough to grab him. He was unsuccessful, but at least we knew Bozley was alive and not injured. Amazed at our pet's resilience and resourcefulness for having survived in the wild all on his own for three long days and nights, we prayed for success in bringing him home.

On Friday, the fifth day of Bozley's disappearance Don and Reg, buoyed by their sighting of him the day before, headed west of our home to search once more for our Shih Tzu. Don had a juicy ham bone tucked in a bag in the back seat of his truck. He hoped the smell of it would entice Bozley to come close enough that Don could catch him. They went directly to the same grassy knoll where they spotted him the day before.

Don and Reg walked around, calling the dog's name. Eventually, Don caught movement out of the corner of his eye. Quickly turning, he saw Bozley running through the pasture's low grass. My husband called to him in soft, convincing tones, holding a ham bone in his outstretched hand. Don knew he had Bozley's attention when the small dog edged closer. Terrified and spooked, the dog scampered a few feet back before stopping and turning to face Don again. Bozley did this several times before his extreme hunger finally got the best of him. Bozley crept toward the ham bone in Don's hand, allowing Don to grab him. We had our dog back. Don raised our pet in the air so Reg, who was on the distant ridge, could see he had him. Reg let out a whoop as he came running to celebrate Bozley's capture. The men returned home with our Shih Tzu. I arrived home after work that day to join in on the celebration as we gave thanks for our dog's safe return.

Shocked at Bozley's appearance, I noticed his long, wavy hair was now matted and tangled with weeds, twigs, and thorns, making him almost unrecognizable. I tried petting his head, but he cringed, cowering away. The once perky and friendly Shih Tzu now shied away from human contact, refused to drink water, and ate very little. His trembling and shaking went on for weeks. A visit to the vet and groomer did not provide any relief. The vet compared his condition to one suffering from Post Traumatic Stress Disorder (PTSD). He told us that Bozley might never recover from this disturbing experience. The vet prescribed pills for parasites, a stomach disorder, and ointment for his dry, scaly skin covered in insect bites. For hours, the dog groomer tried to shave off his enormous mass. The shaver caught in the twigs and burs in our dog's hair. Finally finished, she pointed out all the abrasions and insect bites that tormented Bozley during his time on the run. We also saw how skinny he had become. We resolved to nurse him back to health.

The vet and grooming bills climbed as we tried to restore Bozley to his former self. Over the ensuing months, it became very costly, and, at one point, we discussed whether to sue these careless people who had inflicted so much pain on our beloved pet. After careful consideration, we decided not to. It would cost us more money and, from what we could see, even if successful, Carol and Lloyd would not have the means to make good on any court orders. Reluctantly, we cast that notion aside.

* * *

"Not again, Bozley," I cried several months later, noticing another yellow stain on my cream-coloured living room carpet.

Bozley, his head down, slunk away to hide under the side table next to the couch. I immediately felt sorry I had raised my voice. Since his time in the wild, Bozley remained reluctant to go outside alone. Our previously well-trained house dog now had accidents all over our house. Don came into the living room and coaxed Bozley out from under the coffee table.

"Come on Boz, let's go for a walk," he said as he snapped the leash to Bozley's collar. Our dog obediently trailed behind Don. They left the house together.

I glanced out the living room window that faced the street and saw Don and Bozley heading down the sidewalk. It saddened my heart to see the change in Bozley's demeanour. Before losing him, Bozley always walked proudly ahead of Don, his head high as if to say, "Look at me. I'm taking my dad for a walk." Now, Bozley walked behind Don, his leash sagging as he trailed along with his head lowered – no dignity, no delight, no vitality. Our dog, once proud and joyful, was now robbed of his spirit. All that remained was a shell of a dog. Bozley never fully recuperated from his ordeal and, sadly, faced medical and psychological afflictions for the rest of his life. He remained a pared-down version of his former self.

The Break-In

"Someone was in our house!"

I only got a few sketchy details from my agitated husband about someone breaking into our house before he hung up. The police needed to speak to him. All he told me was that it was bad. Extremely bad.

In my District Branch Manager role, I had plans to work the week in Lloydminster, three hours away from our Rosthern home. I scrapped that idea. Instead, I checked out of my hotel, pointed my rented car east, and headed home. Don's voice indicated the seriousness of the situation.

On that day, February 15, 2012, the drive seemed endless as one kilometre after another slowly ticked by. My mind raced. I considered all the unknowns. I didn't know what had happened, what damage they'd caused, or what they stole. I did not know if they had caught the culprit. I knew nothing except that I had to get home. I sped along, topping 140 kilometres an hour, sometimes higher. I told myself to slow down, easing up on the gas pedal. It wouldn't help to get a speeding ticket or, worse yet, get into an accident.

Around 6 p.m., I pulled into North Battleford. After filling the car with gas, I grabbed some pop and chips even though I wasn't hungry and headed for the road. I called Don, who still sounded dazed. I knew he needed me there.

The last splashes of the sun's orange and pink rays slid onto the horizon in my rear-view mirror. Grateful for the dry highway, but on a stretch well known for the wildlife that roamed indiscriminately, I reminded myself to slow down or risk hitting a deer or a moose. Alert, I scanned the ditches on both sides of the road, watching for anything that moved, anything jumping out in front of my speeding vehicle.

After what seemed an eternity of travelling through the dark, I finally saw the early evening lights of Rosthern twinkling ahead. My foot, again heavier on the gas pedal, had me propelling my SUV those last few kilometres. I reached Rosthern and pulled into our driveway. Everything seemed normal, just as I'd left it. The lights shone brightly inside our house, and for a moment, I felt reassured. I struggled with my suitcase, briefcase, laptop, and purse. Don hurried outside. He had been watching out the window for my arrival and wasted no time getting my car unpacked and my cases carried into the house.

Once inside, everything seemed as it should. It got worse as Don led me through the house. Mud tracks crossed our cream-coloured carpet in the living room, leading up to our big-screen TV. Those same muddy footprints led down the hallway to our bedrooms. The upheaval in our master bedroom showed the intruder spent most of his time here upturning dresser drawers, throwing things out of our closets, and rummaging through our lives. The entire room seemed dumped upside down. Plywood covered our bedroom window. I looked questioningly at my husband.

"What happened here?" I asked. "Why is the window boarded?"

"I'll tell you everything in a minute, but first, come with me."

He took me down the basement stairs. I gasped as I saw all of Don's gun safes toppled over. The offender tried prying these vaults open to get at the contents. While he damaged many safes, only one, less sturdy, lay open. An avid hunter and past firearms instructor, Don abided by the laws regarding the ownership, storage, and safety of guns in Canada. His face registered the devastation he felt.

"Did he get any guns?" I asked in a quiet voice.

"We think only one."

I closed my eyes, too rattled to say more.

We made our way back upstairs and sat down at the kitchen table.

"OK. Start at the beginning. Tell me everything that happened."

"I walked uptown to get a few groceries. Daniel saw me leave."

Daniel, our next-door neighbour, sometimes knew our comings and goings better than we did. I nodded for Don to continue.

"It only took me forty minutes. When I returned, Daniel ran over to tell me he saw someone in our house. He didn't recognize him when the man stuck his head out our side door as though looking for someone."

"Did he call the police?"

"No. He knew I would be home shortly. He waited and watched our house. I put my groceries down and snuck up to the side door to peek inside." Don stopped for dramatic effect.

I signalled with my hands for him to continue.

"The guy had piled a bunch of our stuff just inside the door like he was waiting to haul it all out of the house into a truck or something."

Don continued, "I ran back to Daniel and called the police. It took them about fifteen minutes to get here. We knew the guy to be in the house because we didn't see him leave."

"What happened then?"

"The police told Daniel and me to wait. They drew their revolvers and stormed into the house. We could hear them yelling commands as they moved from room to room."

"Did they catch him?"

"No. He smashed the bedroom window, jumped out, and escaped across our backyard. Neighbours saw him running, carrying a rifle. He disappeared through the evergreens at the back of our property and the police lost him. The culprit dropped the gun and some of our belongings that he carried because the police found them later in the trees."

The doorbell rang, interrupting Don. We cautiously opened the door, relieved to see a young RCMP officer with a smile on his face. We invited him in. He stopped by to update us on the investigation and to see if we needed anything. Struck by his youth and caring manner, I immediately liked this man.

He told us that a rash of break-ins had occurred in Rosthern that afternoon, but ours was the most serious because of the time the culprit spent in our house. The RCMP suspected the same individuals had committed all the break-ins. He asked if we would be all right staying in our house that night and we assured him we would. He advised that we not go into the main bedroom because they wanted to "process" it in the morning.

After he left, Don and I spent a long night huddled in the unfamiliar bed in our guest room. We held our breath at every little creak in the house, waiting for the next sound. After all, the infiltrator still had our house key, the one he discovered rummaging through our garage. We could not help but wonder if he planned to come back to finish what he'd started. Often throughout the night, we got up and crept around our house, not knowing if we were there alone or if someone was in our home with us.

When morning finally shook off the cloak of darkness, we rose feeling exhausted and waited for the police. Word circulated in the community as friends came by to offer help. Some came strictly out of curiosity. The phone continued to ring with much of the same. We learned of other break-ins and thefts, how he stole a young woman's jeep, how the culprit walked into the house of an elderly couple and, upon finding them at home, made an excuse and left. Another neighbour told us how she had seen the police running through their backyard with guns drawn. The entire community, abuzz with the goings-on of the preceding day, seemed unsettled.

During occasional lulls, I called our insurance company to advise of our break-in, gave our statements, made lists of what we needed to do, and provided lists of stolen or damaged items.

The forensic expert, a stalwart man in his 50s, finally arrived from Prince Albert. He performed most of his investigative work in our bedroom, the living room, and the basement. He took fingerprints around the house, studied, measured, and used certain chemicals for different tests. The black chalky powder he used left a residue on everything he processed. After about two hours, he announced his job was complete. We could now begin putting our lives back together.

Picking through the strewn objects in our bedroom, I grasped the reality of it all. I picked up my two broken jewellery boxes, remembering all the expensive pieces my husband and children had given me as gifts over the years – the gold, the diamonds, the rubies, and the sapphires. He stole the sentiment behind them as well. My husband's coin collection was missing, along with our birth certificates, social insurance cards, and blank cheques. Realizing the extent of this robbery, I needed to make more phone calls to the bank, the credit card companies, and the credit bureaus. Oh, my Gawd. Thoughts of identity theft and fraud became apparent. I sank to the floor in shock and disbelief.

Don found me sitting in the middle of my ruined life. It felt as though the glass shards from the broken window had pierced my heart. He helped me to my feet and said we were going out for lunch which granted me a much-needed change of scenery and an escape, if only for an hour.

At the small local restaurant with the '60s-style decor, we saw the same smiling constable that had stopped by the evening before. When he finished his meal, he came to our table to check on us. He assured us they had some leads and promised to keep us informed. He asked if we needed anything. I mentioned that the insurance company required a Police File number to substantiate our claim. The officer told us he would provide that number when he returned to the office.

Back at our house, we began collecting the pieces of our lives and putting them back together again. We spoke to police, insurance representatives, contractors, and each other. We eventually felt we had regained control.

A few days after our break-in, the police officer phoned to ask if he could come over to speak with us. In the past, he just showed up at our door unannounced. We felt a little uncertain as to why he called ahead this time. When he arrived, another officer accompanied him, whom he introduced as his replacement. They had transferred the smiling young man. He was leaving in a day or two.

The constable wanted to tell us personally that they had the man who had broken into our house and vandalized our home. He said the perpetrator stole a jeep in town and fled east of Rosthern. Before doing so, he broke into another person's house, a retired police officer vacationing in Arizona. The felon consumed a bottle of the homeowner's heart pills before going to the bar to have a few drinks. They believed the consumption of medication and liquor caused him to lose control of the vehicle, ending up in the ditch. The driver wore only a hoodie and jeans when he got out to walk. The police found his body a few days later, not knowing if the potentially lethal combination of pills and liquor killed him, if he froze to death, or maybe both. A sense of relief washed over me at that moment. We thanked the police for stopping by and wished the smiling officer well in his new post.

The following week, the local newspaper came out. Flipping through the pages, I saw a picture of the man who broke his way into our lives. He appeared so youthful, so innocent-looking.

The article sought the public's help in locating a missing man. His family hadn't seen or heard from him since February 15. Because of the delay in receiving the newspaper, we already knew the outcome of this story. Such a waste of a young man's life. While initially feeling a sense of relief, knowing he could no longer inflict any further harm or trouble on us, I now felt grief for the family who had lost a son and a brother. I cut out the newspaper article. Don and I recovered or replaced most of our belongings. The man's family will suffer their loss for the rest of their lives.

Going Home

It had been a long week of back-to-back bank meetings in Toronto, rushing from one venue to the next, taking in the jam-packed agenda with little time for decompressing, my feet aching, head pounding. My purse and briefcase seemed incredibly heavy as I trudged through the airport crowds, stepping this way to avoid someone, mumbling apologies if I bumped into another. I found a place to sit on a hard plastic-moulded seat and momentarily closed my eyes. I wished I could vanish, disappear where no one could see me. I wanted to be home in my little haven where I could strip naked, sprawl out on my bed with legs and arms spread wide in starfish style, and forget about the day. I wanted to feel the scalding water from my rainfall shower head beat on my weary body, pounding the exhaustion out of me with one relaxing pulse after another.

I sighed as I studied those around me – the suit across from me wearing no socks. Really? No socks. The Asian woman advancing toward me, speaking into her phone, brushing her hair back with an impatient hand as she bent to pick up a bag she dropped, the young man in sweats carrying a laptop in a bag, practically jogging through the crowds. Was he late for a flight? So many looked like I did and felt as I did. Tired from a week away on business, wanting to be anywhere but here, hoping flights were on schedule, praying there wasn't a screaming baby or an overly talkative senior who wanted to visit on the flight home.

I got up and made my way to the washroom. Once inside the stall, pants down, I relaxed on the toilet. No one could see me now. I wished

I could stay there forever, a bathroom of all places. But here alone, I felt unseen, unjudged. I didn't have to wear my business smile. I wasn't on stage. I was unequivocally me. I rested my head against the partition wall until noises from the line forming outside made me feel bad for occupying the stall longer than I had to.

I got up, adjusted my clothes, washed my hands, and returned to the same hard seat I had occupied earlier. I glanced at my phone to see if I had any messages, then returned it to my purse.

Finally, the attendants announced my flight. A flurry of activity erupted as people rose from their seats, stretched, gathered their bags, and began forming lines to board the plane. At least the flight was on time. That was something for which to be grateful. I boarded, then walked down the plane's aisle and found my window seat, scrambling over the travel-weary man in a business suit. We smiled and acknowledged each other with a nod before I settled for the three-hour flight home.

The attendant approached with pillows in her arms. I made eye contact with her, letting her know I would like one. I grasped the small, perogy-shaped cushion, placed it between me and the window, and sank my head into its soft comfort. Thankful for small favours, I positioned myself for sleep.

The next stop. Home.

The Man In The Van

Morning, my favourite time of day, had just rubbed the sleep from her eyes and drawn back the curtain of darkness to reveal the splendour of the day. Having moved back to Saskatoon and freshly retired from my job, I began a new regimen of eating healthier and going for daily walks. Three blocks from home, I headed toward the park's walkways. I loved watching the rabbits frolic in the lush green grass.

Normally, at 5 a.m., I was the only one out.

But not today.

On a stretch of the street where the houses had few windows and faced opposite directions, a white van inched down a back alley in front of me and turned left. It made its way slowly to the intersection. Here it made a U-turn and crept up behind me. I felt uncomfortable as it edged along, following me. I turned to look at the driver, but the sun on the windshield prevented me from seeing his face. The van picked up speed and drove on.

I didn't realize I had been holding my breath.

My heart began pounding when I saw him make another U-turn at the end of the street, coming toward me again. I did not know what to do. His actions were deliberate. I felt so alone. So vulnerable.

The man in the white van made another U-turn and slowly came up behind me again. I kept walking, picking up my pace and praying he would move on and leave me alone. My heart thumped wildly in my chest. What did this man want? Why was he purposely following me?

I neared the approach to the park, uncertain if I should enter it or stay on the street. I took my chances and headed for the secluded walkways.

Previously, the park was my haven, the place where I connected with nature, where I always felt safe. I hurried along the path, glancing back over my shoulder. The man in the van had made another U-turn and headed in the opposite direction, away from me. I kept looking back as I hurried along. He drove off, and I breathed easier.

The following morning, I debated what to do. Was my encounter with the man in the white van an isolated incident? Or would he be there again this morning, waiting for me? I decided not to go for my usual walk. During the day, I worried about what I should have done, never having encountered anything like this before.

By the following morning, I convinced myself I had imagined it all, blown it out of proportion to something much bigger and more sinister than it was. I slid my feet into my runners, striking out down the street. With fierce determination, I moved further from my home. As I approached the empty part of the street where the white van had shadowed me two mornings earlier, I began walking faster, glancing around to make sure he wasn't there. All too late, I saw a white van turn the corner a block ahead of me. My breath caught. Oh, no. Not again.

As he had done the morning before, he drove toward me, inching past me before making a U-turn. He came up behind me. I clutched the cell phone in my pocket that I had brought with me this time. I could take a picture of his license plate or his face. I'm not sure what good that would do if he had ill intentions toward me, but it offered me a little comfort as I kept walking and wishing he would go away. Once again, I escaped to the park. He left.

I felt trapped. I did not want to give up my newly established exercise routine. I also did not want to relinquish control to this individual who harassed me. In my mind, I played out my right to come and go as I pleased versus being too foolhardy in the face of potential danger.

The following morning, I had my cell phone in my pocket, but I opened my kitchen drawer and took out a paring knife. The small weapon was in my hand. I put it back. The knife I took out instead had a longer blade. I put it in my pocket. The blade almost stabbed my stomach when I bent over to tie my shoelaces. It reminded me of how lethal it could be. I hated what this man had me doing. The fear he invoked in me drove me to actions I would never have previously considered.

I hastened down the street with the morning air brushing my face, he was not there. My fingers relaxed their tight hold on the knife in my pocket. He wasn't there the next day either or the day after. My fear and anxiousness slowly subsided.

Several days later, I turned the corner, crossed the street, and found myself on the abandoned stretch of road on my way to the park. I saw the white van edging toward me. He slowly rolled to a stop and parked in front of me. Walking toward him, I saw him in his van, watching me approach. My mind raced. What should I do? Turn and run? Keep going? Confront him? I reached for the knife in my pocket. Too late, I realized I had not brought it. Instead, I felt the leather case of my cell phone. As the only defence I had, it provided little comfort in the face of imminent danger.

Approaching the van, I stared directly at the driver behind the wheel. He appeared to be in his 50s and had a round brown face. His eyes stared back at me as I continued to meet his gaze unfalteringly. I mustered up significantly more courage than I felt and continued walking toward his vehicle. My heart pounded. I held my breath as I strode past the van, half expecting the side door to fly open and someone to pull me inside, thus making me another statistic adding to the number of missing women in Saskatoon. I hurried past the van, clutching my cell phone. I debated if I should turn and snap a picture of his license plate; however, I thought that might make him angry and incite him. I kept walking.

That was my last encounter with the mysterious man in the van. I walked with the long-bladed knife in my pocket for the rest of the summer. I hated what he had done without even laying a finger on me.

He had robbed me of the peace I had always felt and the freedom I always enjoyed.

Despite that, I spread the word in the neighbourhood, warning fellow walkers, women, and children, to be aware of the stranger who lurked on vacant streets, hidden behind the windshield of a slow-moving van. I refused to let my fear of this person take over my life, choosing instead to educate others on being alert in the neighbourhood and not walking alone. I felt comforted by the extra vigilance as our community pulled together to keep one another safe. Something positive had come from this threatening situation. We became more aware of our surroundings and the need to protect each other.

On a hot summer evening, I smiled and waved to our neighbours across the street. Don and I walked hand in hand strolling toward the park, eager to breathe in the fresh air and listen to the birds sing. We smiled at the rabbits romping in the grass. Once again, I felt safe.

Pandemic Christmas

Christmas 2020 was like no other.

A year earlier, news circulated of a highly contagious, fast-spreading virus called COVID-19 that was infecting people. It was the worst virus the world had seen since the Spanish Flu one hundred years before. At the start of the epidemic, the average person in Saskatchewan remained calm because it seemed a world away from our quiet, uninfected province. Like a python, the virus crept closer. By March 2020, the snake tightly wrapped us within its confines, constricting us. Restricting us. The government introduced masking and social distancing. They also encouraged people to work from home. Businesses closed or had to find new ways to stay afloat, and curbside pickup became a means to limit personal interaction. During the controlled lockdown, Don and I drove through Saskatoon's downtown area.

"It's like we're entering a war zone," I commented.

"Yup. Most businesses and malls are closed. The streets are vacant, no people. No cars. Ours is the only vehicle I can see." Don looked around, up and down the streets. Nothing. So eery.

People became pandemic-weary after eight long months of this. We longed for personal contact. We missed not being able to see our loved ones. We could only connect through front yard visits or peering through windowpanes at family members we longed to embrace. Like everyone else, our family needed each other. Knowing we could not physically be together, we made plans to share Christmas in unique ways. We had to become creative.

Don and I did all our Christmas shopping online. Courier drivers traipsed up our sidewalk to drop off packages and scurried away before we could open the door. We ordered our gifts early to beat the Christmas rush and avoid delays. Already, some companies experienced backlogs, unable to bring in select merchandise. People began to hoard with impending shortages on the horizon. Toilet paper became a precious commodity. Empty store shelves fuelled people's hunger to stockpile when they finally found what they needed. It was very much an "every man for himself" environment.

After months of being secluded, our family needed to come together. If we couldn't do so in person, we would find another way. Don and I delivered wrapped presents to each of our children's houses. We dropped off the gifts on the front steps so our kids could bring them inside once we left. Our grandchildren stood in the open doorways asking why we didn't come in or why we couldn't hug them. Don and I stepped back, smiled, and waved. We needed to keep each other safe as we wiped away big tears that slid down our cheeks behind our masks.

Our three children and their partners tried to make this a memorable Christmas for their families. At 3 p.m. on December 24, we all signed onto a video call. This is how we came together when rules and a deadly virus kept us from meeting in person. Via technology, we joined each other in our respective living rooms. We stared at the computer screens, our smiles flowing into our loved ones' households and watched as our grandchildren took turns ripping open gifts, we had lovingly wrapped for them.

Eventually, everyone opened all their gifts, but one package remained. It had Don's name neatly printed on it. In front of our laptop screen, so everyone could see, Don carefully pulled back the wrap and lifted the lid to the small box he held.

"What's this?"

"Take it out and hold it up," I told him.

The kids demanded that he hold it up to the computer screen so they could see. Obliging, Don pulled a neon green outfit from the box. He struggled with all the narrow strips of cloth, soon becoming apparent that it was a Borat swimsuit. He laughed out loud, and the kids and grandchildren joined in. Don always teased that he wanted a Borat bathing suit for the beach. I made sure he had one. The gag gift proved to be a great way to end the video call. We all wished each other a Merry Christmas before signing off.

Don and I sat down to a quiet Christmas Eve supper by ourselves, grateful our family was healthy and safe even if we could not be together.

The next day, we had more plans. I went to Ilarion Senior's Residence to visit my mom. We knew she would be lonely having to spend the day by herself. I chatted with her for an hour, knowing our children and grandchildren were gathering outside. When they were ready, Sara texted me. I asked Mom to grab her coat as we walked to the exterior side door of the senior's home.

Once outside, Mom and I saw my children and grandchildren holding posters and singing. We serenaded her with the Christmas carols our grandchildren had specially selected to sing for Great-Grandma. They had brought musical instruments, drums, bells, horns, and tambourines to accompany them. The children had helped make posters that read "Merry Christmas" and "We Love You, Grandma" that they lit up with mini-Christmas lights. The enormous smile on Mom's face said it all. Pleased, she clasped her hands together and sang along. Of course, we all kept our distance. The children smiled and waved to their great-grandmother, and she smiled and waved back. Once again, there could be no hugs.

Too soon, it ended. Mom said goodbye to all of us. I know she treasured that day because we found a unique way to spend time with her on Christmas Day. She felt loved and cherished. We came together as a family for a few brief moments outside a senior's home. Standing in the cold winter air singing Christmas carols gave Mom something to converse about with her friends for weeks. She showed off the children's posters by mounting them in her suite's window.

I hope we never have to spend another Christmas like the one during the 2020 pandemic. But even through it all, our family showed our love for each other during one of the most challenging times. The pandemic raged for another year, but for the following Christmas, we once again gathered as a family, as it should be.

Road Trip

When we lived in Meadow Lake, I always felt comforted by the forest where nature's arms reached out, embraced me, and kept me safe. Travelling the three and a half hours from where we now lived in Saskatoon, I wanted to floor the gas pedal to get to the forest quicker. I longed for the tranquillity and oneness with nature. Heading north of Glaslyn in mid-September, I soaked in the allure of the golden aspens, their leaves trembling in the brilliant autumn sun. Splotches of dark green spruce trees permeated the yellow sea of poplars painted against the azure sky.

Here, I felt protected, like I was coming home. No one knew where I was. That is just how I wanted it. I needed to get away. There had been too much lately. Too much COVID, too much isolation, too much divisiveness, too much not speaking. I was tired of it all and felt drained from trying to keep the peace among family members arguing their opinions on vaccinations. I hated wearing masks and practicing social distancing and wanted it all to be over. We needed time to rebuild as a family and as a society. How had we become so distant, so divided? I thought adversity was supposed to bring people together.

"Could you fill it with regular, please?"

I had pulled up to the gas pump at the little convenience store and gas station at the midway point between Glaslyn and Meadow Lake.

"Nice to see you back," Wayne, the owner, acknowledged me with a quick smile. He was a quiet man now in his 60s wearing charcoal pants and a matching grey shirt with sleeves rolled up to his elbows. He was a man of few words, few judgements.

It pleased me to know that in the thirteen years since we moved from Meadow Lake, he still recognized me, even behind my face mask. He pumped gas, eking out a living and I felt encouraged and delighted that some things had not changed. The pandemic had left this isolated business alongside the highway untouched. Or so it seemed.

Wayne filled my SUV with gas and held the store's door for me. I entered, noticing the iron grates on the door and windows as they had been all those years before. Nothing much had changed inside either, still dark and dusty. The sparsely stocked shelves taught me long ago to watch for expiry dates when I purchased anything here. I guess items didn't move too fast in a northern convenience store where travellers primarily stopped to use the washrooms and nothing else.

I paid for the gas and bought a cup of coffee that I knew I would throw out because it had probably sat all day. I wanted to support this man who quietly went about his business in a small world, somewhat excluded from the rest of civilization.

Back in my SUV, I turned north onto Highway 4, scanning the ditches for wildlife as I drove. I knew that moose, deer, bears, and wolves abounded in the area. The last thing I wanted to do was hit one of them. Further down the road, a lone, greyish-coloured whitetail doe grazed on the grass. She casually lifted her head to glance at me as I drove past. She didn't move and I didn't slow down, as though there was a mutual understanding that we weren't a threat to each other, but I was glad I saw her.

I sped along the resurfaced highway, smooth as an airport tarmac. I sailed through the sea of blue and gold, the sky and the trees in perfect harmony. Ahead to the left, the shining, silver beams of the communication towers glinted and pierced the ultramarine sky high above the trees. I knew I had reached what the locals called "the height of the land." From here, the land sloped north toward the gentle valley that cradled the city of Meadow Lake.

My SUV crossed over a little creek, and I glided into town. On the right, the familiar grocery store and strip mall, and on the left, the car dealership, the hardware store, and the new eateries. It was still the same town I remembered. The auxiliary roads ran on each side of the highway like a ribbon from the south end of town to the north, where it led to the beauty beyond.

Rather than checking into my hotel room, I kept driving. The afternoon was young, and I was eager to get to the provincial park. I surveyed the farmland where some fields, already swathed, stood next to crops that waved in the sun. On my way to Dorintosh, the muskeg became more prominent as the terrain became boggier. Creeks and streams monopolized the landscape.

I followed a winding road to Meadow Lake Provincial Park, the sun flickering through the leafy canopy. Driving past Greig Lake, I kept going west until I reached Kimball Lake and pulled into the empty parking lot.

I opened the car door and climbed out, stretching my stiff legs and arms. I wandered down the pathway through the trees and ended up at the beach. The waves calmy lapped at the shore, dragging weeds onto the beach and then washing them out to the lake again. I found a park bench and seated myself. There was absolute silence. No people noises, no cars motoring by, no planes circling, no voices. Nothing. I closed my eyes in repose, letting the quiet and the nothingness creep into my brain, my soul, my being. I don't know how long I sat there, feeling like I was rocked in the boughs of the spruce trees that whooshed and comforted me. Gradually, I felt my body relax, my mind empty of all the clutter that crowded its recesses. I could breathe again.

The eerie and melancholy call of a loon broke the silence, reminding me it was time to head back to town. I realized I must have sat on the bench for almost two hours, soaking in the tranquillity, absorbing the peacefulness. I felt happy once again.

I meandered back up the path to the parking lot, climbed into my vehicle, and drove off. Cranking up the radio, I sang along to the songs as I cruised toward Meadow Lake. Encouraged, I knew the area still had a therapeutic effect on me. I felt re-energized, ready to face the world once again.

Martins Lake

I checked the rear-view mirror of our GMC Acadia, glimpsing the city of Saskatoon sliding away as we headed north over the Highway 11 overpass. Don gazed out the window as our picnic supplies rattled in the back of the SUV. The highway took us through fields of varying green crops, maybe not as thick as they should be for the second week in June. Lack of moisture will do that. We continued north, reaching the Petrofka Bridge and continued to Blaine Lake and north.

"Which lake are we going to?" Don overcame his curiosity enough to ask.

"You'll see soon enough."

In 2021, the pandemic slowly released its paralyzing grip on society. Kept apart for the past two years, our family wanted to be together. Don and Brenda shared a birthday, and both celebrated a momentous one that year, Don seventy years old and Brenda thirty-five. The family and I had a surprise day at the lake planned. Don knew we were going to a lake since he helped me load our vehicle, but he did not know which one.

We drove some distance before I noticed the Martins Lake Regional Park sign and turned off the main road. We had arrived. After speaking with a man who seemed familiar with the park, he encouraged us to use a campsite since there wasn't an overabundance of campers yet in June. That would change come the July 1st weekend.

Glancing at Don, I saw the eager look on his face, knowing he loved any opportunity to go to a lake and drink in the purity of nature. I hoped he and Brenda would enjoy our birthday surprise for them. It was a chance for our family to be together in the splendour of the great outdoors.

One by one, the other vehicles arrived. Sara, Reiss, and their daughter Adara arrived first. Adam, Christy, and their sons Harmon and Quillan arrived next, followed by Brenda, Nathan, and their daughters Helena and Archer. Everyone was there, each having brought food to contribute to the day. Vehicles were unloaded. Eager to explore, the five children aged three to eight ran off to discover what the park held in the line of activities for them.

The combination of the tree shade and the gazebo we had mounted sheltered us from the sun's direct rays. A slight wind rustled the aspen leaves, making them tremble like silver coins. Flies and the odd mosquito buzzed lazily, sometimes coming close enough for us to swat at them. The peacefulness was captivating. We all lounged in our chairs, absorbing the warmth and serenity, no one wanting to make the first move to begin lunch preparations. We listened to the far-off laughter and joyful screams of the children frolicking in the playground.

Don lifted his cap and scratched his head, placing it back in place.

"I'm going to stretch my legs and check out the lake," he said, rising to his feet.

In a moment, he wandered around the bluff of trees that enclosed our picnic site and was gone. I saw him later on the horizon, scanning the lake. I knew he wondered if there were fish in it. Don loved fishing. It was one of his favourite summer pastimes. All those summers he had worked as a crop adjuster and was on the road, Don never had time for fishing. Now retired, he hoped to change that.

With time edging closer to noon, the men assembled the portable barbeque. Once it was hot enough, they slapped hamburger patties and wieners on the grill, along with butter and onions wrapped in tinfoil. The girls and I began digging through coolers to produce salads, veggie trays, buns, and condiments. We called the children who were still playing and watched as they came running toward us with smiles on their faces and sand on their feet.

Don arrived back at camp just as we served lunch. The parents helped their children with their plates. They prepared hamburgers and dished out veggies and salads. The kids on the picnic bench had a solid table in front of them to reduce the chance of their food falling off their plates and hitting the ground. They chattered to each other, more like siblings than cousins.

I watched and listened. The little ones shared stories in their child-like fashion while cramming food into their mouths and asking for a drink. I dug in the coolers and produced mini juice boxes that they eagerly slurped, trying to quench their thirst. Some asked for water instead. They were all thirsty from playing in the blazing sun for over an hour.

The eight adults took turns filling their plates and sitting back in the lawn chairs to enjoy the tasty meal. Everything tastes better when cooked outside. The kids finished the main course and then asked for watermelon or grapes. I helped them as their little hands, still covered in sand, reached for my offerings. They grinned at each other, biting into the juicy watermelon that left red traces on their cheeks.

"Are we going to sing Happy Birthday?" Helena asked.

"Yeah!" Archer supported her sister. "We have to sing Happy Birthday to Mommy and Grandpa."

Harmon amused himself by slapping a tree twig into the ground. Quillan crawled onto his mother's lap for reassurance and comfort after a busy morning without her. Adara did cartwheels as she always did.

"OK, let's sing Happy Birthday," I agreed with the girls, whose faces beamed as we crowded around the table. Our voices all blended by singing the time-honoured traditional song. When we finished, Don and Brenda made their wishes and leaned forward to blow out the candles. Everyone clapped and cheered before eagerly devouring the cake placed before them.

"Now can we go swimming?" Harmon asked.

"Maybe wait just a little for your food to settle," Brenda answered.

The kids, restless from waiting, moved around the camp, looking for things to do. Brenda relented. Soon the kids had all their swimming gear packed in beach bags and had sunblock re-applied, grabbed the floating toys and headed out for a swim. The sapphire arms of the glimmering lake beckoned them with gentle waves washing up against the shore. Soon I heard splashing and gleeful shrieks as the children romped in the cold June water.

Eventually, the parents headed to the lake to watch their children play. Don and I sat at the abandoned campsite, taking in the quiet, smiling at each other, feeling content. I closed my eyes and inhaled. The lingering smell of barbecued meat overrode the craggy whiff of the lake and the insect spray that hung in the air. Children's laughter and parents' voices calling out to them filled the air with sweet music. Timeless.

"You want to go for a walk?"

Don stood in front of me, holding out his hand. I placed my hand in his as he pulled me from the chair. Together, we made our way to the beach. We watched our family at play for a few minutes before turning and strolling down a path. We walked, not having to talk. Being together was enough.

By the time we returned to camp, some kids were already back, grabbing for food that we had left on the table. The grandkids, filled with boundless energy, had stomachs that were bottomless pits.

"Can we go to the playground?" one child called out.

"Sure. Go. You know the way. You all stay together."

"We will," the chorus rang out as they ran towards the swings in their bathing suits, sand clinging to their wet feet.

Once again, the adults collapsed in their lawn chairs, a drink in their hands, contentment on their faces. We made idle conversation, knowing the day was coming to an end.

"This was fun. A great day," one of my adult children said. "We'll have to come back again."

Everyone nodded.

Shortly after, we began packing up, everyone pitching in to help as our family always did. It was our custom. I learned it as a girl from my family and my children learned it from Don and me. Hopefully, their children learned it from them. I knew deep inside that they would.

It had been a perfect day. The weather cooperated, and the park and lake were lovely. But the time spent together as a family, three generations bound tightly by love, made it special. I smiled, thinking how not one of our grandchildren had come to us today stating they were bored.

Farmhouse Window Reflections

It was beautiful! Awe-inspiring!

Don and I stood before my childhood home. This house had always been charming to me in its appeal, representing a haven while I navigated life's challenges as a girl growing up on a farm. This craftsman-style house with the unique half-hexagonal-shaped roof and gables was no longer perched on a hill in the centre of a farmyard. Now, it rested on a high point back from the shores of Wakaw Lake. No longer a farmhouse, this house had retired to the beach for an easier life. The poplars shaded and protected it from the strong winds that blew off the lake. It was magnificent in its serenity.

The current owners were not home, so I walked around the property feeling the love that had gone into restoring this splendid abode. Gone was the white and grey stucco of the house I remembered, replaced with greyish-olive green rounded siding that resembled logs. Stained decks stretched the length of the house. Pots overflowing with flowers, a multitude of colours, were everywhere. I noticed the old windows had been replaced and French patio doors led off the deck into the house. I could not go inside. This was no longer my home. Glimpses inside showed me the same care and attention had gone into designing the interior. It looked bright. Inviting.

Glancing in the window, I caught the reflection of a young girl. Mesmerized, I stared at her. For a moment, I heard my mother and father calling and children laughing as they played. I heard the familiar clang of the dipper as it fell into the metal water pail that always stood on the counter of the porch. I smelled bread baking and pork chops frying. Reaching out to the little girl in the window, she did the same. Our fingers touched the glass but could not touch each other. We were ages apart.

The sun shifted, hidden behind a cloud. The reflection dimmed, faded, and was gone. A woman with chicken-feet wrinkles around her eyes from smiling and short grey hair stared back at me. Her skin sagged but her heart was full.

Don wandered away, giving me time to reflect. I remembered him coming to pick me up for dates and us returning in the wee hours of the morning, sharing an embrace and kisses before he had to leave. Mom came out of her bedroom to talk with me after he left. I shared my evening with her before we both headed to bed, happy that I was home safe.

Safe. Here in this house, I had always felt safe.

Don shuffled his feet in the gravel beside me. I turned to face him. He was my constant in life, always beside me through the good times and the bad, never flinching.

"Ready to go home?" he asked.

I nodded. Walking to our SUV, I cast one last glance over my shoulder at the house, happy to see it in the hands of someone who loved it as much as I did. We climbed into our vehicle, and I backed out of the short driveway. We were going home.

About The Author

Marilyn Frey is published in *Chicken Soup for the Soul, Our Canada, Fun on the Farm 3, Folklore, Canadian Stories*, and the *Saskatchewan History* website. Marilyn feels her life and the lives of the people around her are rich with moments of immense sadness, challenges to overcome, funny situations, and some of the happiest times ever. These circumstances illustrate life's complexities and are the basis of great stories, ones to be told and shared. She is a long-time member of the Saskatchewan Writers' Guild and when she's not writing, she's reading.

Marilyn and her husband reside in Saskatoon, close to their family.

www.ingramcontent.com/pod-product-compliance
Lightning Source LLC
Chambersburg PA
CBHW031411290426
44110CB00011B/337